ACID
DROPS

by Andy Roberts

First published by
Psychedelic Press
Falmouth, Cornwall

Copyright ©2016
Andy Roberts and Psychedelic Press

ISBN: 978-0992808860

Cover art: **Ciaran Shaman**
Design and typesetting: **hobgobgraphics.com**

Printed in Cornwall, United Kingdom

For more information:
www.psychedelicpress.co.uk

Acknowledgments & Thanks

Many people, music and forces, dead and alive, directly and indirectly, bizarre as some of them might seem, have contributed to or heavily influenced the content of *Acid Drops*. You know who you are and why…

Albert Hofmann; Mandy Roberts; Lyndsay Walker; Andy Holroyd; Helen Roberts; Graeme Hartley; Nicky Hartley-Martin; Chris Bland; Dave Lee; Tim Goulding, Tim Booth and Ivan Pawle of Dr Strangely Strange and *Heavy Petting*; The Brotherhood of Eternal Love; Mike Heron and Robin Williamson of the Incredible String Band and *5000 Spirits, Hangman's Beautiful Daughter*, *Wee Tam & the Big Huge*, *U* and *Liquid Acrobat as Regards the Air*; The Grateful Dead; Gavin Lodge; The Ultimate Force of Evil; Liz Elliot; Gregg Hermetech; Allen Ginsberg; Tim Leary; Alexander Shulgin; Kevin Ayers and *Bananamour*; Jeff Dexter; Mr Natural; Andrew Kerr; John Michel; Breaking Convention; Michael Hollingshead; the *genius loci*; David Crosby and *If I Could Only Remember My Name*, my favourite album of all time; Aldous Huxley; Ronnie Sandison; Alan Watts; The Great Mystery; Casey Hardison; Andy Munro; Richard Kemp; C.J. Fish's *Electric Music for Mind and Body;* Stephen Gaskin; The Big Beat; Ramsey Campbell; AOS3; Martin Izat; the Doo-Dah man and my amazing parents, Pat & Derek Roberts, without whom I would not be possible!

Special thanks and a debt of gratitude to: Robert Dickins for his vision and enthusiasm in creating Psychedelic Press and for his faith in *Acid Drops*; Nikki Wyrd for her peerless proof reading skills and patience with my torture of the English language; Julian Vayne and Ben Sessa for being opposite ends of the same spectrum and blessing me with their Fore and After Words; and to the talented and visionary artist Ciaran Shaman who knew *exactly* what I wanted and worked tirelessly to create the cover art.

This book is dedicated to all those students and graduates
of Dr Hofmann's School for the Incurably Curious
and to Mandy, who knows

CONTENTS

I will lift up mine eyes unto the heavens

Garden of earthly delight

Where time delivers a handstand

And the colours are ever so bright

And I'll worship the seas and rivers,

Mountains, planes and skies

And I'll travel with time and tide

To sing you this advice…

– Tim Goulding

1

Foreword

by Ben Sessa

L et us, for a moment, consider those three little letters: L, S and D. Or perhaps, three more, say, D, M and T. Or even the peculiar, simultaneously scientific and druidic-sounding word, psilocybin. Until a few years ago these words were primarily something to do with the 1960s; an archaic throwback to a distant cultural revolution of which your father—or even your *grand*father—could have been part. But that is no longer the case. LSD, DMT, psilocybin (and their new cousins MDMA, 2C-B, 5-MeO-DMT and the rest) are suddenly very *now*.

A lot of swirling, multicoloured water has passed under the bridge since our ancestors' psychedelic culture exploded, burned, died down and then, from the general public's point of view, appeared to go almost entirely cold. Unless you were lucky enough to be hanging around Esalen, or were prepared to live on the edge of society in a Peace Convoy bus in Wiltshire, then since the early 1970s psychedelics were largely absent. Good, as far as I am concerned. A hiatus is exactly what was needed. The gap in societal interest in psychedelics has left space for a new way of looking at these wonderful chemicals; an opportunity for unbiased explorers to reflect without the vacuous distractions of contemporary fashion. The result, however, is that many of today's kids reaching out for understanding of the historical significance of the psychedelic experience are drug-geek, mouse-clicking introverts; hungry for digestible knowledge of their forefathers' exploits whilst concurrently trying to maintain coolness with their Facebooking peers. And who better to indulge their green gills with thought-provoking bewilderments that Mr. Andy Roberts: contemporary society's premier Thinking-Man's Hippie.

Whilst thoroughly modern, psychedelic culture is also unmistakably ancient. The 1960s, for its inspiration, drew heavily on scripts of the pagan and Eastern religions. But for the average 21st century Wi-Fi kid the 1960s are *so* last century, man. Which means the modern psychedelic culture has a history of its own that requires just as much explaining as the shamans of old. Embedded in myth and magic, psychedelia simply doesn't work without the drawl of armchair hippies misquoting at dawn, not knowing their Abbie Hoffman's from their Albert Hofmann's. It is a subject in dire need of journalistic accuracy. Enter Andy Roberts' *Acid Drops*.

Within the pages of his book you will find plenty of well-sourced data on all the standard psychedelic stories of old—and all the usual characters and heroes are here: from Leary to Laing to Hollingshead, Ginsberg, Grof and Jung. But under Roberts' beady, newspaper-reportage eye no mere myth is submissively accepted without distinctive examination. Andy is the man in the background, the fly agaric on the wall, breaking bread with the hippies of old but always prepared to see things his own way; asking with his quizzical frown, "Really? Was it *really* like that?". So the classic stories and dogmatic legends are left dangling tantalisingly—a literary device that allows the author and the reader to form their own opinions. If, by this process, heroes find themselves vilified, or villains rise to the fore as shining beacons of bohemian lava light, then so be it. Only through such a practice do we get anywhere near 'the truth'; if such a thing is ever possible in the history of psychedelics.

In highlighting his stubbornness it is clear from his writing that Andy Roberts is no dippy hippie. Nor, however, is he a straight-laced square with a distrust for pixies. Far from it; Andy is an anti-authoritarian, free-thinking individual who has happily nailed his colours to the weirdness mast without being lost in its sea of ethereal fluffiness. Here is a man who, when he mentions the pineal gland, does so in reference to what it actually *is*. Because despite what you hear on the podcasts of today's ayahuasca-dipped communities, the pineal is *not* a supra-dimensional portal to a world of entities modulated by DMT. It is, in fact, simply a part of the brain that modulates wakefulness in response to light via the hormone melatonin. And with that keen eye on the difference between myth and science, Roberts, to me at least—with my need for neurophysiological accuracy—is bang on the button. He draws on modern and ancient literature, augmented with illuminating self-hand accounts from interviews, fireside talks and, perhaps occasionally, from some of those passing entities. This is scrupulous journalism.

It is these organisational skills and gently sensitive approach that have made Roberts' a firm favourite at the *Breaking Convention* conference since its inception; exactly what is needed when it comes to shepherding around 800 psychedelic cats between visio-aural delights. *Breaking Convention* blends ancient with contemporary, and who better at the helm than Roberts? In *Acid Drops* he drags willing interviewees back to older, and perhaps better, times. He gives them the platform to waffle so the younger generation can judge for themselves what to believe and what to revitalise. And Roberts always crafts his process of analysis without a hint of patronisation. Whilst there is no hiding his fondness for the tepees and music of old he clearly loves *all* the generations of psychedelia, because psychedelia is about the here and now, as he states when reflecting on LSD's non-evidence based banning in 1966, which resonates cruelly with the grisly *Psychoactive Substances Bill* of 2016.

The Jeff Dexter interview is a trip historian's dream; dropping all the right names and all the right acid. Roberts places us at Dexter's sandy feet as we sit on the beaches of Ibiza with Soft Machine, or stand behind the turntables at the Roundhouse amongst the freaks of the time. Roberts gives us Liz Elliot, speaking candidly about her experiences in 1960s London, and on the run with Leary. Using his interview manner of inquisitive regard we lounge beside her in Algiers and Switzerland, surrounded by suitcases of acid, guns, CIA henchmen and hash oil motorbikes. Who wouldn't have wanted to be part of such things? Clearly Andy would have liked to be there, and his neck-craning curiosity and respect for these times keeps the reader in the Kasbah throughout.

The genre of Trip Lit/Psychedelic Fiction is thankfully rather sparse. If not can you imagine the sort of trip-report dross we would have to endure? Roberts showcases the best, in his interview with Ramsey Campbell, with horror, beauty and LSD in equal dreamy measures. But it is Roberts' own pieces of eerie fiction and poetry that stand out. With steely prose he carries us into his fantasies and reveals his vulnerability as much as the next Elfin explorer. And why not? His delusional, drug-addled, creatures are as valid as anyone's. I can see him now; barefoot in the 1970s, traipsing the corridors of alteredness, looking for his other shoe, babbling profundities into the pungent incense-air beneath peeling rock posters as he attempts—better than most—to describe in detail just what the fuck is going on, for us to voyeuristically appreciate in the misty morning gardens all wet with rain.

Who needs Haight-Ashbury when one has a panoramic view of the Huddersfield ICI factory? Andy takes us on beach walks searching for plastic ducks, on which to hang his coincidences. And with acid brother Graeme Hartley we go "into the dreamery, the shape-shifting scenery", amidst forest sculptures from that shaman David Kemp. Graeme sounds cool.

Any conversation with Roberts soon turns inevitably to music. And it seems we share at least four of our top ten best albums of all time—which must mean I am not such a nutter after all. Or perhaps I am; I couldn't care less which. His love of psychedelic music is the closest Andy ever gets to being a dealer. He positively pushes the stuff. On reading the *Acid Drops* review of the *Incredible String Band*, you will be going out (or more likely staying in with one's computer, alas) and buying their albums. This magical band come alive in his words. It is the sort of music that makes you yearn to be damp in Scotland or Wales. And if that ever happens, be sure to drop in on the Roberts' household for tea—of sorts.

Contemporary psychedelia is treading an uphill path; constantly striving to keep our minds open in this quagmire of pseudoscience—but not so wide that our brains fall out. Fundamentalist psychedelic soothsayers are everywhere, with their dogmatically held falsehoods. It is hard to move through the protoplasmic slime without tripping over their delusional machine elves. Yet Roberts, with his dry humour and eye for detail, can see for miles and miles where others are left struggling several bardos behind. This is a man who keeps his chakras clean and third eye well-watered. Although his subjects (UFOs, ESP, Tarot) are tricky things to discuss, he nevertheless bravely carries us to these places, being neither overly ironic nor sycophantically delusional; and always dropping us safely back down to ground in the wholesome goodness of Welsh mushroom gatherings, where police dig trenches for hippies to back-fill, and kettles of bubbling goodness light the Devil's skies.

But *Acid Drops*, for all its professionality, is not merely an unbiased commentary. Roberts is a believer; not necessarily in the erroneous mythologies themselves, but as a passionate devotee of the people behind the stories. A visionaries' visionary; the man on the sidelines with the microphone giving us a grandstand view of the freaks drifting by. With deep regard for the participants, he tells it like it is, or might be, or even isn't. He would make a great psychiatrist, in fact, having mastered the knack of nodding and smiling, respecting the warbling of his psychotic clients without either disagreeing or disbelieving, but rather being alongside, holding their hands as their trip progresses, and in doing so drawing more colour into all of our lives. Because it is from these naïve dreamers that ideas are born, which Roberts—like everyone else in this field—is clever enough to recognise. If we can't see past the end of our stethoscopes because of our materialistic approach to culture, we are missing a trick—not to mention the best parties. One just has to have enough nouse to know on what side one's cerebral cortex is buttered.

So, back to those three little letters, L, S, and D, and all the storming heaven they have created. It's a mind-feeled out there and I personally owe so much to Andy Roberts. When I first tentatively published in the doubting medical press he was the first to critically appraise my work in print, which inspired to me to continue my research of psychedelics. But then, Roberts has a habit of doing this. He helps people form their own opinions, put aside psychedelics' negative bias, and encourages crystallisation of one's thoughts into a narrative worth fighting for. Rather than simply telling them, Andy helps the reader to ask for themselves whether there is a magical universe or not. And in doing so, his influence has kept me looking at the skies—whether to see some real magic or simply prove to myself there is none, I cannot tell. But one way or the other I just have to keep looking. And this book is certainly a good place to start.

2

Introduction

'And my soul has been psychedelicised'

'Tell naught but what was seen by one man in a vale in Albion...', wrote Beat poet Allen Ginsberg in *Wales Visitation,* his 1967 poem written during an LSD trip in the Black Mountains of Wales. *Acid Drops* also draws from the LSD experience, and is my personal view of psychedelic culture in Albion's dreaming. It is intentionally neither an academic treatise nor a scientific analysis of LSD, as the oft dead hand of academia and the stark reductionism of science is antithetical to the exploration and celebration of the psychedelic experience.

In 2008 I published *Albion Dreaming* which detailed the social history of LSD in Britain. *Acid Drops*, however, is more personal, less formal. Through personal experiences, historical research, interviews with some of psychedelia's movers and shakers, some speculation and fantasy, I hope to give the reader a glimpse of the hidden history of the culture behind Albion's dreaming.

Before we go down the rabbit hole, please note that I am not advocating anyone breaks the law! To question it, certainly, but not to break it. The current psychedelic paradox is that although the psychedelic *experience* is not illegal, many of the substances used to access it are controlled by law, with draconian penalties for manufacture, supply and possession.

My psychedelic education began at the age of sixteen. I had devoured Leary's *Politics of Ecstasy* and puzzled over Hendrix's deceptively simple questions 'Are you experienced, have you ever been experienced?'. The only certain way to answer them was to take LSD. But how? The answer came in the form of hippie acid aphorism which whispered you shouldn't *try* to get LSD; if you were destined to take it, it would find you.

Acid found me at a rowdy party in 1972. In the thick of the evening I was offered two green microdots. Uncomprehending of the multiverses they could unlock I took one. Less than 30 minutes later, having felt nothing, I took the other. What could possibly go wrong?

Suddenly, for no discernible reason, I was punched in the face by someone with whom my relationship was antithetical. In that moment my tiny world exploded and my course in life irrevocably altered. As the high dosage LSD kicked in, the room and I disintegrated in a swirl of auditory and visual sensation. I was hurled into an intense psychedelic experience of the worse possible kind.

My next recollection was of being in the kitchen, trying to put my head inside the oven. Why, I had no idea. Those around me, ignorant of my situation, presumed I was trying to kill myself. I was a ten stone weakling but it took several people to restrain me as I struggled in terror. Then I was in the back garden, gulping the cold night air and fighting to prevent further restraint. I looked up and to my astonishment the heavens were filled with Ice Warriors, fictional characters from Michael Moorcock's Eternal Champion books but now real, multi-dimensional in appearance and beyond physical measurement. Their armour, weapons and spectral steeds were resplendent in rainbow hued glittering hoar-frost as they rode imperiously toward some cosmic destination. I was mesmerised with awe, transfixed by the simultaneous terror and beauty of the spectacle.

If my well-meaning but ignorant friends had known of my wonderment they might have let me be and my trip may have resolved into the more typical, and anticipated, 'everything is beautiful' first time LSD experience. It was not to be. The restraint, and my struggles, continued as the acid tsunami surged through my central nervous system, rearranging all in its wake.

The being known as Andy Roberts was gone. There was no 'I', no ego or personality, just a maelstrom of sensory information. Retrospectively I realised I was resisting my subconscious which the LSD was allowing to flood my conscious mind. My experience was of kaleidoscopic thought forms comprising my biographical and ancestral history, hopes and fears about my sexual, social and intellectual identity, existential terror and much more. All notion of time was gone, the past, present and future all existed *now*. An overpowering dread that I would die—or worse, might have already—rose and fell within me. At one point I was sure my parents and the police had arrived, and I was suffused with guilt and shame. Then suddenly all that was gone. Had it happened? Was it going to happen? And if so who to? Then, nothing.

Time, whatever that was, must have passed. I was now in the lounge again, with vague flashes of self-awareness. Although I sensed the party had long since finished I remained motionless, terrified of further restraint. The few who remained were crashed out on floor and furniture, eerily delineated by the neon glow of a streetlamp through the curtains.

Aeons of thought cascaded through me as awareness slowly seeped back. I became intensely conscious of the thrum of electricity in the bungalow's wiring and the watery babble of the plumbing. I looked at the sleeping party goers and sensed the *whoosh* of blood in their veins and the imagery of their dreams.

Then I saw them. Actually, I heard them first. Random *fzzts* and *zzzzzzips*, the staccato sounds of *things* falling to the floor. I looked up. Through the dense mandala-like atmosphere I saw the inverted glass bowl of the ceiling light shade was full of tiny iridescent *things* which were boiling over the brim, dropping to the ground, dropping on me.

I tore at my clothes, ripping my shirt off, and must have screamed because people woke and turned the light on which instantly banished the dripping evil. I was calmed and my clothes restored before the room was again plunged into gloom. I remained motionless, still very turned on and very tuned in. But tuned into what? The writhing *things,* I sensed they were maggots or maybe silverfish, continued to fall but not on me, now scuttling across the ceiling before dropping elsewhere in the room. The multiverse darkened and pulsed with growing portent, my awareness becoming gradually saturated with a very real but not corporeal 'presence'.

Knowledge, from somewhere outside of me, now manifested in my mind and through every cell of my body. The written word is an inadequate vehicle to describe the experience. It was, perhaps, the reverse of a religious revelation, in which I was 'told' that by taking LSD I had 'sinned' and I was now at the mercy of an entity representing the ultimate force of evil. This entity was timeless and way beyond any simplistic Christian notion of the Devil and more akin to a Lovecraftian entity, one of the Elder Gods I had been reading about.

Author Allen Holub gives a good approximation of the entity I experienced: 'By Elder Gods I mean the dark primal forces that reside deep within the sub-consciousness. They are the raw unnamed energies existing since the icy cold of the fabric of space emerged from naught. They pre-date the coming of space itself, and of time, of the aethers, although it can be said that they represent the process of formation itself.'

Crikey!

Once again my awareness was returned to a multiverse of pure information, this time all of it malevolent. I was 'told' my existence, my experience and perception of the world was completely false. Every material thing, every person, every situation, every relationship had been fabricated purely for 'their' entertainment and at the expense of my soul. The world and everything in it was revealed as a sham in which I was just a plaything. I was theirs now. Worse, in my ignorance I always had been. By dabbling with LSD I had sundered the veil and glimpsed the truth of what was *really* going on.

I was given a choice. In retrospect I believe this was my slowly returning ego putting up a defence, but I was far too high to grasp that glimmer of hope. I could remain in that room and be slowly consumed by those *things*, subsumed into evil, with my soul damned for eternity. Or I could go on, burdened with the revealed hollow sham of my existence, the caveat being that eventually I would be back in this situation to face my destiny. This was a choice? I was damned if I did, damned if I didn't.

I cried as I had never cried before.

I was back in the room. In the granular light of an impending dawn I looked at the sleeping partygoers. I now knew their true nature and as the horror of my revelation sunk in I fought the temptation to run screaming from the building. I used what reflective thought I could muster and chose the second option, snuck past the sleeping demons and walked home in the jingle jangle morning trying to make sense of the night's events. I was still so high when I reached the *cul de sac* where I lived with my parents, I had to sit in the fields until I could be certain which the right house was! Plucking up courage, I took the plunge and knocked. The door was opened by strangers. I *knew* they were my parents, but at that moment in time they were alien to me, clearly just another component of the cosmic illusion I was trapped in. Mumbling pleasantries I quickly headed to bed.

The reverberations of that archetypal bad trip echoed in my psyche for decades. For months afterwards I remained convinced my revelation and its implications were true. Paranoid and mistrustful of everyone, including myself, I did all I could to see if I could catch 'them' out, asking friends and family what must have seemed stupid questions about the known and the obvious. Had I explained my mental state to a psychiatrist I am sure they would have diagnosed some form of mental illness, but I had no intention of verbalising the experience to anyone, not least a psychiatrist. After all, they were part of the set up too!

That first trip was atypical of the psychedelic experience, but not uncommon. I offer it here as a cautionary tale of the potency of psychedelic drugs and the dangers of their cavalier use. Since then I have met others who have had similar profoundly negative psychedelic experiences. Some received psychiatric help, others turned to religion for comfort, meaning or certainty with which to re-vivify what they perceived as a tainted and futile existence. Many just stopped using acid altogether and kept the horror to themselves, finding deluded solace in the numb abstractions of drink or hard drugs.

Luckily, I wasn't religious, at least in the formal sense. Belief in a deity whose earthly representatives controlled its worshippers by fear and promises of salvation was patently ridiculous. Besides, their deity was powerless in comparison to the forces I had experienced and, like everything else, was probably just a front organisation for 'them'! I had no intention of using drink or drugs to wipe or repress the experience because I doubted they could. Instead, I took refuge in the lyrics and music of the Incredible String Band and Dr Strangely Strange, and the restorative power of nature. Following months of severe panic attacks and an all-pervading sense of existential terror, I made a decision. Bad trip and subsequent paranoia notwithstanding I reasoned that I'd chosen the psychedelic path of my own volition. And, if the psychedelic experience could be so profoundly horrific, then the opposite must also be true. I couldn't change what had happened; therefore I must go forward and break on through to the other side. And so I did.

Fast forward to 2016, when Britain is currently undergoing a psychedelic renaissance of an unprecedented magnitude. Barely a week passes without a positive story in the media about some aspect of psychedelic drug use, where psychedelic discussion groups and societies have emerged in major cities, and Britain has its own dedicated journal dealing with psychedelic culture. Most significantly, since 2011, Britain has hosted a biennial three day multi-disciplinary conference dealing with all aspects of psychedelic drugs and their culture. This revolutionary event, Breaking Convention, created by David Luke, Ben Sessa, Dave King, Cameron Adams and Anna Waldstein now provides a crucial focus for Britain's psychedelic community.

At the root of this renaissance and one of its primary drivers, is the dedication of a handful of people in the scientific/medical community who believe in the potential of LSD, MDMA and psilocybin etc. to heal. It might seem odd that drugs vilified for decades and still heavily controlled are now the subject of medical trials and positive reappraisal by the media. To explain why we must return briefly to the 1950s.

Between 1952 and the late 1960s, LSD was widely used by psychotherapists in Britain. Thousands of patients were treated for a broad range of psychiatric problems and there was great media excitement about what appeared to be the 20th century's wonder drug. Labour party politician Christopher Mayhew took the psychedelic drug mescaline live on BBC TV, fascinated by how it altered his perception of time, and how relaxed it made him feel. Heavyweight intellectual polymaths such as Aldous Huxley appeared on TV and radio extolling the virtues of LSD, psilocybin and mescaline, suggesting they were revolutionary tools for examining what it means to be human and alive in a world of unfathomable mystery. When asked what he thought of mescaline Huxley summed up the paradoxical nature of the psychedelic experience with, 'It is neither agreeable nor disagreeable. It just is.'

Despite the encouragement from both medical and academic establishments, legal use of LSD in Britain soon came to a halt. Lurid scare stories in the American media about LSD use among young people cast a long shadow over the drug's medical potential. But it was too late, the cat was out of the bag. Beatniks and the emerging hippie movement took to LSD as a consciousness expanding drug, and began to use it to examine their lives and their spirituality. In addition, although this aspect of psychedelic drug use is often played down by both its proponents and detractors, people were using it to have multi-dimensional *fun*! Bob Dylan was correct when he sang 'The times they are a-changing', as LSD users realised everything; the material world, consciousness, religion, consumerism and the personal, social and political games we all play, are not exactly as they appear. LSD showed that other ways of experiencing, of living, of being, were possible.

Harmless psychedelic fun was being had. But for staid and conservative Britain, the aftermath of WWII still rumbling in the nation's psyche, this was too much. Using drugs to help people medically was one thing, using them for enjoyment and awareness enhancement (never mind spiritual enquiry), was beyond the pale. The possibility LSD could undermine the consumerist Protestant ethic of birth-school-work-death was unconscionable and so, without recourse to any scientific or medical evidence, legislation against LSD was rushed through Parliament. Hansard, the official record of Parliament, reveals that the debates leading up to LSD being outlawed in October 1966 were rooted in prejudice and ignorance rather than reasoned and evidenced argument. As just one example, in June 1966 Lord St Just, offering no evidence, asserted, 'No drug has been produced which has caused greater trouble in this world than LSD'. St Just's political hyperbole epitomised Timothy Leary's statement that 'LSD is the drug with the most unusual emotional and psychological effects when compared to any other drug because just the idea of the drug is enough to cause terror among those who have never even taken it!'.

Quite!

Set against this political backdrop of ignorance and behind a smokescreen of nervous bad jokes from legislators, one of the most potent substances discovered was driven underground. This hysteria spread quickly, the prestigious *British Medical Journal* campaigned against the use of LSD in psychotherapy and that avenue of treatment ground to a halt. For several months Morning Glory seeds (which contain a chemical related to LSD), were banned, and removed from sale in garden centres. The British political and social Establishment, it seemed, were determined to deny the public access to a drug which had the power to change people's lives. This denial of cognitive liberty, the right of an individual to alter their consciousness in accordance with their will, is at the heart of the ongoing debate around psychedelic drugs.

Decades of prohibition and persecution of LSD and other psychedelics followed. Users of LSD and later, MDMA, became folk devils. Visible demonstrations of LSD and MDMA culture, such as the LSD driven Free Festival movement of the seventies and the MDMA fuelled raves of the eighties and nineties caused moral panic. With vigorous and disproportionate support from a hysterical media, the political Establishment did everything within their power to eradicate use of psychedelic drugs, and the cultures they spawned.

Evidence, both medical and political, is now emerging that the public have been lied to by governments about the perceived problems with psychedelic (and other) drugs. Take the so-called 'war on drugs' for example. Coined in America during the Nixon administration, this clichéd soundbite has been used worldwide by politicians and police to marginalise and persecute those who wish to make an informed decision about what substances they choose to put in their bodies. The phrase itself is meaningless, there can be no 'war on drugs', only on lifestyle choices, and this artificial conflict acts more as a form of social engineering than a meaningful attempt to protect people from harm.

Although still in widespread use the real motivation behind the 'war on drugs' was exposed in 1994 when former policy advisor to Richard Nixon, John Ehrlichman, revealed the political thinking behind the term:

> *We knew we couldn't make it illegal to be either against the war or black, but by getting the public to associate the hippies with marijuana and blacks with heroin, and then criminalizing both heavily, we could disrupt those communities. We could arrest their leaders, raid their homes, break up their meetings, and vilify them night after night on the evening news. Did we know we were lying about the drugs? Of course we did.*

The downward spiral of negativity about psychedelic drugs in Britain might have continued had it not been for the pioneering work of Dr Ben Sessa and colleagues, who are responsible for spearheading a major element of the psychedelic renaissance. In 2005, Sessa's 'Can psychedelics have a role in psychiatry again?', became the first paper about clinical psychedelic therapy published in the British medical press since the 1960s.

Sessa's paper acted as a rallying call, and other medical professionals with an interest in psychedelics quickly emerged. In 2009 as part of Robin Carhart-Harris's investigation of the possible uses of psilocybin, Sessa became the first person in over 30 years to be legally administered a psychedelic drug in Britain. Further medical trials in Britain have taken place with psilocybin, MDMA and LSD. Sessa, now a qualified MDMA therapist, hopes legal therapeutic use of some psychedelics may be licensed in Britain within the next decade.

If Sessa's dream becomes reality, he and his colleagues will have the potential to reduce the emotional suffering of an incalculable number of people, helping change the world for the better. Sessa and many of his colleagues also believe in the individual's right to legally and responsibly use LSD and other psychedelics for whatever purpose they choose. Sessa believes that the hippie counter-culture has failed to challenge the laws against psychedelic drugs using the cognitive liberty argument. Thus, he believes, the only successful route to achieve legislative change is by using the weight of successful evidence from medical trials as leverage to first bring about legal psychedelic therapies and then to work toward legalisation for personal use.

The Establishment-forged canard that all 'drugs are bad' was demolished in 2009 when scientific evidence clashed publically with political hypocrisy. David Nutt, the Chair of the government's Advisory Council on the Misuse of

Drugs was asked to resign after he claimed in a lecture that some drugs were less harmful than others. Nutt refused to resign and was summarily dismissed from his post. When the background to Nutt's claim was revealed a media furore ensued, revealing the fundamental ignorance inherent in political thinking about the effects of drugs on individuals and society.

In 2007, Nutt, drawing on the expertise of 14 experts with specialisms in all aspects of drug use, examined nine of the alleged 'harms' of 20 drugs. These potential harms included the physical, psychological and social consequences of drug taking and his study was the most detailed study of drug harms conducted in Britain. Nutt's evidence based conclusions were startling. Out of the 20 drugs examined alcohol was ranked as the most harmful, above heroin, whereas LSD was ranked 17th, MDMA 18th and psychedelic mushrooms 20th. Tobacco came in at 6th place.

Of course *all* drugs are harmful to some degree but Nutt's table of relative harms brought into question why drugs causing the most personal and social harms are legal to use, while those with no potential harm other than to the user are strictly controlled. It is difficult to believe, considering then Home Secretary Alan Johnson's weasel words of justification for his action, that Nutt was sacked for anything other than because his findings clashed with the prejudices of the government. Prejudices that clearly demonstrate that the government was not interested in basing law and policies about drugs on evidence.

Prior to his sacking, a telephone conversation between Nutt and Alan Johnson's predecessor, Jacqui Smith, epitomised the simplistic reasoning used by politicians to defend their refusal to base drug laws on evidence.

> **JS:** *You can't compare harms from a legal activity with an illegal one.*
> **DN:** *Why not?*
> **JS:** *Because one's illegal.*
> **DN:** *Why is it illegal?*
> **JS:** *Because it is harmful.*
> **DN:** *Don't we need to compare harms to determine if it should be illegal?*
> **JS:** *You can't compare harms from an illegal activity with a legal one.*

Lewis Carroll would have been proud! None of the psychedelic drugs examined in Nutt's study had legislation applied as a result of any studies of their benefits or harms. Indeed, Nutt was not suggesting that any drug is safe or that one drug should be chosen over another. He was doing his best, using the scientific method, to bring some much needed clarity to a subject mired in confusion and prejudice.

The punchline to the bad joke of Nutt's sacking for offering evidence-based facts about drug harms came in 2011 when Liberal Democrat politician Tom Brake asked David Cameron if he believed in evidence-based policies in relation to drugs. Cameron responded, 'That is a lovely idea'.

Bearing in mind the present government's belief that successful medical trials of LSD, MDMA and psilocybin might lead to an easing of legislation regarding personal use of psychedelics, must be balanced against the progressive tightening of drug laws. MDMA (Ecstasy), enjoyed with little harm by millions of Britons, became a Class A controlled drug in 1977. Cannabis (which has psychedelic qualities) was re-graded from Class C to B in 2009 and so called 'magic mushrooms', which had enjoyed a quasi-legal status prior to 2005, were then designated a Class A drug.

The political thinking behind these restrictions was clearly stated and amplified in the government's still current 2010 Drug Strategy document. The whole document is worth reading but one key sentence stands out as indicative of the government's position: 'This Government does not believe that liberalisation and legalisation are the answer'.

The cynical reader might wonder if the government is trying to outlaw the psychedelic state *per se* by criminalising all chemical substances used to access it. Is there an unspoken witch-hunt against the idea of getting high? If that is the case then any argument for the legal use of psychedelics must be based on the principle of cognitive liberty as much as on the medical model.

The considerable grass roots support for the cognitive liberty argument was boosted in 2015 when the European Convention on Human Rights released a report suggesting that drug taking should be a human right. In response, and somewhat predictably, a spokesman for the British government commented *'This Government has no intention of decriminalising or legalising drugs'*. We live in a world where several countries, including Portugal and Uruguay, have decriminalised psychedelic drugs and have seen no detrimental effect to individuals or society, quite the reverse in fact. In denying the right of individuals to take any consciousness altering substance it is possible we are, as a society, making a grave mistake.

No drug or alcohol prohibition has ever been successful. The evidence from the American prohibition of alcohol to the present day shows that attempts to restrict and criminalise the individual's right to choose what consciousness altering substances they wish has failed and continues to fail. If we are to act on the scientific evidence, rather than prejudice, and the informed choices made by millions of people each day there can only be one meaningful solution—the legal, taxed and regulated freedom to use all drugs, not just psychedelics. The only meaningful way of punishing people for drug taking would be for criminal or anti-social behaviours displayed as result of being under the influence of drugs, as is the case at present with alcohol.

As *Acid Drops* is such a personal view of Britain's psychedelic culture I'd like to underpin it with what the psychedelic experience means to me, although set against the often complex theories and philosophies espoused over the years by drug researchers and psychonauts, my beliefs might seem simple. My view is that psychedelic drugs are nonspecific sensory amplifiers and the content and quality of the psychedelic experience is determined by the set (state of mind, beliefs, fears etc.) and setting (physical comfort and location) of the individual multiplied by the dosage of the drug. Of course that's where simplicity ends as there are infinite combinations of those factors, and therein lies the conundrum for those who would tread the psychedelic path.

If I were to sum up in one word why I became a devotee of the psychedelic path, it would be *curiosity*. Most people who have used psychedelics tend to be extremely curious, driven by wanting to know more about themselves and the multiverse they find themselves inhabiting. Thus psychedelics become a tool of existential enquiry. Whereas drugs such as alcohol and heroin are anaesthetic, greatly reducing the intake of information at all somatic and psychological levels, psychedelic drugs such as LSD vastly increase the amount of information received. Once again simplicity ends and complexity begins.

The psychedelic experience taught me that *all* experiences, from thinking to blinking, from falling in love to filing for divorce and from landing on the Moon to rock pooling at the beach are amazing, multifaceted mysterious wonders. This Great Mystery we are all part of, the multiverse or whatever you choose to call it, is constantly revealing itself second by second and we should be as aware of this revelation as possible, by whatever means possible.

Of course it is quite possible to experience this mystery without the aid of psychedelic drugs, but the evidence suggests that they can play a crucial part in what Julian Vayne refers to as 'intensifying the normal' and examining what it really means to be human, alive, here and now. As such I believe the psychedelic experience is of incalculable meaning and value in all areas of our lives and at all adult ages. That said, writing about the psychedelic experience, trying to explain what it is actually like, is almost impossible and it can only really be understood through the interaction between the molecules that bring it about in the organism it is taken. Hopefully some of the essays and interviews in *Acid Drops* might offer a glimpse to the uninitiated and a wry smile of acknowledgement to those who responded to Hendrix's question.

There are thousands of books dealing with the psychedelic experience. Everyone will have their favourites depending on their own experiences. I believe there are just a handful of books which capture the profound and ineffable nature of the psychedelic experience. My favourite by far is Alan Watts' *The Joyous Cosmology*. The second is Aldous Huxley's account of his mescaline and LSD experiences in *The Doors of Perception: And Heaven and Hell*. The third is the much maligned Timothy Leary's *Politics of Ecstasy*. All those books are an intelligent and multi-layered exposition of the psychedelic experience and the potential it offers humanity. For an authentic account of someone who lived a truly psychedelic life, learning how to work with the potency of LSD I urge you to read Stephen Gaskin's *Amazing Dope Tales: Haight Street Flashbacks* (the original edition). A beatnik turned hippie in the acid filled crucible of San Francisco in the 1960s, Gaskin was skilled in guiding people through psychedelic experiences and enabling them to integrate their psychedelic thinking into daily life.

Gaskin is also worthy of mention because, as with Watts, Huxley and Leary, he realised the insights gleaned during the LSD experience could be translated into positive values and actions in everyday life. Through his psychedelic ministry Gaskin was responsible for individuals changing their lifestyles to healthier ways of living and better ways of relating with each other. Eventually realising he no longer needed psychedelic drugs, Gaskin and his tribe opened health food shops and eventually founded large communes based on the principles of sustainable living and non-violence. Gaskin is well worth reading about!

Taking Gaskin's principles further are schools of thought that believe the positive benefits of responsible psychedelic drug use, translated into psychedelic thinking and action, have the potential to impact on the future of life on earth. Scepticism of these claims should be balanced against the comments of innovative thinkers whose psychedelic experiences have led directly to discoveries that have massively enhanced life on earth.

Here are a few examples which are just the tip of the iceberg. It's no secret that the early days of the computer industry, an industry that revolutionised all aspects of live, were driven by a group of hippie tech geeks who believed in the merits of LSD to enhance thinking and solve problems. Anyone sceptical of this claim should read Professor John Markoff's book, *What the Dormouse Said: How the Sixties Counterculture Shaped the Personal Computer Industry*.

Founder of Apple Computers Steve Jobs said, "Taking LSD was a profound experience, one of the most important things in my life. LSD shows you that there's **another** side to the coin, and you can't remember it when it wears off, but you know it. It reinforced my sense of what was important—creating great things instead of making money, putting things back into the stream of history and of human consciousness as much as I could."

Maverick scientist Kary Mullis also used LSD as a problem solving tool in his development of the polymerase chain reaction (PCR), which helps copy a single segment of DNA into millions of identical copies. His work on PCR is regarded as one of the key scientific discoveries of the 20th century, for which he received the 1993 Nobel Prize for chemistry. The focused use of LSD enabled him to experience the bizarre sensation of sitting on a DNA molecule watching an enzyme called 'polymerase' float past, enabling his discovery. Mullis believed his use of LSD was 'certainly more important than any courses I took', and doubted he would have made his PCR discovery had he not used LSD as a creative tool.

Away from LSD's influence in the world of science, evidence suggests the psychedelic experience has played a significant part in raising awareness about the environment and personal health. The compassion and reverence for all forms of life often felt during a psychedelic experience led to an explosion of interest in vegetarianism, veganism and organic foods in the sixties and seventies, which continues to this day. The wide appeal of bodywork such as yoga, tai chi and other physical techniques that allow one to become aware of and maintain the body, is also rooted in hippie counter-culture. And to amplify Ben Sessa's belief that psychedelic drugs can be of psychotherapeutic use, the co-founder of Alcoholics Anonymous Bill Wilson believed that LSD could give alcoholics insight into their addiction and a way of freeing themselves, and it was once considered for use in AA. These examples are not to suggest that LSD bestows a miracle quality that can increase intelligence or compassion, rather that it appears to enhance those qualities, can increase creativity and may be able to assist 'thinking outside the box' of our limited consciousness.

I am not an LSD evangelist, far from it. Like all drugs, all activities of any kind, LSD use carries a risk. Miscalculations with set, setting and dosage, as my bad trip demonstrated can cause the experience to spiral out of control. People with mental health issues, children, and those with little self-awareness should not take psychedelic drugs. But as David Nutt has shown their *actual* harms are minimal and can be reduced further by careful knowledge and preparation.

Which brings me to my views on the practice of the psychedelic experience. There is no 'right' or 'wrong' way, but anyone who has used psychedelic drugs for any length of time will have formed their own ideas of how that strange territory should be navigated. Whether you follow the highly structured approach to psychedelic voyages as suggested by Tim Leary or Ken Kesey's more adventurous approach, if a few simple guidelines are followed the risks can be minimised and the experience enhanced. It might sound obvious but before undertaking any psychedelic experience you should be absolutely certain you want to do so. Don't be coerced or otherwise persuaded, the decision to play with your perception can only be yours. Careful attention should be paid to set and setting and all that entails. I won't dwell on this as there are many excellent books and internet resources that explore set and setting in detail, but their importance is ignored at your peril. Whenever possible try to factor into the experience encounters with the natural world, and music designed for the psychedelic state of mind. Know exactly what drug you are taking and if possible its potency. Listen to and have regard for what experienced psychonauts tell you. Even if they are old hippies. Especially if they are old hippies! Adjust your dosage to set and setting. By that I mean if you just fancy an enhanced wander round Kew Gardens or the British Museum a low dose is probably more appropriate than a heroic one. All these factors require careful balancing. A blasé approach can sometimes pay off but can also result in at best a waste of time and at worst an immersion in the kind of cosmic horror I witnessed on my first trip.

The psychonaut should have a humbleness of spirit and a flexibility of belief coupled with a willingness to 'go with the flow' yet be able to take decisive action to change the course of the experience if required. If taking psychedelics with others then everyone must accept responsibility for each other's well-being and be prepared to do whatever necessary to minimise problems and maximise the quality of the experience. If you are with someone having their first psychedelic experience it goes without saying they should be your responsibility and focus of attention at all times. Be prepared to experience everything, especially music, the natural world and other people in a phantasmagorical new way. It's also useful to have a keen and surreal sense of humour when dealing with psychedelics, to be able to laugh at yourself, your thoughts and beliefs and the cosmic absurdity of what Robin Williamson referred to as the '*sheer unspeakable strangeness of being here at all*'. In fact I'd go so far as to say that those with no sense of humour should be advised against taking psychedelic drugs!

Helpful advice can be gleaned from books, notably by Tim Leary, Robert Anton Wilson, Aldous Huxley, Alan Watts and other early psychedelic explorers. Their timeless advice can be augmented by contemporary writers on the psychedelic experience. Of these the most useful writings come from individuals involved in a metaparadigm known as 'Chaos Magick'. Forged in the 1970s by occultists who stripped away artifice and pretension from conventional magic, chaos magicians created a constantly evolving system of occult technologies which distilled magical practise to the manipulation of belief, combined with gnosis (unity with the underlying 'spirit' of the universe), to achieve a desired outcome. A skillset relevant to several walks of life, but especially when treading the flowery path of psychedelic exploration. Many of the founders of chaos magick employed psychedelic drugs in their rituals, some still do. And while many involved in chaos magick do not use psychedelic drugs, those who do are using them in innovative and experimental ways to enhance consciousness and effect change in themselves and the multiverse. The entire canon of literature produced by those involved with chaos magic has broader relevance for those who have answered Hendrix's question and want to explore further.

Intent is the final, often overlooked, but crucial element in preparing for a psychedelic experience. One of the founders of chaos magick, Dave Lee, offers these pertinent suggestions.

>...*I think it's a very good idea to go in with intentions, even if they're broad ones, and totally mystical. It doesn't have to be sorcery—you don't have to go, "Right! I'm gonna do this acid and do a spell to get myself a new job!" I think that'd actually be rather silly. But if you say, "Right, I'm gonna do some LSD and heal a particular aspect of myself, confront a particular demon and sort it out..." Under the right conditions of course—don't do this at home, kids! Your unconscious will give you all the experiences you require to lock into that intention. But of course you have to flow with the details. It's not a good idea to have preconceptions about the actual details of what will happen. You will be taken on a journey, and you'll find yourself coming out the other end of it with a good result. You can't force each stage of the journey, but you can put an overall intention in there. In fact, I would say that a lot of time, the problems people have with psychedelics are to do with the fact that they don't have any intention at all. That doesn't matter with low doses, recreational doses.*

*But when you take a high dose, a truly psychedelic dose,
if you don't have any intention whatsoever, you can get
locked into confusion until your psyche actually goes to
a deep enough, sometimes dark enough level to find an
intention. The intention might be as general as to have
a good time, it might be as general as to feel a taste of
oceanic bliss.*

There is, sadly, no emblem signifying the psychedelic egregore. If there were I believe it would be a variant on the ancient glyph of the eight-rayed star, consisting of eight projections, usually arrows, emanating from a central point. Originating in the iconography of Eastern religions it was popularised in the early 1960s in Michael Moorcock's Eternal Champion books and later co-opted by the founders of Chaos Magick.

Psychedelically I interpret the central dot as representing the psychonaut at the centre of their multiverse, with the projections signifying their enhanced and questing awareness. This glyph occurs at the end of each chapter in *Acid Drops*, its form enhanced with interlocking grains of ergot-infected Rye to reference LSD's origins. You never know, it might just catch on!

Psychedelic culture is constantly evolving. We can all play a part in its development and make a difference to how psychedelic drugs are perceived within society. Current legal psychedelics aside, the past 60 years has seen the almost total freedom to use psychedelics withdrawn until currently they are restricted to almost total prohibition. In the future, when you are asked 'What did you do to support the right for people to alter their consciousness by the psychedelic drug of their choice?' what will be your response?

There are several ways to make a difference. If you have the scientific or political skills to become involved in psychedelic research or political lobbying then do so. Lobbying for change in laws relating to psychedelic drugs is no different to lobbying for a change in any other law. Ask your MP what their views on the drug laws are, educate them about the scientific and medical evidence of their potential to heal psychological and emotional trauma, addictions and PTSD.

To sum up, *celebrate* the potential of psychedelic substances whenever you can. Celebrate psychedelic culture in all its forms. Celebrate your positive psychedelic experiences and bear witness to the changes they have made to your life and times. Testify!

Look around you. We are here, now. This is it. We live on a planet which, if we act sensibly, can sustain human life indefinitely. We can be individually and collectively happy with the common purpose of celebrating our awareness and our existence. We can seek ways of improving the human condition and reducing suffering for all living things. Of course this is all possible without the use of psychedelic drugs, but increasing scientific and anecdotal evidence suggests they may be able to help us toward that goal if used responsibly and with intent. American musician John Stewart sang, 'We are living in the heart of a dream in the promised land' . I believe that to be true and all we need to do is to experience, acknowledge and act on that simple fact.

I appreciate you buying and reading *Acid Drops*. I hope you enjoy it and at the very least it makes you think, if not act. If you have any comments or criticisms about the book please contact me at the email address below.

Happy Trails
Andy Roberts

meugher@gmail.com

March, 2016

3

Season of the Witch

1966 and the vilification of LSD in Britain

Certainly no drug has been produced which has caused greater trouble in this world than LSD.

– Lord St Just, 30th June 1966[1]

Prior to 1966 the British government's attitude toward LSD was largely one of ignorance. The Secret Intelligence Services had conducted experiments with the drug during the 1950s, and the MOD followed suit in the early 1960s. Little useful information about LSD was gleaned from these trials other than the drug was too unpredictable for use either as an interrogation tool or battlefield incapacitant, its effects differing according to the mind-set of the subject and the setting it was used in. Government files dealing with LSD for the period 1952-65 suggest that no research took place which would have any bearing on how or why LSD would be criminalised in 1966.

LSD was virtually unknown to the British public until 1966, after which it became a household name, with rarely a week passing without a press story about the drug. Yet until 1963 the few media stories referring to the drug were, without exception, positive, and referred to the use of LSD in a medical context. In 1960, one journalist even suggested that a cocktail of LSD and Methedrine would be used to "Curb the boss's tantrums"![2] At least 50 psychotherapists had begun to use LSD in their practice since the drug's arrival in Britain in late 1952, and a dedicated LSD therapy unit, under the auspices of Dr Ronald Sandison, existed at Powick hospital in Gloucestershire.

During a discussion in the House of Commons on 11th December 1958 the Secretary for State for the Home Department was asked if he was aware of the properties of LSD and other drugs and whether he proposed to bring them under the Dangerous Drugs Act (DDA). R.A. Butler's response was that there was no evidence LSD was addiction forming and thus it was not appropriate to add it under the DDA. Butler also raised his concern that to place LSD under law would only serve to draw attention to it and stimulate demand.[3]

Until 1966 LSD was listed as a poison under Part 1 of the Poisons List and could only be sold on prescription. This however did not restrict its use to psychotherapy if you had a friendly doctor, and author Michael Moorcock recalls being able to obtain LSD this way for recreational use in 1956.[4] More widespread black market distribution and use of the drug in Britain was well underway as early as 1959, and throughout the early 1960s a small but rapidly developing British LSD subculture became established in London.

Intimation of what was to come started in 1963 when a steady trickle of lurid LSD stories in American newspaper and magazines began to reach Britain, and *The Times* reported that a London doctor had drowned while under the influence of LSD.[5] Wider global medical and political reservations were raised in 1964 when the World Health Committee's Expert Committee on Addiction Producing Drugs expressed concern about the increasing recreational use of LSD.

This disquiet may have prompted the brief House of Commons debate on LSD and other hallucinogens in May 1964 when Mr George Thomas stated in the House of Commons that there was "no evidence at present of misuse of these substances, but a close watch was being kept on the situation".[6]

As yet no-one in Britain had been arrested or charged with any offence connected with Albert Hoffman's potent discovery, and the early 1960s was a halcyon period for the British LSD subculture. It was a time when good quality LSD could easily be obtained and appreciated by those who wanted to experiment, without fear of legal repercussion or social opprobrium. LSD was being used recreationally for a variety of purposes, from experiencing the sheer synaesthesic joy of the psychedelic experience, to deeper explorations of the human psyche and the spiritual realms, all of which seemed accessible and limitless when under the influence of this enigmatic drug.

This situation prevailed until 1966 when, suddenly, it radically changed. By October that year a swarm of political, media and social forces, unwittingly aided by the folly of ingenuous elements within the LSD sub-culture, had conspired to demonise LSD, with the result that the drug was made illegal, outlawed for personal use and disapproved of as a psychotherapeutic aid.

Just how that situation came about is difficult to answer. No government file exists to explain the reasoning by which LSD was made illegal. Therefore the drug's vilification and its path from obscurity to illegality must be traced through contemporary media, and such official documents that are available. It is also necessary to posit the existence and influence of 'The Establishment', a term coined in 1955 by British journalist Henry Fairlie to refer to a dominant group or elite that holds power or authority in a nation. "By the 'Establishment', I do not only mean the centres of official power—though they are certainly part of it—but rather the whole matrix of official and social relations within which power is exercised. The exercise of power in Britain (more specifically, in England) cannot be understood unless it is recognised that it is exercised socially."[7]

The cumulative evidence indicates that it was the British Establishment (leading politicians, senior civil servants, police chiefs, governors of the BBC, media moguls and journalists) who exerted influence in order to create a political and social climate in which LSD could be swiftly legislated against in 1966.

By the autumn of 1965 Timothy Leary's emissary to Britain, Michael Hollingshead, had established his World Psychedelic Centre (WPC) in London's Pont Street. The flat was a focus of LSD use and sale, visited by the movers and shakers of London's psychedelic scene as well as pop stars who were flirting with LSD including Paul McCartney, Donovan and Julie Felix. On 25th January 1966, the police began their assault on London's psychedelic culture and raided the WPC. Any hopes they had of finding a psychedelic session in progress or a huge quantity of LSD waiting to be distributed were dashed, but they did arrest Hollingshead for possession of heroin, morphine and cannabis.[8]

Police action in early 1966 was much too late to prevent the spread of serious recreational LSD use. The drug was now so embedded in some elements of society that references to it were appearing in pop songs. The Rolling Stones' 10th British single, *19th Nervous Breakdown*, released on 4th February, 1966 was a song about an ex-girlfriend featuring the words, "On our first trip I tried so hard to rearrange your mind". To those in the know the meaning of the lyric was obvious but, unlike later records which referred directly to the psychedelic experience, it evaded the Establishment's attentions.

On 22nd February the police struck again and were successful. Flying Squad officers stopped Russell Page in Covent Garden and found him in possession of four LSD laced sugar cubes. Page was dealing, buying the cubes for £1 and selling for £1.50. He told the police his supplier was poet John Esam who lived in South Kensington. There, they found Esam and Frederick Klein hiding a tin containing LSD. All were charged with conspiring to distribute LSD.[9]

The media too now had LSD firmly in its sights. In mid-March, *London Life*, the quintessential swinging London magazine, heavily trailed its forthcoming LSD expose in garish half page newspaper advertisements and a TV campaign featuring cheap psychedelic visual effects, and a voice-over intoning: "LSD—the drug that could turn on London. Read the exclusive story in next week's London Life". The editor had secured an exclusive interview with Desmond O'Brien, Hollingshead's WPC co-founder. Both men saw this as their golden opportunity to expound their LSD philosophy to a wider audience. But they were naïve and failed to understand that the press, no doubt emboldened by lurid American media LSD stories, now wanted sensationalism, not philosophy.

The *London Life* interview was published on 19th March. "The Drug That Could Become A Social Peril", opened with O'Brien rather unwisely introducing himself as "Mr LSD" and boasting he and his colleagues could take control of London and the country in under eight hours by putting LSD in the water system; "…10 grams introduced into the water supplies at Buckingham Palace, Whitehall and other key centres in the country would enable us to perform a *coup d'etat* in Britain." Elsewhere in the piece "a leading psychiatrist agreed" that LSD could be a weapon in the hands of anarchists.

O'Brien's attempts to describe the positive effects of LSD use, its potential for causing individuals to change, and the WPC's philosophy, were all subsumed by this threat of psychedelic terrorism and *London Life's* accounts of LSD users imagining themselves to be Robin Hood in Sherwood Forest. O'Brien's comments possibly did more damage to the reputation of LSD than many of the subsequent media assassinations. The editorial helped to further taint the drug's reputation: "In these days of instant trends there is a very real danger of this dangerous drug spreading, as purple hearts did, among wider sections of the population. Who knows what moral lethargy could result?"[10]

Other publications had clearly been biding their time and gathering their own evidence. On the day following the *London Life* expose, the *News of the World* and the *People* entered the debate. *The People* had infiltrated Hollingshead's WPC and, far from finding it a peaceful and purposeful acid ashram for the transformation of minds, portrayed it as a degrading centre of chaotic drug use with, "...hypodermic syringes, empty drug ampoules and a variety of pills" scattered around the floor.[11]

The News of the World's Charles Sandell claimed liaison with the police and noted that Scotland Yard's Drug Squad had been compiling a dossier on LSD use in West London. An unnamed detective was quoted as saying LSD, "... presents a much bigger threat than marijuana and purple hearts", although just what this threat was remained unclear. Sandell also indicated that Home Secretary Roy Jenkins was going to bring the drug under "strict control", although as yet there had been no indication of this resolve in either the press or in parliament. It is hard to avoid the conclusion that in the first half of 1966 there was considerable behind closed doors communication, if not actually collusion, between the press, police and politicians with the intention of undermining LSD and the subculture that was using it, to prepare the way for draconian legislation. The Establishment appeared to be at work.

In an attempt to trace where the supply of recreational LSD was coming from, Sandell contacted Sandoz, the Swiss chemical manufacturer who supplied the British psychotherapists with the drug. A spokesman confirmed that although they had tight controls of their product he believed "there are unofficial supplies coming into Britain."[12]

What Sandoz thought was, by now, immaterial. As yet, no underground British LSD laboratories existed, but substantial quantities of the drug was now coming into Britain by post and by couriers. LSD could be bought easily in London at clubs, coffee bars and from drug dealers. Mainly available on sugar cubes, the drug also came on blotting paper and a powerful dose of around 200μg could be bought for between £1.50–£5.00.

Concerns that LSD use could be promulgated via the medium of pop music arose in late March when the media alerted the public to the B side of The Pretty Things single, Baby I'm Your Man, called LSD. The Pharmaceutical Society commented they were "hoping this kind of thing would not happen. We are actually very much opposed to the idea of publicising this drug, which we consider is one of the most dangerous and frightening to date. It is wrong that teenagers should go to the extent of singing about LSD." Once again the negative aspects of LSD were being stressed, by elements of the Establishment with no clear justification as to why.

Phil May, the song's co-writer, responded: "The words have a double meaning and if you take them to mean pounds, shillings and pence, then it's all right. If you understand them to mean this drug which everyone seems to be talking about these days, then you obviously know about it anyway we have done no harm to anyone."[13]

The lyrics were rudimentary, and ambiguous, opening with "Everybody's talking, about my LSD", with a repeated chorus of "Yes I need my LSD". May's ambiguity aside, a glance at a YouTube performance of the song leaves one in no doubt that it is the drug he is singing about. Pressed by the media for a statement a Home Office spokesman opined, "We cannot comment on the implications of it at this stage, but we are keeping ourselves informed of its progress." A few days later the Home Office clarified its position. "Following a report in the Evening Standard on Wednesday we have contacted Philips Records and they are sending us a copy of the words."[14]

Although it had not yet been made public, increasing governmental concern about LSD was evidenced when the Home Secretary, Roy Jenkins, asked all suppliers of Morning Glory seeds to suspend sales while tests were carried out to determine whether the lysergic content (the active constituent of LSD) of the seeds could be dangerous. Seeds were removed from sale in shops and garden centres and much was made of an Easter greetings card containing a packet of Morning Glory seeds. "More than 100 salesmen employed by Hallmark Cards" were despatched to tour shops and remove the cards from display. The ban was lifted on 21st June but the press furore and the government's hysterical reaction only added to public fears about LSD.[15]

Left wing journalist William Connor, writing as Cassandra in the *Daily Mirror* was one of the first heavyweight journalists to attempt serious analysis of LSD and what its impact might be in Britain. Connor had clearly read extensively about the drug and listened to what pundits such as Timothy Leary had to say about its potential for transforming consciousness. Nevertheless his interpretation of LSD's effects was angled toward the negative. "The mind, not the body, is the victim…The person under the influence of LSD becomes withdrawn and will crouch or huddle on the floor staring at any commonplace object like a chair, an electric lamp or the pattern of a carpet, and perceives in their shape and design a triumph of exquisite achievement."

Connor went on to suggest that "… murders and suicides and acts of total recklessness, regardless of the consequences, have occurred". He also suggested that a complete change of personality, for the worse, was an automatic consequence of taking the drug and that LSD users saw "ordinary life" as "like death (and) normality is unendurable".

But Connor also caught a glimpse of the potential and far reaching changes

LSD could cause when he quoted Leary, "present social establishments had better be prepared for the change. Man is about to make use of that fabulous electrical network he carries round in his skull. Our favourite concepts are standing in the way of a floodtide, two billion years building up. Head for the hills…". Leary—and by extension the increasing number of young acid heads—and Connor's views were diametrically opposed, and in his closing comments on LSD Connor put the seal of doom on LSD with "They don't mention the epilepsy, the convulsions, the lunacy and the final extinction that can be released within the sweetness of a lump of sugar". Connor presented no evidence to substantiate any of his assertions.[16]

He didn't need to, because April 1966 also saw the publication of several more LSD 'scare' stories from America. In one, a five year old girl was said to have accidentally eaten an LSD soaked sugar cube, and in another a man claimed he had been on LSD when he committed a murder. These and other similar stories made national headlines which, coming on the tail of the British press exposes, only added to the rapidly forming popular opinion that LSD was a dangerous drug that would forever change the lives of the nation's children.

These media exposés and minor panics all influenced the public perception of LSD. A once obscure drug now enjoyed notoriety. World War Two had only ended 20 years earlier, and Britain had successfully re-built its economy and society. The future looked bright economically and socially, and the last thing Britain's average family unit wanted was a drug influencing their children to turn on, tune in and drop out, as Tim Leary invited. And while the media stories might have turned public opinion against the drug, they had also alerted thousands of young people to an experience and a culture they now desperately wanted to be part of.

On 15th April, after considerable deliberation and sensing their reputation was at stake, Sandoz announced that due to "unforeseen public reaction" they had decided to stop selling the drug.[17]

The People ran another exposé in April when it gatecrashed an LSD party at London socialite Christopher Gibb's Cheyne Walk flat. The party, filmed for the BBC's 24 Hours programme, was described as being a bacchanalian orgy, "men danced with men —women danced with women", "a mass of male and female forms lying on the floor…. Many of them were embracing". The implication that LSD caused immoral behaviour was clear and if some of the alleged quotes—"I'm high on LSD. I'm a baby again"—were genuine, once again the LSD users had not done themselves any favours. In the eyes of the public this could well have represented the beginning of the "moral lethargy" which the *London Life* editorial predicted.[18]

Police action continued against this backdrop of media panic about LSD and Britain saw its first successful LSD related prosecution in late April. Roger Lewis received a conditional discharge for possessing 13 sugar cubes containing LSD, and a £25 fine for aiding and abetting the sale of LSD. Interestingly, although probably disingenuously, Lewis blamed the influence of the *London Life* article for getting him interested in the drug.[19]

In the House of Commons on 11th May the Joint Under-Secretary of State, Lord Stonham, was queried whether LSD was to be brought under the Dangerous Drugs Act. Stonham's answer was that it could not be, as any additions to the Act were contingent on the decision of the United Nations Narcotics Commission. Interestingly in light of the growing media calls for LSD to be banned, Stonham commented "we have no evidence ... to suggest the matter has got out of hand, whatever may have been suggested in some press reports. We are watching the position very closely..."[20]

This lack of any evidence that LSD was harmful had already been raised in May when, at Bow Street Magistrate's Court, John Esam and his co-accused were committed for trial at the Central Criminal Court. Mr John Ryman, for the prosecution, made it clear that the government were quite ignorant of LSD. Addressing the magistrate he noted, "We are dealing with the use of a type of drug not considered by the courts to any great extent."[21]

Other representatives of the Establishment lent their weight to the slowly mounting campaign against LSD. The influential British Medical Journal (BMJ) ran an editorial calling for LSD to be outlawed, citing cases where users had developed prepsychotic states or definite psychotic attacks after taking LSD as being "enough to warrant the proscription of so dangerous a drug".[22] Subsequent editions of the BMJ published letters from psychotherapists using LSD to successfully treat psychiatric patients, which criticised the editorial, but the BMJ's point had been made. It was taken seriously by the medical establishment and used in parliamentary debates as evidence that LSD was dangerous.

The subject of LSD was raised again in the Lords on 30th June when, in the context of a broader discussion on drug misuse, Lord St Just made the astonishing statement, that; "Certainly no drug has been produced which has caused greater trouble in this world than LSD". This was, it should be remembered, June 1966 when apart from handful of media stories the world knew very little indeed about LSD. Lord Stonham appeared to contradict his colleague by stating, "There is no reliable information about the extent of its use in the United Kingdom", noting that the Home Secretary was considering whether to bring LSD under the control of the Drugs (Prevention) Act

(1964) or the Dangerous Drugs Act (1965).[23] This exchange, the equally contradictory debate in the pages of the BMJ, and the stream of sensational press articles underline the fact that opinion and not evidence appeared to be driving LSD's journey toward legislation.

On 21st July the Home Secretary laid before Parliament a draft Order which, when approved by the Houses of Commons and Lords, would bring LSD under the Drugs (Prevention) Act (1964) in the form of the Drugs (Prevention of Misuse) Act 1964 Modification Order, 1966. The Order was approved in the Lords on 4th August amidst a discussion about the imagined effects of LSD. The general consensus was the LSD was a drug of illusion and hallucination, taken by people who wanted to forget their circumstances. Reference was made to dubious media stories about people re-living their births or wanting to fly. Lord Stonham commented, to much laughter, "LSD is not the only substance that can create that illusion: I have known people who thought they could fly on four pints of bitter." The Order was approved a day later in the Commons, once again in the context of a discussion that mixed half facts with full fictions about LSD's effects and usage. LSD's fate was now sealed and the press moved in to deliver the final blows.[24]

On 8th September, the eve of LSD being banned, London's *Evening Standard* ran a feature titled *To LSD and Back Again*. The rather weak pun was probably lost on most of its readers. Journalist Jonathan Aitken, later to be a disgraced Conservative Member of Parliament, took 200µg of LSD and recorded what he experienced. Aitken did not take well to the drug and after a period of heightened awareness, colour intensification and other usual symptoms of the onset of a dose of LSD, his subconscious threw up images of war and bloodshed. He had previously covered the conflict in Vietnam and Biafra, so this was unsurprising and shows Aitken's ignorance of what LSD was likely to do. He did acknowledge the LSD had given him insight into himself and doubts about his future, but the whole experience was communicated as being primarily negative. Leading phrases from his trip were quoted in the *Evening Standard*, notably "Get the message across that no one must ever use this drug again... it's terrifying what I'm seeing... this drug needs police, the Home Office and a dictator to stamp it out."[25]

October's British edition of *Reader's Digest* (on sale in September), the conservative populist magazine, published a damning swansong to the drug's impending criminalisation. Sweeping and unsubstantiated statements such as "LSD often gives people a powerful urge to jump out of a window, perhaps under the impression they are snowflakes or birds", along with references to incidents in which people were alleged to have murdered or committed suicide under the influence of LSD formed the bulk of the article. Although some of the drug's effects considered positive by users were mentioned, they were re-framed in a negative context. With a British circulation in 1966 of 1,350,000, and a significantly larger readership, *Reader's Digest's* pejorative and uninformed opinion of LSD would have influenced many people to form opinions about the drug as it passed from quasi-legal status to full illegality.[26]

On 9th September 1966 LSD became illegal in Britain. Manufacture, distribution and possession of the drug was now punishable by fines and imprisonment. The opinions of LSD psychotherapists who were achieving success with their patients were not sought. The Establishment's hounding of LSD eventually led to the cessation of legal LSD psychotherapy in Britain in 1967. Yet legislation did not deter those people who believed in LSD as an agent of personal and social change from using the drug. Its new status merely made the process of acquisition riskier and more complicated, and affected supply and quality. The Establishment's unspoken fears about how LSD could affect individuals and society were borne out in the years following 1966 when, despite the draconian legal strictures on manufacture, distribution and possession, an underground LSD subculture arose in Britain. This informal subculture, through its network of squats, communes, events and communications formed the basis of the 1970s Free Festival movement. This LSD fuelled culture was also targeted by the Establishment and persecuted throughout the 1970s, resulting in the smashing of the Operation Julie LSD manufacture and distribution network and the eventual outlawing of the free festivals.

Whether the burgeoning psychedelic community could have prevented or minimised LSD's fate, had it been more organised or coherent, is unlikely. It was inevitable that LSD would be criminalised. Contemporary society legislates against all drugs which affect consciousness. But the manner and haste with which LSD was brought within the law in 1966 indicates how much the drug, with its potential to radically change consciousness, was feared by the Establishment. Opinions, and subsequently laws, were formed without recourse to fact or due consideration of the rights of the individual to alter consciousness in accordance with choice. An air of mystery will forever attend the Establishment's attitude to LSD in 1966, perhaps best summed up in the words of William Braden, journalist and author of *The Private Sea: LSD and the Search for God* who, in his essay on LSD and the press commented, "You can't reason people out of an opinion they did not arrive at by reason to begin with".

4

Two Days After

About seven months after my first, catastrophic LSD trip, I decided to try it again, on the reasoning that if it could be so devastatingly mind-melting then the opposite must also be true. I had by then met Lyndsay who, for the next few years, was to become my acid mentor and this was my first trip with him and another friend and psychonaut, Andy Holroyd. This short, stream of consciousness piece was written two days after the event.

May 1973:

I remember the music with no impression that I remembered and liked, a badger leading us through the fields to hug trees who love us with their breathing, watching the lites in the valley and realising how stupid it was that the lites lit the pollution up for us to see and realise its stupidity. The sign with Pink Floyd written on it dropped by the Intergalactic Drug Squad to freak and puzzle us. Houses with lites on—who could be up at that time of night but people tripping? Raw toast and broken biscuits of which life is one long broken biscuit and I couldn't find the one I liked until the morning. An overcast dawn that I had waited to see that didn't matter when it arrived. My pineal gland being opened to the white lite by an earth creature with earth force who could crush my head with his power that no wizard could equal 'til now and only if he tries and he will because it's a path of many goals and he might find his source through it. And walking home through GREEN fields—om-ing at the grave yard with little response from the dead who were tripped out on another plane above even the OM. The grass running across the field and each noise separate until he looked into the mirror and realised his eyeballs were oh so huge and wondering what mother would say and she wouldn't understand it was good.

5

Queen of Hearts:

Liz, Leary, and LSD

The history of psychedelia, particularly the British experience, has been almost totally written by men. Of the women involved, especially those who were in the thick of it, little has been written either by or about them. A notable exception is Liz Elliot, former partner of Brian Barritt, who was a friend and associate of Tim Leary and author of *Whisper: A Psychedelic Time Script,* and *The Road of Excess.* The full story of Liz's remarkable life will hopefully be revealed in her autobiography.

Among many other exploits and adventures, Liz hung out with the Liverpool Poets, was an early sixties London Beat Girl living in squats, explored heroin and the seamy side of London's drug underworld, and counted the likes of Alex Trocchi and Lemmy among her friends. In Edinburgh she mixed with the emerging strange-folk scene that included Robin Williamson, Mike Heron, Licorice McKechnie, Bert Jansch and Anne Briggs, being first turned on to LSD when Robin Williamson decided she was 'ready'.

With Brian Barritt, one of the first recreational users of LSD, she travelled to Algeria to meet Timothy Leary, before moving to Switzerland to live within Leary's inner circle, where she and Tim fell in love. Afterwards Liz and Brian lived in Amsterdam where they dealt large quantities of psychedelics and other drugs. Also, she knew Michael Hollingshead, had adventures with the Hog Farm, the Brotherhood of Eternal Love, met Burroughs and a kaleidoscope of other psychedelic luminaries. Liz's story, here focussed on her time spent in Leary's orbit, is above all else a story of a life well lived and exudes a humanity not often found in other reminiscences from the psychedelic heyday.

Andy Roberts: *When did you first take LSD, Liz?*

Liz Elliot: In 1965. I knew the Incredible String Band, when I lived in Edinburgh, and they gave me my first acid, through a guy called Vern. Me and my future husband went up to Vern's and he said the Incredible String Band had decided we were 'ready', and he gave us this white powder to lick off a record sleeve and told us to go out and enjoy ourselves, cos it was still legal then. Vern lived in a flat that Clive Palmer, and before him, Spike Hawkins used to live in.

What did you think of the experience?

I thought I was in heaven. Before I first took it I'd only ever had marijuana or heroin or speed and I thought it would be a bit like that. Me and Tam, my first husband, went out and raved around Edinburgh, it was the most amazing thing. I walked along going 'I'm in heaven, this is heaven!' My mind was completely blown! I was just *so* happy to find something *so* wonderful! From being a sort of underground beatnik I felt justified that things had to change and that straight society was not something I wanted to be part of but before I felt a bit guilty about not being part of straight society.

Liz lived in Edinburgh for about six years before moving back to London and living in squats where she eventually got together with Brian Barritt. He was an early adopter of LSD and one of the first few recreational users of the drug in Britain in the early sixties. Barritt spent four years in prison after being caught smuggling four pounds of hash through customs. He was released in 1969, with plans to publish his legendary psychedelic book, Whisper.

How did you and Brian get together, and who had the idea to get in touch with Tim Leary?

I'd met him years before, through the heroin scene, but we didn't really know each other. Brian had just been released from prison and I met him at a squat party—he helped me find my son's scooter. We went for a coffee and that's how I met Brian again. One night when he was staying with me a friend came running in saying 'Tim Leary's escaped from jail and he's with the Black Panthers in Algeria'. So I said, 'Let's go, Brian, come on!'.

In January 1970, Tim Leary was sentenced to ten years in prison for possession of a tiny quantity of marijuana in 1968, later increased to twenty years for a 1965 offence. Following a daring escape in September 1970, planned by the notorious political group the Weather Underground, Leary fled the US and was offered a kind of sanctuary in Algeria by militant US Black Panther leader Eldridge Cleaver.

So it was your *decision, not Brian's, to seek Leary out?*

Yeah, because I knew Brian had taken his wife Paula to India and I was fascinated by this because I wanted to travel, but I needed someone to go with. I'd been pestering Brian to take me to India and this was a reason to make him take me somewhere. Brian told Dave Ball, who was helping Brian publish *Whisper*, and Dave said well you could maybe get Tim Leary to write a Foreword. So now we had a reason to go and I remember saying to all my friends 'you can have whatever you want from my flat!'.

How did you get to Algeria?

We hitchhiked, which was an adventure in itself. Brian and I set off with a duffel bag each over our shoulders with the plan being we would go for three weeks.

What happened when you got to Algeria?

Well, it took us three weeks just to get to Tim because the Black Panthers

were blocking us getting through. We got there on Christmas Eve 1970 and
it was pouring down with rain. I had no presents whatsoever for Davie, my
son, so I pretended Christmas Day was the day after Christmas Day so I had
time to go out into the Casbah to find some toys!

Where did you stay while you were trying to get in touch with Leary?

We only had my dole money so we were staying in the cheapest hotels in the
Casbah, they had no heating. In the end the Black Panthers let us contact Tim.
I was doing the phoning because I spoke quite well and I told the Panthers I
was from the Pan-American Embassy and so the Panthers finally let me speak
to Tim. I said 'we're from England and we've come to see you because we
want you to write a Foreword for this book, *Whisper'*.

What was your first meeting with Tim like?

He invited us up to the place he was staying, where Elridge Cleaver virtually
had him in prison with someone watching him all the time. Tim and Rosemary
were very isolated at the time, they really had nobody so we got on really well
with them and they were pleased to have us there. We had dinner with him
and Rosemary, and he gave us a matchbox full of acid! That was Orange
Sunshine. We ended up staying there for a year!

What was that year like? What did you do?

Took acid, in the most incredible surroundings. Tim and Rosemary moved
out of the place at Rue Lafayette and into a beachside hotel at Madrag. We
used to go round there for breakfast more often than not and often for dinner
as we had fuck all money. We spent a lot of time talking and I remember we
got into some very deep discussions. The hotel had paper table cloths and
they used to get covered in designs and diagrams and then at the end of the
conversation Tim would neatly fold the table cloth up and send it off to Mike
Horovitz at his archive in San Francisco.

Leary clearly had the sense to archive as much as he could.

Yes, because he'd already ended up in prison and by carefully packaging and sending everything he could to the archives he knew he could keep it out of the hands of the Feds.

Where was Leary's acid coming from at this time?

It was almost certainly brought over by Dennis Martino, one of the guys from the Brotherhood of Eternal Love and his partner Robin. Two other guys from the Brotherhood brought some acid over to us when we were in Switzerland, hidden in the speakers of a portable cassette player.

What was it like taking acid with Leary?

Well, I didn't quite understand just how famous he was. I didn't know he'd written so many books, for a start, other than *The Politics of Ecstasy*. I just thought he was as famous as some of the other people, like Trocchi, that I knew. So taking acid with Tim was just like taking acid with a mate! Which I think he appreciated because we weren't there for the money or the fame, just because he was a good guy.

Was he at that time expanding on his ideas about how acid should be spread widely throughout society?

Not at all. He was a bit confused—as confused as Tim ever got—at the time. Cleaver was making him carry a loaded gun—though he secretly removed the bullets—threatening to grass him up to the Algerian government and have him thrown out of the country and back to Folsom prison. So Tim had all that paranoia and Rosemary was paranoid as hell, so that didn't help. Cleaver was trying to get him to use 'shoot to kill' as a motto and Tim was changing it to 'aim for life', and all this was being reported in the American press.

A total clash of ideologies then?

Yeah. They thought, well, we're both underground figures, we're both anti-establishment, it'll work, but you couldn't have met two more different people!

How would you describe Tim's personality as you saw it then?

You know that record My Sweet Lord by George Harrison? We listened to that on an old radio while we were in Algeria, coming through the static, when we were tripping, and I heavily associate that record with Tim. He had a charisma that I'd never come across before and I thought he was absolutely amazing. He didn't really expound any theories as such but over those dinner conversations we'd go into all kinds of things. He never laid it on you what you should believe or anything, but he always had loads of really interesting information of all kinds. Lots of scientific stuff, information about stars, because we could see so many where we were because there was no street lighting.

How did Eldridge Cleaver treat you?

Eldridge kidnapped me, under the pretence of giving me some weed, and then interrogated me for hours about Tim, asking me what acid he was taking and so on. He took me into his pad and put all these locks on the door. The room had a thick pile carpet and a huge marble table and all these pictures round the walls of Black Power people pointing guns at police and at this point I started to think he hadn't got me here to give me the bit of weed he'd promised me.

He got me very, very high on very, very strong grass which didn't help because all I wanted to do was lay down. I was kind of beyond scared, the whole thing was surreal! He was really playing mind games with me.

At that time I wasn't exactly sure about the relationship between Tim and Eldridge and how Tim had really been kidnapped, so I didn't know where I stood or how much of the questions I should answer; if I lied would Cleaver know I was lying and think the rest of what I said was lies. It was a proper interrogation. I was kidnapped off these streets and kept in a room where a bright light was shone in my face as the questions were asked and Cleaver's right hand man, DC (who had hijacked an American plane and landed it in

Algeria) was taking notes. It lasted for hours until for some reason they asked me about my passport and when they realised I was British they very quickly let me go after that! The way Brian described it was they had visions of English gunships coming into the Port of Algiers. But Cleaver could have done anything because nobody, not even Brian knew where I was.

Were you involved in the magical rite that Tim and Brian took part in?

No. What happened was Tim said he was going to go into the desert and trip with Brian. I think they wanted to get away from the women, Rosemary and I, and have a man's trip together. So they drove into the desert and had to go to a place called Bou Saada because Tim and Rosemary had been staying in a hotel there for a while and they'd left something there they needed to pick up. It was acid, wrapped up in something, clothes probably. So they went into the desert and although they didn't know it at the time it was the very same place and probably the very same river bed where Aleister Crowley and Victor Neuberg had carried out their mescaline fuelled full moon ritual in 1909. And it was a big, big, trip and they kind of basically channelled Crowley and Neuberg.

> *We touched base at Bou Saada. We did not realise until Brian Barritt told us months later that we were following exactly the route which Aleister Crowley took on his search for illumination. The eerie synchronicities between our lives and that of Crowley, which were to preoccupy us, were still unfolding with such precision as to make us wonder if one can escape the programmed imprinting with which we are born.*
> (from *Confessions of a Hope Fiend* by Timothy Leary)

Ah, so, at the time they didn't know it was the same place used by Crowley and Neuberg in 1909?

No, no, no. I was reading something later, one of Crowley's books, and I said to Brian, isn't that the place where you and Tim took acid? That's where Crowley and Neuberg were channelling John Dee and Edward Kelly!

How did you come to leave Algeria and where did you go next?

We saw Tim one day and he said he'd been invited by a group of students to speak at a university in Copenhagen and he asked us if we thought he should go. We were worried that the CIA might be waiting for him at the airport, but off him and Rosemary went, to Copenhagen, and we were expecting them back, but they didn't come back. Then there was this big thing in the Algerian newspapers saying everyone had been waiting for Tim Leary at Copenhagen airport—including the CIA!—but he'd disappeared while on this airplane flight. It turned out the plane had landed in Switzerland, but we didn't know this and we were really worried for three weeks or so because we had no idea what had happened. Then we got a postcard from Tim saying 'We're in Hesse country, come and find us'. So without Tim it was time to leave Algeria, as we had no money. We hitched to the coast, got a ferry across the Med and ended up living in a squat in London for about six months.

How did you re-forge contact with Tim?

We ended up talking to Tim on the telephone, he contacted us via *Whisper* and Dave Ball. It was amazing. We were trembling and I remember Brian saying to me that it was like talking to a lover. Brian said he'd go over and leave me in the squat with Davie because we only had enough money for him to go, and I thought, oh, that was it. But then a friend told my story to Dr. Jean Hoerni, one of the inventors of the micro-chip and he gave me £500, a lot of money in 1972, to go over and join Tim and Brian. So I got on the phone to Brian, and then Tim came on and said 'why aren't you here? I would have paid for you to come'. I didn't know anything about networking then but I realise now that Hoerni was expecting me to tell Tim about the microchip.

> *Liz and Davie arrive in Switzerland. We meet at Lucerne railway station. Liz, red-hair flaming, yellow bell bottoms…*
>
> (from *The Road of Excess* by Brian Barritt)

Were you still involved with heroin at this time?

Yes. I got on the train, and I had a lot of heroin on me. Brian and I had got a habit after going back to London again. So I got back to Switzerland with it and Brian had some and so did Tim. I was the first, and probably only, person to give Tim a heroin fix—and he *loved* it!

Why did he not pursue that kind of drug experience then?

Because he knew that it wasn't a good way to go!

> He appreciated the buzz and analysed it quicker and more accurately than anyone I have known. It was classified before he took it in fact and just filed in the space waiting for it at the first level of his system as a 'euphoric downer.'
> (from *The Road of Excess* by Brian Barritt)

Where were you living in Switzerland?

We had several places to live in Switzerland. We had the chalet by Lake Zug in Ticino canton, loaned to Tim by Bobby Dreyfus and his wife. We had another place in Vaglio and another in Bern. This was after they'd sold the book. Tim had been writing *Confessions of a Hope Fiend*, using Brian as a sounding board.

Who actually wrote Confessions of a Hope Fiend, *was it Tim who actually wrote it or Brian who ghost-wrote it for him?*

It was Tim who wrote it. But Tim used bits of *Whisper* in it and they made up a bit of a story between them about Tim having come across *Whisper* in prison—it's all in *Confessions*, but the story was made up. Tim wrote it on his own but was getting ideas off Brian.

How much was Brian paid for his contribution to the book?

What happened was, to stay in Switzerland a French arms dealer, who was in exile in Switzerland but who had strings he could pull in the Swiss government, a guy called Michel Hauchard, helped Tim. Tim was arrested at one point because the Americans were trying to extradite him and Hauchard visited Tim in prison and said he would get him out as long as he signed over all the rights to all the books Tim wrote in the next ten years!

Obviously Tim agreed to this just to avoid being extradited to America. But he told Hauchard Brian had co-written *Confessions* with him, so it meant Hauchard could only get half the money for that book and we could get the other half. Tim went with Brian to open a bank account and initially we got $40,000 and Hauchard got $40,000, but Tim hadn't read the small print which said that the next amount of money, the next $80,000 was to go to Hauchard and he would give Tim half—which, of course, he didn't. It was costing a lot of legal fees to get a lawyer called Hebe, who'd also been Solzhenitsyn's lawyer, to try and get the money back from Hauchard. Hauchard did a bunk back to France so we never got that money.

So we had three places to live in and we were giving permanent acid parties in all of them and driving between them. People were visiting from all over the world; guys from the Brotherhood who were coming through the desert from Afghanistan with hash oil in the frames of their motorbikes, and lots of important friends of Tim's. Brian and I went over to London and brought a load of good hippie clothes back, Biba and so on. So we were all strutting around in furs and satins.

Tell me about the Krautrock record you were involved in...

We made it with this guy in Bern called Rolf Kaiser, who came over from Germany, to ask Tim to make a record, so we had to decide what to make it about and it had to be the Seven Levels of consciousness—it was seven then, not eight—that we'd talked to Tim about in Algeria. So Ash Ra Tempel, a German band, very sweet little hippies, came over and we made the record in this tiny little studio in Berne. The drummer was too stoned, because we'd had acid in a bottle of 7 Up, which was why the album was called Seven Up. Dennis Martino had spiked everybody, and the drummer couldn't do it so he had to be taken out of the eight tracks and replaced, but you could still hear him, and we had just one night to do it, it was chaos!

> *Oh what a night it was, it really was! The crystal acid*
> *that David Solomon laid on Tim... is passed around.*
> (from *The Road of Excess* by Brian Barritt)

David Solomon would later achieve notoriety as a major player in the 'Operation Julie' LSD manufacturing and distribution ring. This LSD was some of the first LSD chemist Richard Kemp made for commercial sale.

I understand you did some backing vocals on Seven Up?

I sang on Velvet Jeans, which Tim wrote then and there. It was terrible because Davie was banging on the studio door crying to be let in so I couldn't concentrate and by the time I'd settled Davie to sleep they'd moved on. The girl that was supposed to sing on Velvet Jeans, either she couldn't do it, or Tim made it so she couldn't do it so I could.

Was there a relationship developing between you and Tim, Liz?

Brian went off to mix the record in Cologne where the main studio was. But Tim hadn't been able to go because the CIA would have got him. While Brian was away, Tim and I took acid together and fell in love.

Do you think you were in love with Tim before you took acid together, just you and he, or did the acid precipitate it?

It was getting that way, we'd taken acid often before that but Brian was there, so I didn't really let it happen. But our acid trip wasn't contrived for that purpose. I went up to see him in the penthouse he was living in in Corona, which was owned by Christoph Wenger, the grandson of Herman Hesse. We were getting on so well, talking, probably talking cosmic talk and I just thought we could expand on it if we were tripping so I asked him if he had any acid, and he went and got some from Dennis downstairs.

Liz later wrote up a comprehensive and eloquent account of her trip with Tim. It is possibly the only detailed account in existence of a psychedelic experience with Tim by one of his lovers. Liz has kindly allowed an edited extract of it to be included as part of this interview:

The Tim Leary Psy-Phy, Hi-Fi, Wiz Trip

by Liz Elliot

We were facing each other on the bed, sitting cross-legged. I bent forward to touch his penis which looked like the fruit of a yew tree or an acorn, and very sexy, but he said, "Let's play." And I relaxed happily, with a sense of relief. It felt good to be freed from the stipulated run-up to copulation expected of a naked woman sitting on a bed with a naked man. Even on acid.

Screwing restricts you to a sexual level and feels animalistic and not very pleasant when you've just taken 500 mics of Orange Sunshine. You're all wide open, and your vagina is no exception, so that there can't be much stimulation there for male or female and the whole thing feels mechanical and boring with an undercurrent of sadness—probably because you're not getting as high as you would be if you weren't engaged in this pointless occupation. Making physical love is best saved for later.

He said, "Let's play." And suddenly I was somewhere else. Did we play physically like children or was it in the ballroom of my mind? He showed me how we could play with each other's brains, stroke mental erogenous zones. Flash electric current between us. Waltz round and round fast and clear and beautiful together in the hilarious rapture of Now. Future and past didn't exist. I was totally turned on!

It was like knowing everything you'd always known—because you were there ahead of yourself before you knew it. All I'd ever experienced or ever would fitted together into a significant, meaningful whole. Did we touch bodies and weave in and out and round about each other?

We'd moved to the other quarter of the bed now, me facing the bottom, he the top. I was cross-legged but balanced high on my knees and toes, straight backed and tall. He seemed to be nudging my thinking with a word here and there. Or was it a thought here and there? He was teaching me to think more intensely than I'd ever thought before and I loved it. It was like being a computer able to access all areas and understand everything when suddenly Saloon Bar doors in my mind flip-flapped open and my consciousness flew out of my head!

'Huxley's Doors of Perception!' —BLAM!—all in one go!

Instantly I was floating in infinite understanding, the full glory of enlightenment. No thought, no time, for ever—but it couldn't have been long because I could still hear the doors flip flapping slightly behind me as they came to rest. I looked round and saw I was floating among stars and planets, purple, blue, pink, dots of light, bright orange light just to one side. Then, for an instant, I grasped the Universe, inspected it, turned it, marvelled and knew it for what it was.

Everything seems to be in order—come on, let's go! And the High Priest of LSD grabbed my hand.

I looked down and briefly saw a green and flowered landscape with pathways below me. I thought of Superman and Wendy. After that there were no more pictures; we rocketed through the stars at light speed. Thoughts and random knowledge slotted into spaces in a magnificent jigsaw to make perfect sense and Tim was showing, guiding, watching and was beloved and beautiful. Revelations reeled forth like an oracle with no restrictions. My understanding was exponential, wide open and everywhere I looked—and nothing was hidden. I was at the centre—everyone's centre!

It would be nice to stay here for ever and ever, floating in total bliss—but that would result in perfect stasis, no changes, there would be nothing new to explore unless I kept moving. I willingly resigned my position but Tim didn't need to take it. He was laughing that I should think, because I had the power to stop time, I was so exclusive. He knew these realms well.

Did I want to catch the big red beach ball he was spinning on his index finger?—laughing, smiling, bronze-chested Tim. Did I want to take on all the responsibilities that it so attractively represented? Could I stay positive for the sake of a world? Of course I can—how could anything possibly go wrong? Are you sure? Of course, I feel completely confident—and I caught it.

I felt he was implanting something in my brain that I would come across later. Something to which I agreed. The mystical, psychologist father-figure was giving me a key, a secret, an initiation. A psychologist guru—perfect! Was he giving me what was in his mind or just illuminating what was in mine? Was he getting as much joy from me as I from him? Was it the same or something completely different?

This was the point where you could brain-wash someone with auto-suggestion—but I trusted him completely. We were in love but I didn't realise it. I was too in love with all creation! I saw myself as a novice and Tim as a benign benefactor doing everything for my benefit out of kindness. I never even considered, until much later, that he was in love with me. That we could invent the future together.

I saw that he knew a way through; there was a round, black hole we could climb through just above his head. I was game—in fact this was the greatest game I'd ever played. Suddenly we were present in the nose-cone of a rocket ship. I understood I was actually in the future travelling through space and therefore time. Tim ESP ace!

There were windows, on the same side as the penthouse ones that slanted above Christoph's bed where we'd started, but these joined in a point forming the nose cone. At the same time I was aware of Tim the pilot, grinning, sitting at a joy stick behind his forehead, in complete control of his own personal time-ship. Was he leaving me to pilot this one? Inside is out. There seemed to be an opaque blue mist beyond the windows—it had been dark night at Christoph's. Perhaps it was dawn, I would have seen more had I really looked through them, but it was all happening here and the windows were there and I didn't want the time-trip to end, so I don't know.

Then I was sitting on the floor, on the edge of the bed platform. Davie had come in earlier, a little distressed, and probably woken by the vibes or the music and wondering why I wasn't in my bed. Re-assured, when he saw who I was with, he'd settled down on a mattress beside the platform and gone back to sleep. As I turned my head after looking down to check on him—so kind and bright and tolerant this four year old I thought—I came face to face with Tim who was lying diagonally across the bed.

Our eyes met and our faces started to change and change and change. I saw him as a boy, a young man, animals—a lion—different nationalities but then he started to crease into an old man. I didn't want to look any more and with a sigh I pulled my eyes away. It was sudden and he said, to smooth it out or to show me that he'd seen it too, "Funny what we can do to each other isn't it?" It was the first time I remembered actually hearing him say anything since, "Let's play."

(Later, as I lay back on the pillows, I looked down at my stomach. It looked very pink, but not unduly saggy I was pleased to see. I was amazed that I hadn't considered it at all during the trip. Only a few weeks previously I had given birth to a still-born little boy at past full term and had been very large. Even as I realized it wasn't quite flat again, yet I wasn't embarrassed by Tim having seen it, I wondered if he'd been trying to help me cope with my loss by tripping with me. Little Davie had helped more than anyone, never putting any pressure on me about there being no longed-for little brother. Even though it was his first brush with death.)

And the day had dawned—grey and overcast to start. A bird was singing on a roof nearby. Our stomachs grumbled welcomes after our long absence. The records that Dennis had been playing for us all night at the bottom of the stairs were silent. I didn't realize, until Tim told me, that he had been doing this. So completely transfixed was I by the total environment of mind, let alone senses and body. But he must have chosen the music well.

As Tim and I lay side by side I felt intensely grateful for such a beautiful experience. I turned and looked at the hair-line wrinkles in the skin of his shoulder and loved him and thought how much older he was than I.

— — —

Wow, that must have been such an intense experience. How did it resolve itself? Did things between you and Tim develop further?

The situation went on for ages. I remember one time driving along with Tim and Brian in the front and Davie and me in the back and Tim turned round and said, 'Look Liz, you're going to have to decide between us sooner or later'. I said, 'yeah, I know', and didn't say anything else!

It's nice to be wanted!

Well, you see, that was the thing. I was having a wonderful time, with two men treating me like I was the Queen of God Knows What! My low self-esteem had disappeared and I felt wonderful, I'd never felt so good in my life and I didn't want anything to change. It was hard to know what to do because I'm really quite a monogamous person and I'd committed to Brian. I hadn't finished the scene with Brian to know that I didn't want him, and I couldn't just abandon him. Davie was starting to regard Brian as his Dad and yet I was in love with Tim, although Tim was so much older than me! On the other hand Tim had bought me a car, got an air-hostess to bring an ounce of heroin through customs for me (the last thing I wanted at the time) bought toys and got a nanny for Davie. And how could I presume Timothy Leary, the famous psychologist, a Harvard professor, would want me? He'd done a good job boosting my self-esteem. He must have been amazed to find it was so low when he was psycho-analysing me. For that's what he must have been doing. But he had such a *good* brain! There was no way to choose between those two at all, I was very confused.

So what happened, how did it end, Liz?

I was supposed to meet Brian in England. Brian had to go back to London to do various things, see about *Whisper*, get some more clothes, and Brian had gone ahead and asked me to come so I said ok I will. But I went with Tim to meet this guy representing the Austrian government —Tim was thinking of moving to Austria—so we went to St Moritz to see him and stayed in the Bridal Suite of the Palace Hotel. We had dinner with this Carlton Smith guy and arranged for Tim to cross the border, and the senator just assumed I would be with Tim and Tim asked me to go with him. But I'd promised to go to Brian in England so got Tim to take me to the airport and at the ticket gate he said 'are you sure you want to go?'. I didn't want to go, but I'd promised, so he said 'I'll tell you what we'll do, I'll toss a coin, you choose'. I think I chose heads and I would stay, tails and I would go, so he tossed the coin and it came out heads and he said 'well, you've got to stay'.

Thanks very much, Liz. Let's stop it there and leave the readers wanting more!

6

No Imperfections
in the Budded Mountain

Allen Ginsberg and the writing of *Wales Visitation*

As an historian of LSD culture in Britain, I can honestly say I haven't come across much LSD poetry. Verse written under the influence of, inspired by, or about LSD is uncommon. When it does exist it is often doggerel, of the you-had-to-be-there kind. There are exceptions, of which doomed Brit Beatnik Harry Fainlight's *The Spider*, about a bad trip, is possibly the most famous. Another excellent example, which accurately and succinctly distils the acid experience, is Roger McGough's dry, witty 1967 koan-like *Poem for National LSD Week*[1]:

> *Mind, how you go*

At the other end of the spectrum is Lancashire poet and former acid dealer Dave Cunliffe's lengthy and descriptive *The Two-Hour Assassination of God*, the first and last stanzas of which are:

At 4am, she entered the brain of God
And stumbled blindly through its convoluted
Swamps until reaching a clearing
In which was reflected the image of everything
That had ever happened
To anyone anywhere in time and space

At 6 am she clearly and directly saw
A myriad living things manifest
In joy and liberation upon the surface
Of a world which didn't really change
Except some skin and scales just dropped away[2]

I know. We've all been there!

Fainlight, McGough and Cunliffe's efforts notwithstanding, the fact is that Britain has only ever produced one *really* great and perceptive LSD poem. And it took the American beat poet, Allen Ginsberg, to create it.

Ginsberg, love or loathe him, was a major influence on the literature and lifestyles of the beat and psychedelic scenes. His story is largely an American one, but he visited the UK on several notable occasions, including giving a reading on the same bill as Harry Fainlight at the 1966 *Wholly Communion* event at the Royal Albert Hall. His most notorious poem, *Howl*, a word jazz paean to a generation, redefined how poets from the 1950s onwards wrote.

Ginsberg liked getting high. Besides experiences with alcohol, marijuana, mescaline, peyote, yage, nitrous oxide, psilocybin, heroin and other mind altering substances, by the mid-sixties Ginsberg was a veteran acid head, having taken it first in 1959 at the Mental Research Institute in California's Palo Alto.

The set and setting for Ginsberg's first trip were odd, to say the least. As Hofmann's potion suffused his being, Ginsberg lay in a windowless room full of medical equipment, listening to Wagner's *Tristan and Isolde* while undergoing a battery of psychological tests. He survived the ordeal, and passed the acid test before it had been invented, commenting, "It was astounding. [I] saw a vision of that part of my consciousness which seemed to be permanent and transcendent and identical with the origin of the universe... this drug seems to automatically produce a mystical experience. Science is getting very hip."[3]

Indeed, he was so impressed with LSD he concluded it to be more powerful and more meaningful than mescaline or peyote, and so safe he even wrote to his father, encouraging him to try it! The experience stimulated him to write the unambiguously titled *Lysergic Acid* which opens:

> *It is a multiple million eyed monster*
> *it is hidden in all its elephants and selves*
> *it hummeth in the electric typewriter*
> *it is electricity connected to itself, if it hath wires*
> *it is a vast Spiderweb*
> *and I am on the last millionth infinite tentacle of the spiderweb, a worrier*
> *lost, separated, a worm, a thought, a self*
> *I Allen Ginsberg a separate consciousness*
> *I who want to be God...* [4]

Ginsberg took to LSD, rapidly becoming something of a psychedelic evangelist. In November 1966 he suggested to a room full of Unitarian ministers in Boston, Massachusetts: "Everybody who hears my voice try the chemical LSD at least once... Then I prophecy we will all have seen some ray of glory or vastness beyond our conditioned social selves, beyond our government, beyond America even, that will unite us into a peaceful community." [5]

Ginsberg first visited Britain in 1965, appearing in D. A. Pennebaker's film document of the Bob Dylan tour, *Don't Look Back*, and in Peter Whitehead's film of the International Poetry Incarnation event at the Royal Albert Hall, *Wholly Communion*. He returned to London two years later in 1967, the so-called Summer of Love.

Infamous psychiatrist, R.D. Laing, and his friends in the Institute of Phenomological Studies (David Cooper, Joe Burke and Leon Redler) organised the ten day long Dialectics of Liberation conference, to be held at the Roundhouse—London counter-culture's iconic venue—between 15-30th July. Ostensibly about social injustice, yet ironically not featuring a single woman speaking in its line-up, the conference featured countercultural heavy-hitters including Stokely Carmichael, Gregory Bateson, Herbert Marcuse and Emmitt Grogan. Ginsberg planned to deliver a paper titled 'Consciousness and Practical Action'.

On confirming the invitation to speak Ginsberg contacted his UK publisher Tom Maschler, asking if he could stay with him in London. Maschler was a high profile literary agent and publisher, noted in a *Guardian* profile as having "re-established Jonathan Cape as the blue chip literary imprint." He was also one of the people responsible for creating the Booker prize.

A young Iain Sinclair, many years distant from his fame as novelist and psychogeographer, was very much into film at the time. Sinclair was offered £2,000 by a German TV company to make a film of Ginsberg's visit to London, filming him at the Dialectics of Liberation conference and in a variety of other settings, both in interview and giving readings. Ginsberg made many pronouncements about LSD use during the course of filming in London, and Sinclair's *Kodak Mantra Diaries* is an indispensable record both of these and of the poet's London visit in general.[6]

Following the conference, Ginsberg took a break from filming with Sinclair and was invited to spend the weekend at Tom Maschler's Welsh holiday cottage at Carney Farm on the slopes of the Black Mountains.

On Thursday, 28th July, Maschler drove Ginsberg the 150 miles or so to his Black Mountain retreat. After the pair had settled in at the cottage they ate and over dinner Ginsberg opened a small tin, showing Maschler two pills wrapped in cotton wool, saying, "These are LSD. I thought you might like to try it." Maschler was an LSD virgin, although he had often considered taking it. "If you don't want to, I won't either", continued Ginsberg, "but you need not be nervous. If you take the pill I will wait to make sure you are OK before I follow you."[7]

Maschler thought Ginsberg's "degree of caring was seductive" and, considering the set, setting and companion to be as perfect as it would get, agreed to the strange invitation. Ginsberg, by now a frequent flyer, knew exactly how to handle a neophyte on the golden road to unlimited devotion and suggested they wait until the following morning, so the drug's effects would have worn off by evening and they would not be kept up all night.

Friday 29th July dawned, wet and humid in the Black Mountains, with cloud wreathing the surrounding hills. Pan had clearly heard the call and was marshalling his elemental forces in order to give Maschler and Ginsberg a day to remember. Maschler took the LSD and, once Ginsberg was certain everything was ok, he swallowed the other pill. In the early stages of the trip, Maschler experienced the usual strong visual disturbances, "I took the pill and looked out of my sitting room window on to the mountainside opposite. The mountain gradually turned a reddish-brown and the earth began to run down the hillside like lava." After three or four hours, possibly at the peak of the trip, Ginsberg wisely suggested they go for a walk, no doubt on the principle that venturing into the great outdoors is one of the best things you can do with a neophyte tripper.

Both men donned wet weather gear and wellingtons and set off up the hillside to the rear of Maschler's cottage, into the great mystery. Maschler was somewhat nervous about the climb. In fact it is neither particularly steep nor dangerous but the amplified sensations of LSD could well have made it appear so. To allay his fears Ginsberg taught Maschler a calming mantra: *Um, Um Sa Ra Wah, Buddha, Da Keen E Eye, Ben Za, Wan Niye, Ben Za, Be Ro, Za Ni Ye Um, Um Um, Pey Pey Pey So Ha.*

Despite being high Maschler had the presence of mind to take a camera with him on their lysergic adventure. He took several photographs of Ginsberg communing with nature on the Welsh mountainside; "the poet in his gumshoes communing with a chunk of nature."[8] Maschler recalled, "The hills surrounding my cottage are dotted with sheep and Allen saw us as just two more sheep under the sky." Away from his home country, the city, the literary establishment, the politics and the weight of his own fame, Ginsberg's trip thoroughly embraced the environment. Maschler remarked, "He was immensely moved by the landscape and in the afternoon, still heavily under the influence of the drug, he began to write a poem called *Wales Visitation.*"

Ginsberg's hand-written first draft is reproduced in the 1968 Cape Golliard edition, the poem at the time of writing apparently have no title other than the date, *Wales 1967 July 29 Saturday.* The astute reader will note that 29th July was in fact Friday and the confusion of dates may have come from the fact Ginsberg was writing as Friday slipped into Saturday or just because Ginsberg got the date or day wrong! The beginning of the first, as yet untitled, draft of the poem is reproduced here, with spelling and grammar exactly as Ginsberg wrote them on that misty mountain day:

Thru the thick wall'd window on vale Browed
White fog afloat
Trees moving in rivers of wind
The clouds arise
As on a wave, gigantic eddy lifting mist
Above teeming ferns exquisitely swayed
By one gentle motion vast as the long green crag
Glimpsed thru mullioned windows in the valley raine

Bardid, O Self, visitacion, Tell naught
But what was seen by one man
In a vale in Albion, of the folk, of Lambs,
Of the satanic thistle that raises its horned symmetry

Flowering with sister grass & flowret's visible
Pink and tiny invisible-small
Budded triple-petalled bloomlets
Equally angelic as lightbulbs,
Remember your day 150 miles from London's
Symmetrical throned Tower & network
Of TV pictures flashing bearded your Self,
Link the lambs of the tree-nooked hillside of
This day
With the cry of Blake and the silent thought of
Wordsworth in his Eld stillness —⁹

Maschler and Ginsberg drove back to London, Maschler still feeling the psychedelic effects of his back-to-nature acid experience, "On the way back to London I had a sense of driving over the earth, the earth that was underneath the tarmac of the road." Once in the city Ginsberg continued to hone the poem as he resumed filming with Iain Sinclair who noted, "He's just been down to Wales, to the countryside, the hills. And has written (is writing) *Wales - A Visitation....* He has drunk of the Black Mountains and is easier for it, is calm and reflective."

Ginsberg later wrote of the poem: "*Wales Visitation* was written on the sixth or so hour of an acid trip in Wales at the house of my English publisher. The word "visitation" comes from the peregrinations of the Welsh bards, who went once from village to village rhyming their news and gossip. The poem uses two thirds of the notes made at that time, stitched together later." In London, as the poem developed, it was later annotated "July 29, 1967 (LSD) – August 3, 1967 (London)." Justly proud of the poem and of how he had captured his psychedelic ramble Ginsberg wrote:

> *I was interested in making an artwork comprehensible*
> *to people not high on acid, an artefact that could point*
> *others' attention to microscopic details of the scene.*
> *They wouldn't necessarily know the poem was written*
> *on acid, but with an extraordinarily magnified visionary*
> *appreciation of the vastness of the motif in its 'minute*
> *particulars' it might transfer the high consciousness of*
> *LSD to somebody with ordinary mind. By focusing the*
> *poem's eye outside of my thoughts onto external pictures,*

details of the phenomenal world, I was able to maintain
a centre and balance, continuing from beginning to end
in an intelligible sequence, focusing on awareness of
breath. It was coherent enough to publish in The New
Yorker, whose editors eliminated the note about acid.[10]

Wales Visitation is regarded by many as one of Ginsberg's best poems, haunted as it is by the observant ghosts of the English Romantic tradition, like William Blake and Wordsworth, "Long-breath Blakean invocations."[11] But as one of Ginsberg's fictionalised contemporaries (Japhy Ryder (Gary Snyder), in Kerouac's *Dharma Bums*) said elsewhere, "comparisons are odious", and poetic analysis is not going to overly concern this writer. The poem's technical merits aside, *Wales Visitation* is, to me at least, a perceptive description of what an acid trip can be like in such wild and numinous surroundings; the elemental qualities of landscape, plants, animals, wind, and rain, intensified and coloured by the drug's effects. Distance from his everyday reality as the counter-culture's poet-in-residence allowed Ginsberg to drop his mask and just let the acid show him what was in the moment. As he later reflected, "for the first time I was able to externalise my attention instead of dwelling on the inner images and symbols."[12]

The poem begins as the LSD comes on, inside Maschler's cottage, with Ginsberg observing the weather and myriad subtle movements of the landscape through mullioned windows. He vows to "Tell naught but what seen by one man in a vale of Albion," although his thoughts briefly flash back to the filming he did earlier in the week with Iain Sinclair, before the trip intensifies and he heads out onto the hillside. Then, a full-on lysergic celebration of and communion with nature takes place, inner and outer sensations mingling as, "Roar of the mountain wind slow, sigh of the body/ One Being on the mountainside stirring gently/Exquisitely balanced from bird cry to lamb to this voice knowing."

As Ginsberg dreams the world alive, the symmetry of flowers suggests to him mandalas, the bleating of newly born lamb sounds recall mantras. He wandered the hillside, Maschler following and snapping Ginsberg in a variety of poses; pensively surveying the valley, lying on the wet grass examining an incised stone, kneeling and gazing into the camera's eye. Aware, thinking, sentient. High. As the poem draws to a close he reflects on the fact that the experience had been about the minutiae of what Irish mythology refers to as 'The music of what happens'—"What did I notice? Particulars!".

Ginsberg had clearly attained that most clichéd but no less valuable of altered states, the sensation of being at one with nature, becoming, "one giant being breathing—one giant being that we're all part of". The imagery of *Wales Visitation* was completely different to that of his first acid poem, *Lysergic Acid*, much softer and pastoral, concerned with observation of the minutiae of right here, right now, rather than the earlier poem's cosmic vision.

Back in London, the first draft of *Wales Visitation* written, Ginsberg's parents, Louis and Edith, joined him, and father and son (Louis being a well-known poet in his own right) gave a reading together at the Institute of Contemporary Arts in Dover Street on 22nd August 1967. His freshly minted lysergically inspired nature poem under its full title of *Wales—Visitation July 29th 1967* had its first reading that night. The reading was recorded and later released on the Saga Psyche record label as *The Ginsbergs at the ICA*.

Iain Sinclair came across *Wales—A Visitation* by accident. During a visit to poet Nathaniel Tarn in Hampstead, Sinclair was given a copy of the glassine-covered Cape Golliard hardback. "Reading it, I found out where Allen had been when he absented himself from the filming: back in my home territory, Wales, climbing the hills behind Llanthony Abbey. Doubling the metaphors of romanticism, a Worsdworthian high on a high ridge. Hallucinogenic tourism in the great tradition. With muddy wellington boots and a camera."[13]

Wales Visitation was first published in 1968 by Cape Goliard Press (London), as a hardback book with illustrated dust jacket, outer glassine jacket and endpapers made of Japanese wood pulp paper. The text of the poem is printed opposite a facsimile reproduction of the heavily edited and corrected manuscript. The edition comprised 300 copies of which 100 were signed and numbered by Ginsberg and included a 45-rpm recording of the poem attached to the inner rear cover.

A further 200 copies were issued by Cape Goliard Press. These were *hors commerce* (not for trade) and the edition was published in small, landscape format, pamphlet size, with card covers and endpapers of Japanese wood pulp paper. The last page was printed with 'An offering for a peaceful summer from Allen Ginsberg & Cape Goliard Press.' These editions have become collectors' items, selling for several hundred pounds.

On 3rd September, 1968, Ginsberg appeared on the conservative US TV discussion show Firing Line, where host William F Buckley Jnr asks him if he has a poem and Ginsberg responds, "An interesting project, which is a poem I wrote on LSD." Buckley: "Under the influence?". Ginsberg responded, as he pulled out from behind his chair the text of Wales Visitation, "Under the influence of LSD", noting it was "a long poem, long enough to be entertaining". As Ginsberg reads the title, Buckley interjects with "w.h.?", presumably thinking, possibly trying for a laugh, that the title was *Whales Visitation*! Ginsberg corrects him and launches into the full poem, with Buckley somewhat inanely interjecting "nice" after the first stanza. Ginsberg gives a spirited reading of the poem, complete with trademark stare and gesticulations. Buckley's rictus grin never wavers throughout, but rather than the expected sarcastic put down, the best he can manage is, "I kinda liked that" .[14]

Ginsberg revised and changed the text of *Wales Visitation* a number of times over the years, most notably on live versions, and the interested reader is urged to locate and compare as many as possible. For copyright reasons we are unable to reproduce the finished version of the whole poem here, but a number of versions can be located on the internet, with the definitive printed version being available in *Allen Ginsberg: Selected Poems 1947-1995*. The poem is also on *Ah!*, CD 3 of the four CD box set *Holy Roll, Jelly Soul* (Rhino Word Beat R271693), where a recording of the poem taken from The Richard Freeman Midnight Show (Radio KPFA, Berkeley, 2nd July, 1971) is used, together with a backing track of Ginsberg himself on harmonium.

In March 2013 a media report announced that part of the original typed manuscript of *Wales Visitation* was to be auctioned at Bonham's of London. Simon Roberts, books, maps and manuscripts specialist at the auction house said he expected the 60-line, hand annotated, manuscript to fetch between £800 and £1,000.[15] At the auction on 10th April the manuscript exceeded all expectations by selling for £3,125. Ginsberg would no doubt have been most amused that the ephemeral material evidence of his psychedelic intimacy with the elemental forces of the Welsh hills had been reduced to the exchange of mere money in one of capitalism's finest institutions!

7

The Acid Test for LSD

The Grateful Dead's LSD telepathy experiments

In December 2000 parapsychologist Richard Wiseman announced he was going to conduct the "world's largest telepathy experiment" in London. Unfortunately Wiseman's experiment, using up to 100 telepathic 'senders', fell well short of the far more Fortean approach taken by a group of parapsychologists and musicians towards the end of the psychedelic era in America.

The real 'world's largest telepathy experiment' actually took place in February 1971 at Port Chester in New York State. Far from being conducted in the psychically arid test conditions of a laboratory, it was hosted by the world's strangest rock and roll band, The Grateful Dead. The Dead themselves are no strangers to Fortean phenomena. The synchronicities surrounding their gigs at the Great Pyramid of Giza, and percussionist Micky Hart's encounter with a cursed human skull drum are the stuff of legend. Unarguably at the cutting edge of genuinely psychedelic music, and all that entails, the Grateful Dead were forged in the crucible of 1960s American West Coast acid culture, playing to huge crowds where band and audience were under the influence of the strongest psychedelics. Their music to this day both encompasses and surpasses all contemporary and historical forms, leading one critic to define their œuvre as "music beyond idiom".

Accounts of the sheer power generated at a Grateful Dead gig are legion, band and followers believing that when they are playing at full throttle a temporary psychedelic psychic 'church' is created in which musicians and celebrants are joined in a sort of 'wholly communion', becoming a single entity with one mind.

Micky Hart puts this succinctly: "Our main focus was the idea of group mind. We saw the Grateful Dead as a group mind and one in which we were able to share with the audience. We were able to take an image and project it into the audience and send it to receptive receivers." With this kind of belief it was only a matter of time before the parapsychological fraternity became seriously interested in the Grateful Dead.

The link came in the form of parapsychologist and author Stanley Krippner, at that time director of the Maimonides Dream Laboratory in Brooklyn, New York. Krippner had been working at the far edges of parapsychology for several years, and since 1964 had been involved in testing the hypothesis "that sleeping subjects are able to incorporate aspects of randomly selected target stimuli into their dreams". Krippner was also a Dead fan and had used their music in previous ESP experiments. The Grateful Dead's biographer, Dennis McNally, described, in *A Long Strange Trip: The Inside History of the Grateful Dead* (Bantam, NY, 2002), Krippner's entry into the Dead's world: "Krippner was yet another of the fascinating people the Dead had attracted, a distinguished psychologist who was comfortable with the rational study of 'fuzzy' things like ESP, or psychedelics, or both together."

Jerry Garcia, the Dead's lead guitarist, and Micky Hart first met Stanley Krippner at a party in 1970. McNally recalls, "Eventually Krippner found himself in conversation with Garcia, who wondered about the potential interaction of various altered states of consciousness, for instance sleep and the psychedelic state, and whether or not that could aid sensitivity to ESP. Their conversation yielded the Dream Experiment, which was deemed worthy of publication in a formal, academically refereed journal of psychology."

Krippner initially conducted a smaller version of the Port Chester experiments, in which ESP, hundreds of people, rock music and psychedelics were brought together. This took place at a Holy Modal Rounders concert on 15th March 1970 where five volunteer telepathy 'receivers' were selected for the experiment. Each receiver was told the geographical location of the concert and asked to 'tune in' at midnight, when certain images would be telepathically projected by the audience. The receivers were situated at random locations within a 100 mile (160km) radius of the concert venue. The target image chosen to be projected was 'birds', and a sequence of appropriate moving images and transparencies was prepared by the psychedelic light show operator Jean Mayo. These consisted of a film about eagles and a number of slides depicting photographs of various birds, together with key symbols such as the Egyptian hieroglyph for bird and phrases such as 'Think birds' and 'fly high'. One crucial slide sequence showed a mythological phœnix appearing and disappearing in flames.

The audience were informed verbally that when these images appeared they were to concentrate on them and 'send' them telepathically. To create the strongest link between the target images, the power of the music and the audience, the images were projected during the band's performance of 'If You Want to Be a Bird'. This song was already fixed in the audience's minds as it had been featured in the 1969 cult film Easy Rider, during a sequence in which Jack Nicholson looned around on the back of a motorcycle.

Midnight duly passed and the audience, high on music and drugs and open to the potential of telepathic contact, did their best to project the chosen images into the collective unconscious. The five receivers reported variously, 'something mythological, like a Griffin or a Phoenix', 'a snake', 'grapes', 'an embryo in flames growing into a tree'. The fifth receiver was singer Richie Havens, who also reported seeing a mythological creature like a phœnix.

Was this experiment successful? Maybe. Interpreting a telepathy experiment can be difficult because, unless the images received are exactly the same as the ones sent, the results are open to scepticism at best, ridicule at worst. However, at least two of the images received appeared to be within acceptable parameters and Krippner felt that with some important changes to the methodology of the experiment he could improve the results.

Buoyed up by the apparent success of the Holy Modal Rounders experiment, Krippner planned something much more ambitious involving the Grateful Dead. This was to take place at each gig of the Dead's six-night run at the Capitol Theatre in Port Chester, New York State, during February 1971. The Port Chester shows themselves have become legendary in 'Deadhead' circles as being fantastic examples of the transformative and redemptive power of music. Listening to them you are aware of a music being created which is truly 'out there', an ideal backdrop against which to conduct a telepathy experiment.

Contrary to the somewhat shambolic psychedelic milieu in which the Grateful Dead existed, the Port Chester experiments were planned in some detail. In attempting to refine the methodology used at the Holy Modal Rounders experiment, Krippner's team made some radical changes. It was decided to make the instructions to the senders (the audience) much more specific, and also to make them aware of the physical location of one of the receivers. To ensure against the possibility of the target images being leaked, either consciously or unconsciously, they were to be selected at random immediately prior to being shown to the senders.

For the Port Chester experiments just two receivers, Malcolm Bessent and Felicia Parise, were chosen. Both were experienced 'psychic sensitives'. For the duration of the experiment Bessent was to be observed whilst under laboratory conditions, sleeping at the Maimonides Dream Laboratory, 45 miles (72km) away. Parise was to sleep in her flat where she would be telephoned several times during the night and asked to describe the content of her dreams.

The audiences on each night were told only about Bessent's involvement in the experiment. This was so that the Dream Laboratory staff could monitor 'intentionality', i.e. whether or not the senders' knowledge of who was taking part and where they were could affect results. In this case, if intentionality was relevant it would be expected that Bessent would have more success in receiving the images than Parise. Conversely, if it were the receiver whose subconscious mind reached out and located the target images, both senders could be expected to score equally well.

Krippner's assistant, Ronnie Mastrian, was in the audience at the Capitol Theatre and immediately prior to each gig selected one of two envelopes by the flipping of a coin. Each envelope contained a series of slides containing images which were to be the focus of the evening's experiment. The selected transparencies were loaded into a projector and shown on the stage backdrop. At 11:30pm when the concert was well under way, the bemused and excited audience read the instruction slides; "1) You are about to participate in an ESP experiment, 2) In a few seconds you will see a picture, 3) Try using your ESP to 'send' this picture to Malcolm Bessent, 4) He will try to dream about the picture. Try to send it to him, 5) Malcolm Bessent is now at the Maimonides dream laboratory in Brooklyn".

One of six randomly selected pictures was then projected onto the stage backdrop for 15 minutes whilst the Grateful Dead played. Unusually for the Dead, there was no psychedelic light show at any of the Port Chester gigs, thus making the projected images the visual focus of the concert.

When Malcolm Bessent had been observed to be engaged in REM (Rapid Eye Movement) activity for ten minutes, he was woken and asked what he was dreaming. This took place several times throughout the night. Felicia Parise was contacted by 'phone at 90 minute intervals and her dreams recorded. On the following morning, both subjects were asked to add any details they had missed, together with any associations they attached to their dreams. Their recollections were tape-recorded and transcribed for use by the evaluators.

At the end of the six-show run, the two evaluators were each given the full receivers' transcripts together with copies of the images used. The evaluators, working independently of each other, the telepathy receivers or Dream Laboratory staff, were asked to read the tape transcripts. They then recorded on a 100-point scale any correspondences between the dream recollections and the images projected during the experiment.

As with the Holy Modal Rounders experiment, the results were encouraging but open to wide interpretation. One example of this dichotomy comes from the 19th February gig where a painting called 'The Seven Spinal Chakras' was projected. This showed a male in the yogic full lotus position, deep in meditation, each chakra vividly illuminated. When Bessent was awakened during this particular experiment he remembered dreaming he was, "very interested in… using natural energy… thinking about rocket ships… an energy box and… a spinal column". This correspondence was classed as a success, although sceptics will have their doubts.

Another debatable success came from the night of 20th February when the surrealist painter Magritte's 'Philosophy in the Boudoir' was selected and projected. The painting is of a headless woman in a transparent robe. This time Bessent dreamed about a "little girl's doll" which Krippner believed demonstrated "a degree of correspondence".

The Dream Laboratory's report on the experiment noted: "The average evaluation of the two judges was computed for each pair of dream transcripts and target pictures. If coincidence, rather than ESP, had been operating, the judges' evaluation of the correct transcript/target pairs would have been higher than all other pairs one time out of six. For Miss Parise, one correct pair obtained the highest rating. In the case of Mr Bessent, the judges gave the highest score to the correct pairs four times out of six… Thus, for Mr Bessent, the ESP hypothesis is supported. Further, some support is given to the position that the agents must know who the target is to be transmitted to and where he is located for telepathy to occur."

So, were the experiments a success? Krippner and his team certainly thought so, although sceptics and debunkers will snort derisively at the lack of rigour in parts of the experiment's design. And, of course, the results were open to interpretation and raised many questions, such as: how clearly and exactly does a received image have to correspond with the image projected? Does the whole dream have to correspond with the target image? —and so on. No-one said parapsychology was easy!

Other rock commentators doubted the psychedelic component of the experiment. Former band manager (and not entirely reliable commentator) Rock Scully, in his book Living With The Dead (Little, Brown, 1995), expressed a jaundiced view of the event; "The results turned out to be shady… the Port Chester audience is 18- and 19-year-old kids who've hopped over the border from Connecticut to get drunk and are all screwed up on beer and hard liquor." Hardly the blissed out psychonauts of mid-sixties San Francisco's Haight Ashbury who were the Dead's original constituency.

In both design and organisational terms, the Holy Modal Rounders and Grateful Dead telepathy experiments probably weren't as rigorous as the parapsychological establishment would have liked. But from a Fortean angle the results are not really the point. No, the point is that all concerned had the courage of their convictions and strength of belief to attempt the manifestation of a wild talent, involving over 6,000 people. These experiments were, to date, the largest telepathy tests conducted outside of laboratory conditions, with over 2,000 people being involved at each concert. They reflected a zeitgeist, rapidly fading from our memories, in which it was believed the human subconscious had limitless potential and could be accessed and directed by drugs, music and intent. Contrast that with the general drabness of psychical research in the early 21st century! Now largely forgotten, the world's biggest telepathy experiment has become just another footnote in the annals of both parapsychology and rock and roll. Ah well, I guess you had to be there!

8

Meddled

S trange things sometimes—often—happen when you take psychedelic drugs. How 'real' these events are is a pointless question. You are experiencing them and therefore they are real to you and to anyone else who shares the experience. These gratuitous mindfucks, to badly paraphrase Aldous Huxley, open one's eyes to the essential strangeness of the psychedelic experience and offer an insight into murkier corners of the multiverse. I've been fortunate to have had several such experiences, of which this was the first, dating back to 1973 and an early encounter with one of the few genuinely psychedelic people I've ever met.

After my first, soul devastating bad trip, recounted in the Introduction, I was extremely wary of taking psychedelic drugs again. But I reasoned that if the psychedelic experience could be so infernally bad, the opposite must also be true. And of course this was supported by the hundreds of accounts of positive psychedelic experiences in the literature. The opportunity came along within a few months when I met the guy who later became my de facto acid guru, mentioned in the piece Two Days After, which I wrote in late 1972 and which obliquely refers to this event.

My good friend and early tripping partner Andy and I, decided to take some acid at his parents' bungalow on a Saturday night. This was the same location as my trip to hell and back, and as a 'setting' for a psychedelic experience was about as unsuited as possible, being a plain, soulless 1960s bungalow. But, it was the venue for many of my early psychedelic experiences. We invited Ageing Hippie, our older and much more experienced tripping friend to join us. There was no pre-arranged plan for the evening, just the idea to take acid in comfortable surroundings with someone more knowledgeable than us and see what happened.

At about four o clock on that Saturday afternoon, I walked the three miles or so from my parents' home in Hightown, to Roberttown, where Andy lives. I didn't drive in those days and so had the choice of several methods to get to Roberttown; walking via a variety of roads, lanes or fields, a combination of those, or by bus or bicycle. I suppose I could have even persuaded my father to drive me there as he had done on other occasions. As it was a warm, sunny afternoon I chose a circuitous route over various fields, paths and country lanes with the final mile or so being across a long series of fields on little used paths.

About half a mile from any road access there was a small wood, a copse of mature deciduous trees, bounded by a low stone wall, with a stile allowing access and egress. I'd been through the wood before many times and knew the path well, passing through it quickly and arriving at Andy's at about 5 o'clock. Ageing Hippie arrived shortly afterwards and we took the acid, a very mellow, floaty, mildly colourful substance, completely unlike the qualities of my only other trip and very enjoyable. Andy and I felt comfortable in the presence of someone we trusted and the evening went well, conversation being interspersed with the usual acid speculation and interesting music.

As was the fashion in those days, late in the evening, just after the gentle, but powerful peak of the trip, we decided to go out for a walk. Prior to doing so we put on one last LP. I decided we should listen to Meddle, by Pink Floyd. I was never a particularly big Pink Floyd fan, then or now, but I quite liked Meddle, particularly the track One of These Days, with its propulsive, almost Krautrock-like riff. After the usual faff, we darkened the room and lay down for what turned out to be a memorable listening experience. When the album finished we put on our coats and blended into the night for a psychedelic ramble. It was a clear, starlit night to rival anything Van Gogh could have conjured with his mind brush, and so we wandered. I wanted to get away from the village, away from the possibility of bumping into other people and suggested we went across the fields to the copse I had passed through earlier knowing it would be quiet, away from any other nocturnal wanderers and with the added promise of a spectacular view over the massive Huddersfield ICI factory (which was brightly and luridly lit, a bit like the Bridge scene from Apocalypse Now!).

As we neared the now darkened copse I had passed through earlier I could see something leaning on the stone stile. I alerted my companions, thinking perhaps it was someone out walking their dog, and we planned a route change if necessary. It didn't look like a person, more like a shape and as we got closer the darkness resolved itself into a piece of wood, about four feet square, with some writing on it. It had not been there earlier in the afternoon, when I passed.

But so what?

The 'so what' factor was quickly revealed when we realised that painted on the board, in pink, art nouveau lettering, was the words 'Pink Floyd'. We stopped. We goggled. We boggled. We muttered in amazement. Several minutes of psychedelic speculation ensued as we mused coincidence, synchronicity, and how the sign must have, in fact, been placed there by the Intergalactic Drug Squad to freak us out. Because how else, why else, would it be there? A bit perplexed and somewhat fazed, totally at a loss to explain the sign, we wandered further into the wood, to watch the colourful light show provided by ICI's chemical pollutants and to hug and listen to the trees breath, as one did in those halcyon, innocent acid daze of the early 1970s.

After 45 minutes or so we returned to the bungalow by the same route and the sign was still there. At least our surreality was consistent! Slightly less high now, we attempted serious scientific experimentation to ascertain the sign's reality status. We banged it, moved it, lifted it and performed various other crude but effective scientific tests to prove its reality in the quotidian world. No doubt about it, the sign was real. But how could we prove it outside of those space-time co-ordinates? We should, I suppose, have taken it home with us. Yet that would have only proved its existence and would have shed no light on why it was there or by what agency it had appeared. So we wobbled back to the bungalow and what was left of the night. The following morning I walked home, this time intentionally choosing the same way I had arrived. It almost goes without saying that while the wood and the stile was still there, there was no trace at all of the Pink Floyd sign. I shrugged to myself and plodded on, pondering the hows and whys of it all.

So what had happened there? This was the first of many meaningful 'coincidences', synchronicities, even, that I have enjoyed while under the influence of psychedelic drugs. It became a story to tell, one of many such tales trippers related to each other about their non-ordinary experiences. To most people they sound like gibberish, drug induced fantasies with no basis in the reality of the man on the Clapham omnibus. But to others who have had similar, yet completely different experiences while high they make perfect (non) sense.

Of course some people I have told about it over the years have just sneered and laughed, stating that it 'must' have been placed there by Ageing Hippie to demonstrate his 'powers'. And yes, that's certainly *possible.* But for that to be the case Ageing Hippie—who I barely knew at that time—would have had to have known I really liked Meddle, which I'm pretty sure he didn't, and would have to have with chosen or manipulated that album to be played, just before we went for or walk, which he didn't and he would have had to have ensured we walked across those particular fields out of many, which he didn't.

The 'acid trickster' scenario is further complicated by the fact that Ageing Hippie had no idea which of the many routes or forms of transport I was going to use to get to Andy's. And of course had he been able to divine all the variables it would have been much easier just to put, say, an empty Meddle LP sleeve on the stile rather than going to the trouble of freshly painting a sign for that purpose, hauling it across half a mile of field (and trusting local youths or a passing farmer wouldn't have moved it prior to our arrival) and then retrieving it again later after our nocturnal mission.

I have no specific belief invested in the why or how of the Pink Floyd sign. It happened. Three people experienced it in exactly the same way and it has given me much food for thought over the years and reminds me that, as the song says, things are not what they appear.

9

An Afternoon with Jeff Dexter

The name might not be familiar to everyone, but Jeff Dexter is a legendary figure in the British counter-culture. One of the original mods, in the early sixties Jeff was a professional dancer for Mecca Ballrooms and sang with Cyril Stapelton & His Orchestra and the Ray McVay Orchestra amongst others before encountering LSD. After taking LSD and becoming part of the early psychedelic scene in London, Jeff helped create the legendary underground club UFO, ran the famous Jeff Dexter Record Show, knew everyone who was anyone and was at most of the key psychedelic events of the 1960s. In 2007 I spent an afternoon of wide ranging discussion with Jeff, focusing on his relationship with LSD and its penetration of mid to late 1960s London.

Andy Roberts: *When did LSD first appear on your cultural radar?*

Jeff Dexter: I first heard about it in 1965. My best friend at the time was called Ian 'Sammy' Samwell, his wife Dolores and her friend Zeluma, and they'd befriended this bunch of people and I remember one of them very clearly, his name was Desmond O'Brien.

Would that be the somewhat enigmatic Desmond O'Brien who bankrolled Michael Hollingshead's World Psychedelic Centre?

Yes. He looked like a doctor though. He seemed very straight, very smart, seemed like a doctor or a business man, not like a freak out of the music business. He was talking about setting up this thing in Chelsea near Sloane Square (the World Psychedelic Centre), but I didn't really get it at the time. Although I'd been in dance bands since the age of fifteen I thought anyone who took drugs was a junky, I didn't know any better. Gradually, between '64 and '65 there seemed to be more and more people smoking dope and doing stranger things and then in '65 this new group of people seemed to arrive in my life through Dolores and Sammy and they were bringing over strange books like the *Tibetan Book of the Dead,* which I didn't understand because it was from outside of my culture. So there I was singing and dancing and doing show-bizzy things, and there was this strange element creeping in.

Were your friends already taking LSD at that time?

I know they started to take acid in '65. The first time I remember hearing about LSD was before the summer of '65 and I heard strange stories about people like Spike Milligan and other comic writers who were doing acid. Then at the end of '65 I know there were regular gatherings where my friends were meeting and having these guided tours beyond their minds. I was still scared, and then a band called the Small Faces came into our lives, Ian Samwell had discovered the Small Faces and got together with a guy called Don Arden. Ian wrote and produced *Whatcha Gonna Do About It?*, their first record that was a homage to Solomon Burke but was also the first intimation of soul going into outer space. It was only later that summer I discovered the Small Faces smoked dope all the time, and I thought what a shame, all these young kids are just junkies, but they said no Jeff, we're just getting high. I didn't even smoke cigarettes!

So you were becoming gradually aware of the developing London LSD scene?

At that time there was a bunch of kids from Purley and that part of the world who were moving into the dandy areas of London, Chelsea and Notting Hill, because that's where everything was brewing and of course there was a very 'high' part of Hampstead, the intellectuals that were also all experimenting and of course there was these oiks from the East End called the Small Faces who were getting loaded all the time, and having a great time. And that's when I realised, before I took the acid, that cannabis was something good, it's not a 'drug', it's a herb so I joined the herb set in the summer of '65. I had really peculiar experiences for months. I really believed every morning that I was going to die because I'd smoked this strange thing that had given me another vision in my life. I was actually quite scared for a while although I knew I'd found something. Don't know what it is, I couldn't quite make out what it was. As a boy I'd been to church every week, two churches twice a week, and I knew every part of the Bible, every part of our religious instruction and I had something there although I no longer believed in God, there was something I was searching for. And I think during that experience of turning onto marijuana and my mind going into another place, it turned me paranoid for a while but then I got where I was going and thought I was ready to move into outer space.

How did your first LSD experience come about?

In the spring of '66, it was still bloody cold out so it was probably February '66. It took place in very controlled circumstances. There was three of us. Ian Samwell sat Peter and me down in his little living room in Gayton Road in Hampstead and we played our favourite music and he would read chapters from Leary, chapters from the *Tibetan Book of the Dead*, chapters from Aldous Huxley's *Island,* and while doing that we went to a new place.

What form did the LSD come in?

It came as liquid, it came in a little test tube and the dose we were told was 250 mics and you just took it out of the dropper. Sammy was very particular that you didn't have too little or too much. It cost £3 10 shillings a trip. There were people selling acid much cheaper but we were always told only take what you knew came from the real source. Acid was also available at that time on blotting paper and people were selling it on sugar cubes too. Blotting paper was around in '66, they hadn't gone into production yet, generally it was the pale green blotting paper you got at school and you could see little stains on it and you'd cut out a square and that would be your trip.

What did you think of the LSD experience?

Well, I flew in the apartment! I levitated. I went from room to room without leaving or using my legs, I saw the most beautiful things in the world. I saw my friends as deities, everything I looked at was immaculate and beautiful, full of life and throbbing and I was just melting into it. But then I think we ate something. It was the most stupid thing to do and I got sick and puked, and I puked bugs—the bugs came out of my mouth and they crawled across the carpet towards me and I freaked out. Sammy said, 'No, Jeff, look at them. What do you see? It's life, it's beauty'. So I looked at what I was seeing as bugs and they were diamond encrusted bugs, they were creatures from another place and the stains on the carpet where I'd puked were psychedelic colours throbbing with beauty.

After a while I felt good again and carried on into a white light experience, and then I lay down and died; the three of us lay down and died together and went on an astral plane, communicated with people from other times and other generations and as we started to land, wow, we're in a better place, we are somewhere else and so we planned the next experience, on the next day we had off, which was two weeks later, which we did and I found my way through it very fast, very easily and knew direction my mind was going, and I wasn't scared of dying anymore, I wasn't having the horrors I'd had before and everything was beautiful.

Then we started sharing the sacrament with women too and of course that made it even more miraculous; LSD and sex and a beautiful woman and the beautiful smell of a woman, and I found my real life inside me. It was a life changing experience. It was a mystical experience and a physical experience.

I was still working for Mecca at that time, and singing and dancing with the Ray McVay Band. We'd been doing the Come Dancing TV shows every month usually from the Orchid Ballroom in Purley, said by Mecca at that time to be England's biggest ballroom. It was very straight but I was having these weird experiences there and things were beginning to be *different*.

Were you aware of any other LSD scenes outside of London?

That summer a whole bunch of friends were going to Majorca, opening nightclubs there and I was invited to go but I was singing and dancing, and doing Jeff Dexter's Record Show and the idea of leaving town when there was so much going on seemed rather odd to me. There were lots of strange new people in Majorca at that time and because of what was happening with the tourist scene lots of the pop and rock bands, who were also beginning to take acid, were going to play clubs there. And there were a lot of new freaks brewing on that island.

Majorca seems to have been a melting pot for the early European LSD scene. Daevid Allen and Kevin Ayers were hanging out there at that time.

Yes, particularly from a place called Deia. Robert Graves was the soulbearer of their little scene on the island, so I planned to take a trip and go and join my friend Peter Sanders who had taken up the post of DJ at Sloopy's Club that was set up by another friend, Brian Mason. I took some acid with me, a test tube full of about 50 trips. That summer in Majorca was quite fantastic. I went with this test tube in my pocket to share it with all my friends there, but on the airplane going I hadn't realised that the pressure of the cabin would pop the cork off the test tube, which it did, inside the pocket of my Mohair jacket and soaked it. So I turned the pocket out and sucked it, mid-flight.

What could possibly go wrong?

As we were arriving I could see huge great arms reaching out of the sea with lights and beams coming off them. The little waves were turning into monsters but beautiful ones and there was this huge arm appeared out of the sea as we were flying into Palma, holding the aeroplane and gently guiding us down to land. I got off that aeroplane and I was higher than I'd ever been in my life, and I'm on my own. And of course you see uniforms and guards and all I could hear was the sound of cicadas and all the stars were twinkling and there were things in the sky I'd never seen before and I had to walk through this line of Garda Civil, through immigration and customs, but I felt very confident, I had no worries about it at all.

Some of what would become Soft Machine hit on me because they'd heard I had LSD. So I went out to see them in Deia and shared it with Lady June and Daevid Allen and a few others. I didn't know the others that well but I became very friendly with that group. There was this whole new life developing there and we had wonderful, controlled, trips, and trips on the beach and going diving and snorkelling on acid. I remember one night, at John Bloom's (the Roll's Razor company guy) apartment where we had a session and spent the night listening to *Pet Sounds*, *Revolver* and *Billy Stewart* and had this wonderful night. As the sun came out we stood on the balcony in absolute amazement, it was a glorious sunrise and all these flying fish started jumping out of the sea. I didn't believe it was true, I thought I was hallucinating! They were real but at first we just thought they were visions. The colour of the sea and the colour of the sky and the smells and Majorca coming alive in the morning was one of the most wonderful experiences of my life.

It must have been a hard come down, returning to old London Town at the end of a summer like that?

I got back to the Orchid Ballroom in Purley where I'd worked for the past three and a half years and the Orchid Ballrooms manager, Dave Preedy, announced I was fire on arrival, they'd got a replacement. I still played at the Hammersmith Palais and was still singing and dancing with Ray McVay's band at Hammersmith Palais and that summer we had the Ike and Tina Turner Revue playing there. I loved Ike and Tina Turner so the night they were on I'd dropped some acid during the course of my second set with Ray McVay's band, to watch their show on acid but then I was told that after their set I've got to come on again. Oh dear! And the dance band at that time were mainly alcoholics and by the end of each night most of them were drunk, very aggressive and quite nasty. I'd watched this fantastic revue with the Ikettes and was in love with them all and then I had to be at the side of the stage as they finished and the stage revolved and I was back on with Ray McVay and the band and they picked up the rhythm of Ike and Tina's band and I have to come out and sing *Up tight and out of sight* in a black Mohair suit and my mind is…. I sang it with all my heart but as I turned and looked at the band they were all wrinkled and their faces were distorted, drunk and nasty and, this is own up time, I never sang again. I quit then. I walked off the stage and that was it.

How did the LSD scene develop in London in 1966, before it was made a controlled drug?

Among this Chelsea gang who had come into my life, there were musicians, Eric Burdon for instance, who I took acid with. But we weren't sort of dropping it and going out raving at that time, we were doing it in comfort in secure places. Dolores and her friend Zelma and Sammy were friends with the Chelsea crowd I mentioned, taking acid but doing it secretly in quiet and controlled situations and reading strange things like the *Tibetan Book of the Dead*. They were taking it seriously, they weren't just dropping acid and going out, they wanted to go further, instead of going out and having fun they were opening the doors of perception.

Did you see a tension between the two schools of thought around taking LSD; the religious angle and the going out and having fun aspect?

Well I did both! I believe wholeheartedly in both because there's only one life! But then we started to experiment with taking it and going out and I started to take it at gigs as well, even taking it in the ballrooms because I wanted a new perspective.

How much of your life at that time was devoted to psychedelics, had you turned into a psychedelic person.

I think I had *totally* turned into, for want of a better term, a journeyman. I was on a journey but the one thing I learned, and this is the beauty of the people we were reading at the time, like Huxley, was 'Here and now boys, here and now boys', it's still clear in my mind. The fact is you're on a journey, but you're also already there and that was dominant in my mind and I'd become very secure in myself about how I thought about things in my life, how I felt about music and in particular how I felt about women. Women were the most important thing in a man's life and there were *so* many beautiful women around, I had the most wonderful time. I'd always been surrounded by beautiful women since I started work at Mecca in 1961 but now I was beginning to experience these things in a deeper way I suppose you could say. It was beautiful. I was in a wonderful place, experiencing wonderful things with the nicest things in the world.

Did you see any harm in LSD?

I saw some people had the horrors and go through dodgy experiences and I was sympathetic to them but I think it was their own, earlier problems in their life which caused them. But out of those bad trips, cos I had two bad trips, they taught me something about myself. The worst part of a bad trip was being paranoid about something that wasn't there or if you had a bad thought or if someone hit you with a bummer you could go down instantly, it was so easy to go down, as easy as it was to go up. But I think some of those bad experiences were great curves in my life that taught me a lot about my mind and my feelings and other people's too. But honestly, my acid experiences filled me with love. I know it sounds really stupid but I wanted to become a 'beautiful person' inside and out, lots of my friends did too and we all adored and loved each other.

You mentioned Huxley and Leary—how influenced were you by their writings?

I found Leary hard going, although I read lots of it. Some of it sounded very good but some of it I found kind of 'American' and a bit falsified in some ways, whereas reading Huxley there was a certain clarity to it that really did me good. Although the chapters in Leary's *Book of the Dead* about turning off your mind, well I found them incredibly useful and my friends were finding them useful too. And some of the singers too—there was of course Donovan that year who I'd always considered to be a dodgy woolly jumper, but what he was beginning to say, and the way he looked, there was *something* going on. And that summer in Majorca was quite fantastic.

Did London have its psychedelic 'happenings'?

When they launched *International Times* in October 1966 at the Roundhouse, Zelma and Dolores said there's going to be this party, we're all going to get dressed up and it's going to be a rave and a happening. I had no idea what International Times was, but the Soft Machine who I had met in Deia that summer were going to be playing along with Pink Floyd . I'd seen Pink Floyd earlier that summer at The Marquee but didn't think much of what they were doing at that time, they were too odd for me; but I was told lots of people were going dressed up so I thought I'd at least experience that, and that of course led onto UFO. I'd met Joe Boyd earlier that year when he was working for Jac Holzman at Elektra and by that time he was looking for new acts for Elektra in England. I invited Joe to a few things and we were always discussing what new bands were on and in the ballrooms and the clubs there were lots of new bands experimenting, doing odd things, plus there were wonderful records coming from America which were soul records but suddenly had a different edge—one called *Sock It To 'Em JB* by Rex Garvin and the Mighty Cravers. It's a soul classic dance record but Part II, the B-side was the same tune where they'd decided to psychedelicise it. It was the first piece of dub, psychedelia, all flanged and phased out, all full of echo; so there was this other side coming from America from the soul scene and the main soul contingent just didn't get it 'cos they were still dressed in their tight arsed clothes.

Did you have much contact with any of the eastern gurus who, in the late 1960s, became popular with LSD takers?

My interest in Flying Saucers, and the Thursday night meetings at Leslie Duncan's flat discussing UFOs and aliens, with Bruce Cathie, the New Zealand guy who had tracked them on radar, with other friends like David Bowie—he'd only just 'become' David Bowie at that time, eventually led me to the Samye Ling monastery and Tibetan Centre with Chogyam Trungpa. He was the real thing, he was wonderful. Anyway, the second time I went up there, in 1969, and you had to sign the visitor book when you came to stay and David Bowie had been there just days before. Trungpa had a strange name for David, it was slightly derogatory too, but warm with it for David, I can't remember what it was, but he called me 'Little Mouse'.

One night there I had some acid and Trungpa said, 'Give me some then'. We'd already been drinking whiskey, he liked his whiskey. Everyone sat round him in awe, because he was like a deity. So I gave him some acid, all three of us in the room took some, and after about 40 minutes this bead of sweat appeared on his forehead and I thought it was a crystal coming out of his skull (laughs) and he went, 'I see, little mouse, this is something quite special. You have to realise that all your answers, anything you're looking for' and he touched me on the shoulder, and of course if he touched anyone people immediately they'd been blessed', 'all your answers are already inside you, you're already there'—and I said, 'but that's from *Island*, that's 'Here and now boy's', and from Ram Dass' *Be Here Now*, that's the journey, that you're already here'. It was quite fantastic really. Well, anytime you take acid it's fantastic. And then we went out for a walk on the moors in the middle of the night, it was dark, pitch black, it was freezing cold and the sky was beautiful and crystal clear. My eyes were seeing beauty, and then all of a sudden there were these lights in the sky—my first thought was 'They're here, man'—then another light, then another and another and it was the Aurora Borealis, and the sky was better than any light show at UFO, better than anything I'd ever put on anywhere in my days as the Jeff Dexter Light and Sound Show.

To get back to the International Times party in October 1966—that party was a *great* party, very peculiar—the giant jelly, the motorcycle, all the weird things. It was the night I became friendly with Syd Barrett. Soft Machine were playing and the Pink Floyd and around Syd were these four beautiful women, one of whom was June Child who would later marry Marc Bolan. So I became friends with Syd cos I wanted to be surrounded by beautiful women and the whole night sort of melted into one strange experience; and I think UFO was the culmination of that night, translated into a semi-commercial basis for a weekly gathering of the tribe. Although it was in a dodgy Irish ballroom, once you were inside you were at home in a different land with 40 per cent or 50 per cent of the people there being on acid, and it felt like home because there were all these other people there experiencing it with you. Everyone who danced and jumped around and made fools of themselves were getting higher. There were lots of stories from UFO such as the one about the guy who stood on the stairs and handed out the sacrament if you handed over a few quid.

In December 1969 Jeff attended a party connected with the launch of the UK edition of Rolling Stone magazine. He went with his old friends Ian Samwell and Marc Bolan, then of Tyrannosaurus Rex (later T Rex), the archetypical hippie band.

The paper had already appeared, headed up by Alan Marcuson and it had attracted a lot of writers from Oz and other underground magazines. Mainly due to Jo Bergman who worked for the Rolling Stones, the Stones wanted to fund Rolling Stone UK. So it was a party to show that the Stones were behind it, and all the straight press and the freak press turned up. I think one of the Stones turned up, I think Keith was there. It was a wonderful room to be in, lots of wonderful food and alcohol and for some reason someone had laced a lot of the food and alcohol with some substances. I started to feel rather odd, and so did Ian Samwell. I was with him and Marc (Bolan) and all of a sudden, Sammy started feel really weird and said 'oh god, someone's spiked us', then Marc said he felt strange and it suddenly dawned on me that we were tripping. Marc started to get in a bad way and then June (Child, Bolan's wife to be) arrived. He claimed he had tripped before, but I don't think he had because of the way he reacted. He was in a bad way and so was Sammy, so June—who was completely straight—drove them home to my house and by that time Marc was going completely crazy and I was holding onto him for dear life in the back seat of a Mini. The acid, or whatever it was, had got to Marc and he was afraid he was a faker.

Did Marc ever take acid again?

No. But it certainly made him think about who he was!

The likelihood that Marc Bolan only took LSD once and that experience was a disaster might come as a shock to many of his fans. Your comment he was concerned he might have been a 'faker' is perhaps validated by the widespread belief that Tyrannosaurus Rex stole many of their musical, fashion and lyrical ideas from the Incredible String Band, who pre-dated Tyrannosaurus Rex and made no secret of their psychedelic influences.

What the Incredible String Band were doing at that time was beyond psychedelia. It was the sound of the earth, for me anyway. The best line they ever came up with was from the *Hedgehog's Song*, 'You know all the notes and you sung all the words but you never quite learned the song to sing/I can tell by the sadness in your eyes that you never quite learned the song'. I use it all the time and still think it is the most beautiful put down line in British psychedelic writing, but delivered with such love.

Are there any other instances of sixties acid weirdness you were involved in, Jeff?

In 1969 there was a strange bunch of people who arrived from America, Babbs and Kesey from the Merry Pranksters, The Brotherhood of Eternal Love people, and an amazing woman acid chemist. They came over and there was this weird scene going on at Apple HQ, or Apple Corps as they called it, and they brought with them thousands of acid tabs and I was supposed to share this with people who I thought would benefit. So I was given this bag of

500 Orange Sunshine LSD pills and I was doing all those shows at that time and whenever I met anyone I thought was deserving I would share it with them, pass on the sacrament to them. It was brilliant, absolutely fantastic. They came over again about a year and half later and gave me another bag of acid and it was great to be a conduit for them, I was very privileged to be given the job of distribution. But I never sold it, I just gave it away! They'd come over to turn on London and because the Beatles to them were the Sun Kings, they weren't just a pop band, they'd changed our culture, so they were obviously very important to the American acid heads. And they had Derek Taylor running the press office upstairs and the office was always full of any freaks who came into town, they'd go straight to Derek's office. They stayed on for the summer of 1969 and Owsley came over for the Blind Faith gig in Hyde Park. I was the MC for that gig and I went on acid...

Thanks for that brief insight into how you got involved in LSD during the sixties, Jeff. I bet you have just as many stories about the 1970s?

Well, I also helped Andrew Kerr and then later Arabella Churchill put the 1971 event together and was the DJ/MC for the event. Lots of acid there!

But that, as they say, is another story...

10

Glastonedbury

The annual Glastonbury Festival has become a unique British cultural institution. Each year, in June, on the weekend nearest the summer solstice, hundreds of thousands of people flock to Worthy Farm in the Somerset village of Pilton to camp for three days. They are there to experience the dizzying kaleidoscope of music, theatre and arts on offer on numerous stages. The festival caters for all ages, cultures and socio-economic backgrounds. It is often referred to by cynics as a holiday camp for middle-class hippies. Yet the origins of this quintessentially British event are rooted deep in the counter-culture and entwined with LSD and other psychedelics. Had it not been for the psychedelic focus of the first major Glastonbury event, the festival would not have developed into the kaleidoscopic, multi-media event it now is.

But why and how did Glastonbury become the spiritual birthplace of the free festival movement? The growing awareness among young people that the LSD experience itself was not the destination, but a catalyst to a spiritual journey, had led to an explosion of interest in a variety of belief systems during the sixties. As we have seen, psychedelic seekers often chose to explore Buddhism, Hinduism and other religions. Others found themselves drawn to the Western Mystery Tradition, Arthurian legend, magic and/or shamanism, wanting to discover at first hand the legacy of spiritual traditions and beliefs of the British Isles. And where better to do this than at Glastonbury?

The Glastonbury area is steeped in myth and legend; it is claimed Jesus visited Glastonbury Abbey, UFOs have been sighted over the Tor, ley-lines criss-cross the area, sending serpent power through the West Country, a terrestrial Zodiac can be discerned in landscape features surrounding the Tor, and so on. In the mid-1960s these and many other legends had recently been re-vivified and re-tooled for the counter-culture by author John Michell in his books *The Flying Saucer Vision* and *The View over Atlantis*. Michell wrote: 'It was, I think, in 1966 that I first went to Glastonbury, in the company of Harry Fainlight... We had no very definite reason for going there, but it had something to do with ... strange lights in the sky, new music, and our conviction that the world was about to flip over on its axis so that heresy would become orthodoxy and an entirely new world-order would shortly be revealed'.[1]

Michell was the counter-culture's resident philosopher, their Merlin; an Eton and Cambridge educated polymath who had taken the side of the hippies and was educating them about their indigenous spiritual heritage. Michell lived in the hippie enclave of Notting Hill Gate, equally as comfortable at counter-culture events as he was hanging out with the Rolling Stones or minor aristocracy. His books were key spiritual guides for the British counter-culture and could be found in every thinking hippie's pad, offering a source of discussion and speculation during those timeless LSD trips toward the dawn.

Michell showed there was no need to take the hippie trail to the East when the West Country was just down the M4. And the visual imagery of Glastonbury was everywhere in the underground press. One very good example is the cover of issue one of the Underground magazine, *Albion*, edited by Steve Penk. Dragons and UFOs teem in the skies over Glastonbury Tor, here stylized as a woman's breast, whilst swords, serpents and geomantic imagery are visible as part of the body of the Earth below. Hippie travellers in search of enlightenment had settled in the area from the mid-sixties onwards, fuelled by Michell's exposition of Glastonbury as a sacred place. It was against this backdrop that the Glastonbury festivals would develop.[2]

The first festival at Glastonbury in 1970 was a low-key, commercial event attended by a few hundred people. Organised by Pilton farmer Michael Eavis, the festival was a financial disaster. To recoup his losses, Eavis left the organization of the 1971 event, known as Glastonbury Fair, to a rather unlikely group of people.[3]

Andrew Kerr first met Arabella Churchill, Winston's granddaughter, while working on Randolph Churchill's biography of the great political leader. In the late sixties, like thousands of others, Kerr was taking LSD and enjoying being part of the counter-culture. The seed of his idea to hold a free festival at Glastonbury was planted at the 1969 Isle of Wight rock festival. Kerr was outraged that large areas near the stage were cordoned off for the press and privileged few, while the foot soldiers of the psychedelic revolution had to pay to stand at a distance to the stage. On the drive back to London he announced to his fellow passengers: 'We've got to have a proper festival and it's got to have at least some cosmic significance. Let's have it at the summer solstice at Stonehenge.'[4]

The pair chatted and a now historic meeting was convened at Worthy Farm. Kerr prepared himself by spending the night before atop Glastonbury Tor on LSD. The meeting was a success. Eavis agreed to the use of his land for a reasonable fee and Kerr, assisted by Arabella Churchill and utilising a small inheritance, formed Solstice Capers to organise the 1971 festival.

Speaking after the event, Kerr acknowledged Glastonbury's place in the Matter of Britain, 'It is the very heart of the body of England...What drew these people to Glastonbury was a feeling that from this ancient, sacred place a new spirit is to spread among men. They were here to bear witness to the birth of the new era, The Age of Aquarius.'[5]

Kerr started to plan his festival in earnest, expanding on the philosophy behind Glastonbury Fayre: 'There seemed to be a need for a truly free festival. All the others had some profit motive behind them-some worthy causes, some for greed, none for love. The bread was made out of the people who least could afford it; it was time they were given a party.'[6]

The 'bring what you expect to find' ethos which permeated all British free festivals really began at Glastonbury Fayre. Another of the core organising group, Thomas Crimble, who had recently stepped down from bass guitar duties with nascent free festival stalwarts Hawkwind, recalled, 'The ethos was, if there's a problem, sort it out yourself, don't expect anyone else to do it, it's your festival'.[7]

The Observer wrote: 'Kerr has the intensity of a man with a deep spiritual obsession. He claims he is trying to recreate a prehistoric science, whose huge energies are not recognised by modern society. His ideas are based on the writings of antiquarian John Michell, who in a book called *The View Over Atlantis*, recently elucidated the spiritual engineering which, he says, was known over the ancient world.'[8]

These ideas were transmuted into the location and design of the stage. Kerr dowsed the site and when he located a blind spring, with Glastonbury Tor in the distance, it was decided to site the stage directly above it. John Michell told him the stage should be built to the sacred proportions of

Egypt's Great Pyramid. This suited Kerr's intention for the festival, which was to '… create an increase in the power of the Universe, a heightening of consciousness and recognition of our place in the function of this our tired and molested planet.'[9] Or to put it more psychedelically; 'Imagine, we're going to concentrate the celestial fire and pump it into the planet to stimulate growth.'[10] Bill Harkin, now a respected stage designer, designed and built the stage and a silver pyramid eventually sprang up among the cows, fields and hedges of Worthy Farm.

Jeff Dexter, veteran DJ from London's UFO club, organised the music, a dizzying line-up consisting of the house bands of the counter-culture which included freak favourites Quintessence, Brinsley Schwarz, Hawkwind, Gong, Traffic and Arthur Brown. These bands were open and enthusiastic about their use of LSD and strove to create a musical environment suitable for those under the influence of psychedelic drugs. Dexter tried hard to get the archetypal LSD band, the Grateful Dead, over from America to play but this didn't come off. They did send a financial donation to support the festival and appeared on the Glastonbury Fayre soundtrack album.

Psychedelics of all kinds, including mescaline, were freely available at Glastonbury, but LSD was by far the most prevalent mind expanding drug on offer. Tim Hargreaves, who was on the road in the early 1970s, eventually ending up in the Free High Church commune on the Isle of Cumbrae, with ex-Learyite Michael Hollingshead, recalls what happened when he and his friends arrived at the gate, 'As we pulled up at Worthy Farm we were met at the gate by a woman who showed us where to park up and make camp. She asked if we had money, we said we had a bit but were setting off on a trip round the UK to visit all known communes. She said not to worry about tickets but did we have food? Saying yes, she told us to share it and then asked if we were prepared… and then dropped near 50 tabs into our hands.'[11]

Hargreaves believes this could have been Anabella Churchill. It's possible. Although she denied indulging in psychedelics herself she was aware '… there was a lot of acid, because this man came up with a large briefcase and said: "This is full of acid, man. I was going to sell it but everyone's doing everything for free so here, give it to everybody." I put it under a bed and I can't remember what happened to it in the end.'[12]

For many festival goers, Glastonbury Fayre was their first experience of the burgeoning counter-culture. The festival made a huge impact on Croatian actress Hanja Kochansky who wrote this fecund account of the event, noting the many different mind altering substances that were available as well as the strong sense of community which underpinned the free festivals:

Thai sticks, Moroccan hash, magic mushrooms, Mexican mescaline and Timothy Leary acid rained like manna from the blue skies. Celestial sounds echoed through the valleys in this psychedelic wonderland, where streams of extravagant humanity had come from everywhere to celebrate life. Flutes, guitars, drums, harmonicas; happy naked babies like butterflies; goats, a calf, horse-driven gypsy caravans. As our eyes met, reflecting open smiles and free love, we sang, danced, embraced, experienced ecstasy.

A drove of timESPace travellers with coats of many colours dwelled in vans, trailers, trucks, limousines and pantechnicons, with their Tarot cards, tattoos, muesli, brown rice, books on mysticism, magic cats, bubbling cauldrons, unleavened bread and video-cameras.

In this microcosmos, where goodwill flowed as naked bodies soaked in the sun I met the scarlet haired Rainbow Gypsies from California who taught me to henna my hair; took LSD with the poet George Andrews; was charmed by Pan-like Heathcote Williams playing his flute to woo his girlfriend, top-model Jean Shrimpton.

Oh how happy was the gypsy in me: washing in limpid streams; cooking on an open fire; joining in musical choirs that went on till it was time to salute the sun with Yoga asanas. As I watched the smoke from chillums sneaking up towards the sky, I wanted to remain in this sweet life, this dolce vita, forever: in this link between me and the Divine.

When the event came to an end we shared our last chillum round the last of the fires with heavy heart. In the morning we packed our tents, cramped our few clothes in baskets and carpet bags and headed back to the city to resume our daily lives. But we were never the same again. We had glimpsed Paradise on Earth and from now on we were to take the road directed towards Eden; the road less travelled.

Author Williams Bloom's impression of Glastonbury was that '… nearly everyone was tripping at one stage or another. Sometimes it was being given away…. The festivals would not have been what they were without hallucinogens.'[13] 'The mixture of very good LSD and very bad scrumpy. Impromtu processions. The frenzy of the underground press to produce newssheets. The good vibe. Bowie waking the crowd playing a foot-pumped organ.'

For his part, David Bowie recalled being under the influence of magic mushrooms as he took to the stage at five in the morning: 'By the time I was due to perform I was flying and could hardly see my little electric keyboard or my guitar.'[14] Bowie's recollection is intriguing, not least for the fact that it is one of the earliest instances of 'magic mushrooms' being used at a festival.

Not only was there a great deal of LSD around, there were many different varieties too, including 'Several thousand so-called 'Sarsaparilla' (sic) pills (each derived from 50 litres of the distilled, concentrated flavouring, along with a touch of LSD and amphetamine) had been shipped to the Festival as "vitamins"', remembers wandering hippie, Nick Butts. 'They made people feel as though they were walking on air, and were an extreme aphrodisiac. They provoked an outbreak of uninhibited coupling all around the site, and throughout the festival cries of "Are we sassed yet?" rippled through the crowd.'

Many clergymen visited the 1971 Glastonbury festival, attracted by this radical youth movement and their alternative brand of spirituality. Among them was the diocesan youth chaplain from Swindon, who took some LSD (whether voluntarily or not is unclear). The confused clergyman ended up rushing headlong down the festival hillside, his cloak flaring like a giant bat behind him. However, his Christian faith wasn't enough to help him navigate the multiverse he experienced under the onslaught of LSD, and he had to retire to the bad trip tent organised by Release where he was gently talked back down to earth.[15]

Though the majority of LSD experiences at Glastonbury were positive there were, as at every festival, some drug casualties. Bad trip tents were to become a feature of the free festival scene, often full of seriously confused teenagers who had been attracted to LSD by peer pressure and expectation, but who were unprepared for the effects of the drug. On one hand these tents were perhaps the downside of the free festival experience, but on the other they demonstrate that free festival goers were prepared to care for those who had overindulged. Quintessence guitarist Allan Mostert remembers: 'A rather shattering experience I had at Glastonbury was while wandering through the audience before our set, I took a look inside the so called 'bad trip tent', where they took the people who had dropped LSD and gone on bad trips. This experience strengthened the idea in me of what we were actually trying to do with our music and 'message'.[16]

Arthur Brown's performance at the festival was also too much for some of those trippers who were focussed solely on love and peace when they were under the influence of powerful psychedelics. His doom laden show which featured band members dressed as monks, flaming crucifixes and Arthur himself with a fiery headdress, was an overwhelming audio visual experience.

'Arthur Brown fucked the festival up that night. He caught a lot of people stoned on acid, and he freaked a lot of people out, and they left the stage area. I think they went back to their tents or hid in the woods, 'cos Arthur Brown appeared on stage with a bloody crucifix—on fire—and it was like the Ku Klux Klan in your head... he gave out this evil presence, and the whole atmosphere became evil from it, especially for those who were stoned or tripping.'

Brown's biographer, Polly Marshall, also noted about Brown's Glastonbury appearance, 'Into this welter of peace, love and LSD, wandered Arthur and Kingdom Come. But what really made their set memorable was their light show, probably dreamt up by Dennis Taylor whilst munching through one of his "small doses" of 500 mics. He set up flaming crosses in front of the stage.'[17] Dennis Taylor was a member of Brown's road crew, notorious for his LSD consumption. The section of the Glastonbury Fayre film that features Arthur Brown shows the acid-soused audience's reaction to Brown's pseudo-satanic performance and stage set; many were clearly freaked out!

Overall, the preponderance of LSD and other psychedelics at Glastonbury Fayre was positive and a combination of the drugs and the general vibe led one attendee to say, 'A sort of constant ecstasy seemed to be the mood of the day. People strode around, often with a lovely look in their eyes, as if they had seen visions and other strange miracles, hard to put into words...'.[18]

The mixture of free psychedelics, along with living out the hippie ethos, made the Glastonbury Fair the prototype for subsequent events. LSD and other psychedelics brought people together around the campfires at night, making the already otherworldly experience appear completely divorced from the 20th century and Western civilisation. Mick Farren summed it up: 'We might as well have been in the sixth or even twenty-sixth century as we told tall travellers' tales of intoxication, of outwitting the law, of the lights in the sky, lost continents, the lies of government, collective triumphs and personal stupidity, while the music of past, present and future roared from the pyramid stage.'[19]

Michael Eavis made a profit on the event but was somewhat concerned. 'There was a lot of LSD around. People were freaking out, wandering into the village wearing nothing but a top hat, that sort of thing. I was all over the place, looking after the villagers and the cattle that were straying. Once it was over, I decided I didn't want anything to do with it again.'[20] His concerns soon subsided and although a number of years elapsed before a festival was again on his land, by the early 1980s the Glastonbury Festival was embedded as part of the English cultural landscape.

Following the 1971 Glastonbury free festival the area became a focus for traveling hippies. Small encampments sprang up in the country lanes, or droves as they are known, and there were almost continuous gatherings on the summit of Glastonbury Tor. In the seventies, there were people taking LSD on the Tor every night of the summer. To visit the Tor, take LSD and watch the sunrise over the Somerset levels was considered a hip thing to do, a psychedelic pilgrimage.

At one stage, the tower on the Tor had been broken into and turned into a hippie crash pad. Free festival poster artist Roger Hutchison and friends travelled to the Tor from Essex. He climbed to the summit at 3 am, to find the inside of the tower bedecked with cushions and lighted tapers with a group of hippies smoking cannabis and drinking wine. Such was the spirit of community and trust in those times that he was immediately offered LSD in blotter form by a colourfully dressed hippie, and settled down to watch the sunrise, accompanied by chanting and drumming.

This type of shamanic activity was prevalent among the mystically inclined at free festivals. Drums, chanting and psychedelic drugs have been used together since prehistoric times, each enhancing the effect of the other. This type of group behaviour not only had a strong bonding effect but served to help individuals navigate the LSD experience, either as participants or observers.

Now that the counter-culture had experienced just what a summer time multi-day free festival, fuelled by psychedelics, could be like it was only a matter of time before other, much larger and more contentious ones would be planned.

11

Mushroom Magic at Crazy Creek

The Welsh Psilocybin Festivals 1976–82

From the late 1960s onwards, Britain was host to a series of open air festivals each summer, organised by the counter-culture and bearing the name 'Free Festivals'. From the 1970's Phun City, through the multi-day events of the Windsor, Trentishoe, Stonehenge and countless other free festivals of the 1970s, psychedelic drugs, primarily LSD, were widely and openly used at these events. It is my contention that these free festivals were events in which members of Britain's counter-culture (heads, hippies, freaks etc.) could come together and take psychedelics in a safe, mutually supportive environment.

The media and police were very much aware of the focus on psychedelic drugs at Free Festivals. But organisers of the events generally played down this aspect to 'straight' society, fearing even more harassment than they already suffered if the truth were openly revealed. But if the use of psychedelics at most free festivals was kept as far away as possible from the public, media and powers that be, the same cannot be said of the Welsh Psilocybin festivals. The clue was in the name!

Psychedelic fungi have been used in religious and cultural ceremonies for millennia by indigenous societies across the globe and continue to be used in the present day. Britain has several genera of psychoactive fungi but other than the little used *Amanita Muscaria*, it is primarily the species *Psilocybe semilanceata* that was used by the free festival movement, and which was the focus of the Welsh Psilocybin festivals.

Evidence suggests that recreational use of *P. semilanceata*, better known as the 'liberty cap' or more popularly 'magic mushrooms', dates to the late 1950s in Britain, when it was used occasionally by the Beatniks. However, its use among the hippie underground was limited and until the mid-1970s, use of any psychoactive fungi among the counter-culture appeared to be limited. Just why this situation changed is unclear. Several factors seem to have conspired to bring *P. semilanceata* into broader usage. It is possible that widespread experimentation with all types of psychedelic drugs, coupled with an interest in drug use by indigenous peoples led the British counter-culture to pursue its native fungi for their own access to altered states. Books by Carlos Castaneda, purporting to be the experiences of an initiation into mid-American shamanism had featured psychoactive fungi, and were popular among British hippies. Another factor in the usage of magic mushrooms was Operation Julie, the smashing by the British government of Richard Kemp and Andy Munro's LSD labs, and the requirement to find alternate sources for the psychedelic experience. Another, much more practical, reason was the cost. *P. semilanceata* was free at the point of picking and if one had access to productive fields it was easily possible to pick thousands of the tiny mushrooms, enough to last a year with enough to sell or give to friends.

As with many aspects of the British counter-culture, we may never know the real origins of the widespread usage of psychoactive fungi, and I thoroughly recommend Andy Letcher's excellent book *Shroom*, for a well-researched and level headed examination of the rise and rise of magic mushrooms. By the mid-1970s references to mushrooms were creeping into the counter-culture's iconography. You have to be diligent to find these references, but as an example several of the promotional flyers for the 1974 and 1975 Windsor free festivals featured a variety of mushrooms. However *P. semilanceata*, somewhat oddly, is not among them. This is perhaps indicative of their still limited use as well as of a general, growing and broadening awareness of the magic mushroom as a consciousness changer. In 1976 Alan Beam wrote: "In Albion Free State there are 1,001 ways to stay high - 'jam open the doors of perception' with chanting, fucking, dancing, dreaming, visions, magic mushrooms, yoga and a lifetime's full of other possibilities." And in 1977 the cat was well and truly out of the bag with the publication of Richard Cooper's *A Guide to British Psilocybin Mushrooms*.

But back to the Welsh Psilocybin festivals. *P. semilanceata* grows in profusion in most areas of Wales from late July onwards, with the peak of the season (dependent on the weather), being in September and October, and ending with the first frosts. *P. semilanceata* can easily be found in most upland areas of Britain on liminal farm land. Why one particular area should have been chosen above another for the Psilocybin festivals is unclear but seems to have come about by a happy accident.

The Welsh Psilocybin festivals are widely referred to as taking place at Devil's Bridge or Pontrhydygroes, about 20 miles from Aberystwyth in mid-Wales. The events *actually* took place in the picturesque valley of the Afon Ystwyth, on a dried out stream bed between the old Grogwynion lead mine workings and the sawmills. Devil's Bridge is several miles away, on the A4120, but the village may have become synonymous with the festivals because its name adds a faintly mysterious air to the events and because the tiny hamlet with its dramatic gorge and forest scenery would have been a memorable road turn-off point for most people travelling to the festivals.

The first Psilocybin festival took place there in mid-July, 1976. According to people who were there, the event came about after the police evicted people from the free festival being held on the moors at the head of the Elan Valley, about fifteen miles away. Janet Thompson remembered, "On the 13th at 6:30am 400 coppers had encircled the site and woke everyone up and evicted us, it was a bit of a shock, most people were still in bed. I think they had bussed in coppers from all over Wales. Everyone got themselves together and moved off 'up the road' to another site which became the first mushroom festival at Pontrhydygroes."

The diaspora from the Elan Valley eviction created the first mushroom festival by default, although due to the time of year it is unlikely there was a large mushroom harvest. A Ceredigion District Council (CDC) document refers to a large gathering of hippies being moved on from the Elan Valley that "...regrouped and squatted for several weeks on the flood plain of the River Ystwyth". The camp was set up near a disused lead mine at Blaen-Y-Ddol. It was an idyllic site; isolated but not too far from main roads or towns, with wood, water and, of course, psilocybin mushrooms.

No event appears to have taken place in 1977, but in 1978 about 300 hippies turned up and held a small festival in the location used for the 1976 gathering. By 1979, however, the festival had come of age and was being widely referred to as the Psilocybin Fayre. Badges were produced bearing the words *Psilocybin Fayre*, surrounding the colourful image of a dancing elemental spirit copied from one of Janet Shankman's paintings on the sleeve of the Incredible String Band's *I Looked Up* album.

The 1979 festival attracted over 2,000 people and ran from the 6-13th of September. The location of the event had moved approximately one mile downstream and west of the previous festivals to a larger area. *Liberty 'trippers' flock to fungus festival* screamed the headline on the front page of the *Cambrian News*. Those present dubbed the site 'The Free State of Albion' or, more colloquially, 'Crazy Creek', and went about their annual mushroom business. Asked by a journalist why he was attending the festival, one attendee claimed it was to, "Worship Eris, the goddess of Discordia", noting that "It was the time of the full moon, which represented the end of the summer and the beginning of autumn." The accompanying photo showed one festival goer clutching a large handful of the fungi.

Jennifer Marigold Wood attended the 1979 festival and, being used to festivals which offered a wide array of entertainments, remembers being disappointed to find "There was no entertainment, just people and drugs". This observation reinforced the idea that the early Psilocybin festivals were primarily about the gathering and taking of *P. semilanceata* and the coming together of the British hippie traveller community, rather than commercialism and performance. And it wasn't just *P. semilanceata* which was being collected. Wood recalls, "Someone had been in the woods collecting fly agaric mushrooms and they duly fried them over the fire and shared them out with the caveat 'they can be poisonous sometimes." Wood ate some but doesn't recall any effect. However, in describing a walk she took later that day, it is possible the subtle effects of Amanita kicked in later, as she remembers "I was not on anything but I felt so high and so much a part of everything in the universe. It was the most wonderful feeling and has stayed with me ever since."

The Dyfed-Powys police fielded a high profile presence and randomly targeted festival goers, mainly on the road as they arrived at the site. The robust stop and search tactic was undertaken because the police believed a reasonable percentage of those attending would be carrying illegal drugs and that a proportion of the drivers and vehicles would be unlicensed or un-roadworthy vehicles. Hundreds were stopped and searched and 90 people later appeared in court on a variety of drug charges, mainly involving cannabis. Despite this, one of the festival organisers was gracious enough to say, "…to be fair to the police they've caused no trouble at all on the festival site itself."

In the aftermath of the 1979 festival Ceredigion District Council vowed the event would not take place again. CDC's concerns revolved more around the potential for fires and their discriminatory perceptions of hippies, than any substantive evidence that the festival had caused problems. As the Psilocybe mushroom was still legal to use in 1979, albeit with a slightly more dubious legal position around its dried or prepared usage, there was little reference by the Council as to *why* the event took place. In fact, the Council's Public Health Department were very impressed with how much help had been given to leave the site as clean as it was before the event, "During an inspection on the day the site was vacated, little refuse was left and considering that some 2,000 people had been through the place, it was remarkably clean." He added, seemingly in support of free festivals generally, "If this fair is to be held again in the future, every effort should be made by the organisers to be on site at least two days before the commencing date, to arrange for toilets, water and rubbish disposal".

In late February 1980 a special Council meeting was held at Aberystwyth Town Hall to discuss the now annual festival. Officers from C.D.C., Dyfed Fire Service, Dyfed Powys Police, the Forestry Commission and the Welsh Water Authority attended, along with representatives from Gwnnws Isaf and Llanafan Community Councils. Local landowners and the public were in attendance too, and all were determined, once and for all, to bring an end to the freaks' festival of fungus.

A report entitled 'Problems resulting from Hippie 'Festivals' in the Ystwyth River' Valley was circulated at the meeting. This document focused on three main issues regarding the festivals; pollution, fire danger and threats to properties in the area. Once again there was no mention of the focus of the festival—psychoactive fungi. This may have been because of the Psilocybe mushroom's quasi-legal status, but it is the author's belief that objections to the festival were more about the lifestyle of those who attended. Mid-Wales was, in the 1970s and 80s, extremely conservative with religious beliefs still playing a strong part in the overall culture of the area and in the lives of many who lived there. The hard core hippie traveller's lifestyle was anathema to the hard working country folk, and Wales' regional and local newspapers regularly featured stories concerning the hippie influx. Rarely a week went by without the *Cambrian News* reporting on a commune, a drug bust or some other aspect of hippie life that many readers would find distasteful and completely alien to their traditional work and chapel centred existence.

This unspoken prejudice was amplified in the report with its assertion that "The small scattered local population is quite at the mercy of a lawless, nameless and at the very least truculent and unsavoury army of occupation… It becomes noisy, filthy, repulsive—something between a fairground and a rubbish dump… We are polite because they seem slightly subnormal, and because we are afraid."

This discriminatory rant at the counter-culture's expense was balanced slightly by a suggestion that existing sites with facilities, such as those used by fairs and Eisteddfods, could be rented to free festival organisers. But CDC was frustrated with its inability to identify organisers or leaders. They simply didn't grasp the loose anarchic 'bring what you expect to find' ethos that underpinned the free festival movement. CDC Officers, steeped in decades of stultifying local government rules and regulations could not comprehend there was no formal structure behind the free festival movement. The following sentence exemplifies the problem CDC faced and their inability to grasp the facts, "Hippie festivals are not spontaneous, they are organised. There must be a corresponding organisation to deal with them?"

The meeting concluded with the agreement that the local authority was impotent to deal with the festival, and new legislation was required. Various measures were mooted to prevent or disrupt the 1980 festival including police action, and driving the hippies away by partially flooding the site. Other suggestions to prevent the mushroom munching hordes included asking local traders to actively discourage the hippies, which nowadays would be a flagrant breach of discrimination legislation.

One suggested solution, to make a Direction under Article 4 of the Town and Country Planning Act 1977 to require planning permission for camp sites occupied for more than 28 days, was taken seriously. Seriously to the point of paranoia, with one internal Council communication requesting, "I am sure that you realise the importance of keeping these discussions as confidential as possible. If the hippies get to know that public bodies had met to discuss this matter they might feel encouraged by such a move and might therefore interpret it as some form of acceptance on our part."

The need for secrecy, lest news of this impending change in legislation get back to the counter-culture, was repeated three times in the report, highlighting a touching naivety in the Council's belief that those who attended free festivals cared anything at all about laws surrounding land access!

Discussions as to how to prevent the 1980 festival taking place continued throughout the spring of that year. The Welsh Water Authority (WWA) were completely against any flooding of the area due to the risk of heavy metal residues from the former lead and zinc mines in the area being washed downstream. (CDC was unimpressed, having pinned its hopes on flooding being the most practical way to deal with the 'problem'. The delightfully named J.H. Stoner noted, complete with unintentional pun, "It seems clear that the Authority wish to wash their hands of this matter and are not prepared to co-operate in any way".

So a change to the law it was, and on 20th June 1980, the local addendum to the Town and Country Planning Act was made law. This revised legislature forbade, without prior planning permission, any camping or the erection of moveable structures in the Gwnnws Isaf and Llanafan areas. That this legal constraint was aimed solely at the mushroom festival was made abundantly clear from the duration of the change, which ran from 20th June until 19th December 1980—essentially encompassing the main mushroom season.

In early August, Dyfed-Powys Police wrote to Ceredigion District Council to notify them that 'leaflets' obtained at a recent free festival held on the Welsh border were advertising the 1980 Psilocybin festival would commence on Friday 12th September. CDC and The Forestry Commission between them arranged for the access road to the festival site to be fenced off, and an eight foot deep six feet wide trench dug, to prevent vehicular access.

These efforts were to no avail, and by 8 am on Saturday 6th September the fence had gone, the trench had been backfilled, and in the words of one local complainant to the police, "the hippies were in". Being proactive hadn't worked and the highly organised Ceredigion District Council had been fooled yet again by a chaotic culture they clearly despised.

Once fully underway, the festival unfolded in the usual way. People went looking for mushrooms, listened to or played music and just generally hung out with their friends; "The main event which usually happened three or four times daily was the arrival of the festival kettle—a blackened industrial sized affair, filled with magic mushrooms. The custom was to throw a few more shrooms inside, make as much tea as you all required, then carry it over to the next camp…". Children were present, as they were at all free festivals, and the Daily Mirror reported with delicious horror that "…many took their children on a four-mile trek to gather dangerous 'liberty cap' mushrooms that give LSD-type hallucinations."

Although largely psychologically harmless, if not prepared correctly, taken on an empty stomach or confused with other fungi, taking psychedelic mushrooms could lead to problems. A roughly handwritten 'bulletin board' on the festival site warned, "Before you take your mushrooms check with someone who knows because we do not want more people with bad guts in the first aid tent.".

Despite Ceredigion Council's negative attitude towards the festival and its attendees, many journalists who visited the site were broadly supportive of the event, and the culture that had created it. A report in *The Observer* noted, "Inside the festival there is a gentle carnival atmosphere. Food and mushrooms are shared… The festival is possibly the only meeting place of the hard core of 'new Gypsies' who travel with horse and cart and erect covered wagon-shaped tents, called 'benders', from bent over saplings.... Many at the festival feel that the magic mushroom could lead to the return of the hippies as an important movement".

This last sentence bore out the increasing confidence felt by the hard core of the free festival travellers. In the early 1980s free festivals had spread and evolved to the point where the committed hippie traveller could be on the road and at a festival more or less continuously from May to October. Thousands of people were now on the road and genuine alternative hippie traveller culture existed with its own fixed calendric celebrations of which the Welsh Psilocybin Festivals were a welcome addition at the end of the festival season.

Free Festival veteran Bev Richardson was in attendance in 1980 and reflected, "A lot of people come here to pick mushrooms to sell... The market for them isn't in this country but on the continent in Holland and Germany. I suppose you could call it a hippie cottage industry."

Although gathering, taking, or indeed selling, Psilocybe mushrooms was not illegal in the late 1970s, the heavy police presence presaged the future for the free festival community. Returning from one mushroom hunt, Keith Mitchell was strip searched by the police operating the road blocks in and out of the site. They found his mushrooms in a tobacco tin, naively enquiring, "Do you smoke those with the stuff boyo?".

The Observer also acknowledged the overzealous police presence. One young drugs squad detective told the journalist he would expose his film if he took photos of uniformed policemen searching vehicles. Road blocks continued to stop and search vehicles entering and leaving the festival site, ostensibly "...to carry out crime checks because of the increased number of petty thefts in that area reported to us since the festival began", but these searches gave the police carte blanch to look for drugs, check documents and vehicle roadworthiness, carrying out arrests if laws were found to have been broken. At least fifteen of those treated in this way made a formal complaint to Aberystwyth police.

Penny Mellor, of the government sponsored Festival Welfare Services commented that many festival goers thought the atmosphere was spoiled by, "the high level of police activity on the approach roads to the festival. Road blocks were set up and virtually every person and vehicle going to the festival was stopped and searched during the weekend I attended. It was felt that this level of activity was sheer harassment of the festival people, on the pretence of searching for drugs, whereas the proportion of those actually found in possession of drugs was very small."

Mellor's observations reinforced the fact that many of those who attended were activists, doers, people acutely tuned into the burgeoning culture they were part of. Psychedelic mushrooms may have been the event's *raison d'etre*, and the drug of choice, but this was no idle gathering of dole scroungers. It was a genuine representation of a new, alternative society; one at odds with the prevailing materialistic culture.

Mellor continued, "The Psilocybin Fair was a festival of doing. Almost everyone on site was trading in some way, mainly in food and crafts. People were very ingenious at thinking up new ways of exchanging money. The trading wasn't worked out on a high profit basis, but more on people working with whatever money and resources they had to generate enough money or basic supplies to live on themselves whilst providing a service for other people at the same time. The variety of food available was very wide. There were tea and coffee, sandwich and homemade cake, soup, vegetarian stews and bean-burger stalls; in addition, some people chose to wander round the site hawking their products—like the wandering samosa seller."

The 1980 event was also the most together of the Psilocybin festivals from an entertainment point of view. There was a generator, a small stage, and several bands and musicians, acoustic and electric, played. But the weather was miserable, and it was a poor season for psilocybin. By Friday 12th September the heavy rain and gales, coupled with the poor mushroom crop, led many to leave the site. Almost 200 remained however, with the promise of more at the coming weekend. 1980's festival ended when the hard core of hippie travellers left the riverside site to travel south to the Meigan Fayre, in Pembrokeshire.

Despite Ceredigion District Council's fear of fire, pollution and pillaging, the 1980 festival passed, as did previous events, with little incident. The council's much vaunted 'secret weapon' of making it illegal to camp on the festival site was ignored and not enforced. And despite the police harassment, arrests were actually fewer that in 1979, with only 40 people arrested and charged, mostly with minor drug offences.

1981 saw Ceredigion District Council even more determined there would not be a re-run of the perceived problems caused by earlier events. Their plans were immediately thwarted in early May of that year when, perhaps hoping to settle there until the autumn festival, 20 hippies set up camp by the River Ystwyth near Llanafan, at the 'usual' festival site. Local residents complained and the police began to patrol the area. CDC were jolted into action by this early incursion of festival goers and reiterated that there would be no festival in the autumn of 1981. Ceredigion District Council's chief executive, J. Kendall Harris, noted that a special council meeting was to be held to discuss the issue. "It is hoped that the small group who have arrived now will move on fairly quickly, but obviously officers of the council will investigate the position at once", Mr Harris confidently asserted.

Once again there appeared to be no real foundation for this panic, to the point where Harris could only offer the somewhat vague claim that, "We have had a number of local residents informing us that they are there and that they are anxious that something might happen in view of past experiences over the past few years". The fact that some people had been "anxious" and that "something" "might" seemed hardly substantive enough to ban the celebratory activities of a bunch of hippies, but apparently it was.

By early September 1981 around 50 hippies had gathered on the festival site, the vanguard of an expected several hundred mushroom munchers. The landowner, carpenter Alan Jones, contacted his solicitors and instructed them to seek an injunction preventing the festival from going ahead. And on 2nd September Judge Michael Evans granted a possession order, meaning the hippies could legally be moved off the land.

A possession order would usually take five days to come into effect but the judge granted it immediately because he "agreed it was urgent". Interestingly, it was revealed that Jones had been unable to take legal action against the hippies in previous years because he could not afford the solicitors fees. But this year he was financially supported by CDC! That a local Council was prepared to financially assist a landowner to prevent hippies from gathering on private land is perhaps a measure of the disproportionate panic caused by the festival.

On 3rd September the police took action, advising the 60 or so advance campers to vacate the land immediately. Bailiffs were standing by to enforce the possession order if required. A few offered token resistance by moving to the adjacent landowner's field, but soon left when he threatened to set a bull loose. So determined was CDC to drive the hippies out of town that those travellers who had run out of fuel were given the cash sum of £25 so they could move on to the Elan Valley where a small gathering of hippies was encamped. This payment, ostensibly an act of charity, could equally be seen as a disproportionate use of public money, showing CDC's lack of understanding, as all this did was move their perceived 'problem' to that of a neighbouring Council. Those festival goers with no transport were picked up in a bus sent by the Elan Valley hippies, and the annual mushroom festival continued untroubled, albeit in reduced circumstances, in a landscape populated by even more of the bone coloured fungi. Following the eviction from Llanafan some hippies, claiming to represent the festival organisers, approached Alan Jones the landowner, to see if it was possible to rent the site; but negotiations quickly broke down.

With the evicted Psilocybin festival goers now in the Elan Valley, within the space of six years the festivals had come full circle, rising from and returning to the same location. This offshoot of the Psilocybin Festival was taking place on Welsh Water Authority land and by 8th September over 500 hippies had gathered and the festival was in full swing. But, as with the 1976 festival, they were forcibly evicted by the police and the festival ended abruptly.

The £25 cash handouts to 'encourage' Psilocybin festival goers to move to the Elan Valley rightly caused a political storm in CDC's narrow corridors of power. Councillor Mike Byrne was rightly appalled that public money had been used to effectively foist CDC's 'problem' on another council. In true political fudgery the Council officials who sanctioned the handout denied they knew where the hippies intended to go and just wanted to help them move on.

In the aftermath of the failed 1981 festival a suggestion was made by members of the Welsh Farmers' Union (WFU) that landowners who had psilocybin growing on their land should spray them with 'poison'. Deputy president R. Hughes referred to hippies as "parasites on society" who could only indulge in festivals because they were on benefits. This priceless piece of prejudice ignored the fact that many travellers made money by trading and, whether illegal or not, by selling drugs. Many of the festival goers who came from across Britain and Europe also had jobs. Once again it appeared it was the hippie culture the Welsh found distasteful simply because it differed from their own.

The 1981 Psilocybin festival was the last such to be held at Llanafan. An event was planned and anticipated in 1982, but was countered in advance by Ceredigion District Council taking out a county court order, enabling them to immediately evict anyone occupying the site. A handful of mushroom aficionados turned up and were promptly told they would be arrested if they did not move on, which they did. The Welsh mushroom festivals were over.

Their demise hardly mattered because word of psilocybin's potent effects had spread like wildfire throughout Britain. People had no need of a specific festival at which to obtain them or to celebrate their use. Many upland areas of Britain played host to the little fungi and they were easily gathered in their thousands or could be bought very cheaply. *P. semilanceata* was now just another widely used psychedelic both in the home and at festivals. In the decades following the 1970s, their use became endemic. Interest in hallucinogenic fungi flourished to the point where in the 2000s one could buy several varieties of Psilocybe mushrooms in head shops or via mail order, or even buy kits with which to grow your own. Of course this widespread case of people openly having fun with drugs was quickly noticed by the Establishment, and laws were brought into service in the early years of the 21st century that outlawed British psychedelic fungi of most kinds once and for all.

12

Have You Seen the Saucers?

Can more than one psychedelic drug user share an identical, and, to them objective experience, one which is not apparent to observers who are not high? I believe the answer is 'yes and I'd like to offer an experience which I believe such states can be accessed under the influence of psychedelic drugs. The 1970s were the heyday of the free festival movement and by 1974 it was growing rapidly. The festivals at Windsor Great Park in 1972 and 1973 were relatively small events but the well-advertised, well-organised 1974 festival marked the beginning of a decade in which there was a free festival underway somewhere in Great Britain throughout much of the summer.

Various psychedelic bands including Hawkwind and Gong were billed to play and festival organiser, Bill Dwyer, was advertising the festival as being in the 'Queen's back garden', due to its being held on land owned by royalty and just up the road from Windsor Castle. The park authorities had pulled out all the legal stops to prevent the event happening, but eventually realised the flood of raggedy hippies arriving from all over Europe on foot, cars, vans and buses proved impossible to halt.

I hitched down from Yorkshire the Thursday before the Bank Holiday weekend and set up camp. It was immediately obvious there were massive quantities of LSD circulating on the festival site, almost certainly emanating from the Operation Julie LSD manufacturing and distribution ring. Rumour had it that this was top quality, very powerful LSD, and not the sort of stuff most trippers were used to. Yeah, right, we muttered to ourselves, we'll be the judge of that!

We didn't trip on the Friday but as a scorching hot Saturday dawned, a guy we vaguely knew came to our tent and asked if we wanted to buy some LSD. Of course we did! We took it around lunchtime and quickly discovered the rumours were correct but had undersold the strength and quality of the drug. The tiny brown microdot was mind-meltingly, soul stretching, powerful stuff. Words danced from the printed page, twirled a merry gavotte before us in colours textures and dimensions that defied name and description as they floated out of our tent to meld with the rainbow filled skies through which cosmic butterflies fluttered by. Music, live and recorded, permeated our being in shimmers of colour and meaning. It was the stuff of legend which only those who experienced it could even hint at its potency. I digress, but the power of this LSD is relevant to what we later saw.

By the time we were coming down it was 2 o'clock on the Sunday morning and I was sat in my tent talking to my girlfriend and some friends. Above the background noise of people having fun we suddenly heard a conversation start up close to our tent.

'Wow, what's that up there in the sky?'

Being curious I opened the tent door and looked out. Three hippies were sat cross-legged outside the tent opposite looking up at the sky. It was obvious from their expressions and general demeanour they were tripping hard.

'What *is* that? Is it a star?'

It seemed that they could all see 'something' in the sky. Something that we and others who were sat outside could not see. It was 2 a.m. and dark, with just a few stars being visible, nothing out of the ordinary even to people coming down from a powerful acid trip.

'It's a very bright light, it's coming closer'.

The conversation went on like this for a few minutes, the same comments and phrases being repeated in different way. I don't recall the night trippers looking at each other during this period of time. They just stared skywards, oblivious to the growing number of people who were now watching them, fascinated. Suddenly one of the trippers said:

'Look it's a flying saucer, it's a U-F-O'.

'Yeah, it's coming closer, it's going to land!'.

The conversation intensified and they rapidly described to each other what sounded very much like a classic George Adamski flying saucer. This kind of UFO has been reported many times by UFO witness worldwide since the early 1950 and consists of dome supported by a plate-like ring, with a tripod structure underneath.

As the trippers, two females and a male, talked they described the craft descending and landing in front of them, their heads and body posture changing as the—invisible to all but them—UFO landed somewhere in front of them. Had they not been under the influence of LSD what they *would* have seen was actually a big field filled with people, sleeping bags and tents with a darkened stage a few hundred yards away. There was nothing that even vaguely resembled what the trippers were clearly seeing and experiencing.

According to their ongoing narrative the UFO had now landed and a light emanated from the inside as a kind of drawbridge door opened. As they continued to comment on their shared experience we learned that a woman figure walked from the craft, her hand held palm forwards as if to denote a welcome. And there it ended, although after 40 years, I can no longer remember exactly how. The 'UFO' might have just faded away or perhaps took off and vanished, but I can't be certain.

Just another hallucination you might cynically observe. Yes, the acid was certainly powerful enough to bring such a hallucination into being. But that isn't the point, which is that to the three anonymous trippers whatever was happening was objectively happening *to them*, but it wasn't visible to everyone else. Moreover it was a shared visible experience that lasted around five minutes or so and each appeared to have seen and experienced *exactly* the same thing. We drifted off to sleep pondering just what we'd witnessed and what it meant for the potential of LSD.

The following day I asked one of the three hippies what had happened to them last night. Had they seen anything unusual? 'Oh yes, we saw a flying saucer land just over there and a Venusian woman came down the ramp towards us'.

Surely, I said, it must have been a hallucination?'

'Yes, it might have been. But we all saw it! It was there!'

I tell this tripping yarn as an example of how a psychedelic drug can be so powerful and have such qualities that it creates a consensus reality between people who have a belief in a particular thing. Of course it wasn't objectively real. Yet to the trippers it was; they had, for whatever reason or from whatever stimuli, talked and believed the UFO into *their* reality. The penetration of UFO/flying saucer lore in Western society runs deep. Carl Jung referred to UFOs as a 'modern myth of things seen in the skies'. Flying Saucers were very much in the news during the 1970s and my assumption is that the saucer spotters, fuelled by the potent LSD they had taken, subconsciously drew on their shared cultural knowledge of UFO mythology to amplify and transform perhaps a star or other insignificant light source into a shared UFO landing experience. To me this is yet another example of the immense power of psychedelics on the human imagination and its ability to be shared on a communal level. Whether, via the LSD, they accessed a collective consciousness or whether it was the skilful talking up of a vision between three people on a powerful psychedelic I don't know. But I do know it happened and I watched it happen in front of my very eyes!

This piece has been adapted from an interview I did with the co-author of many books on UFOs and folklore, Dr David Clarke. It was originally destined for his book How UFOs Changed the World, *but didn't make the final edit.*

13

I Think LSD Gives People Hope

An Interview with Dr Ronnie Sandison

No one knows with certainty when LSD was first brought to Britain. The British Secret Intelligence Services (MI5 and MI6) were aware of the drug's use by the CIA in the 1940s, and it is possible the S.I.S. may have conducted LSD trials at Porton Down years before their 'official' experiments in 1953. The earliest certain date for LSD's arrival in Britain seems to be in 1951 when it was trialled at the Crichton Royal in Dumfries. The first established LSD clinic in Britain was established in 1952 following Dr Ronald Sandison's (then a Consultant Psychiatrist at Powick Hospital in Gloucestershire) return from the Sandoz Laboratories in Switzerland, having been personally given a quantity of LSD by its discoverer Albert Hofmann. Sandison went on to use LSD in psychotherapy at Powick Hospital until 1964. Since then, Sandison has rarely given interviews about his involvement with the drug.

During research for *Albion Dreaming* I visited Sandison at his home in Ledbury, Herefordshire, and interviewed him about his life and times with LSD. At 90, his health was failing, his memory not as sharp as he would have liked, but for me it was an absolute pleasure and a privilege to spend even just a few hours with the man who introduced LSD, and LSD psychotherapy, to Britain.

Andy Roberts: *How did you first become aware of LSD?*

Ronnie Sandison: Really by accident. As you know I worked at Powick Hospital. I got my first Consultant appointment there in 1951 and the following year, in 1952, I got an invitation to go on a study tour to Switzerland, run by a very well-known psychiatrist, Isobel Wilson. Our first port of call was Basel and from there, as an optional extra, two or three of us went to the Sandoz Laboratories and they were absolutely a-buzz with LSD, they weren't doing anything else at that particular time. We met Albert Hofmann and W.A. Stoll, and one or two others who were working in it. The interesting thing was my colleagues seemed rather bored by it, they thought, you know, this was just a chemist playing round with something; but I was immensely excited by it because of some of the things they'd talked about from some of the volunteers. The upshot was, two or three months later I went to Switzerland again and spent more time with Hofmann and brought back a box of ampules of LSD and we started at Powick.

Were they talking about LSD at Sandoz in a psychotherapeutic context at that time?

Not in a psychotherapeutic context as such. What they had done was give LSD to 10–15 volunteers, mostly laboratory workers or people they could easily get hold of. Hofmann had been to Burgholzli Hospital, where one or two patients, I think they were mostly psychotics, were given LSD. It was at a very experimental stage, so I wouldn't say there was any real psychotherapy going on. But therapy was in the air as you might say, and there was a paper by Stoll (1947) you might have come across that probably was the very first paper on LSD as an aid to psychotherapy. Another one was Busch and Johnson (1950). They're a curious pair Busch and Johnson, they never followed up their work. They wrote rather flippantly about it elsewhere and said 'oh well we just wanted to give the patients a big mental kick, and see what happened', which didn't seem to be very scientific or therapeutic. I never met them at any conference and they never did any further work, they just disappeared so we were really on our own at Powick. I had a very able assistant and then we appointed a Registrar to work the whole time with LSD, which was Dai Davies. In the fullness of time, after about two years, we managed to persuade the Regional Hospital Board to build a special unit at Powick which was purpose built for LSD.

How did you persuade them to do that then at that time, it must have been a huge financial investment for a substance that was as yet largely untested?

Yes it cost them in those days about £60,000 [the equivalent of £1.5 million pounds in 2015]. We wrote our first paper, *The Therapeutic Value of Lysergic Acid Diethylamide in Mental Illness* (1954). That tells you how to do it, and I've always valued this paper because although it was the first paper we wrote about LSD it is pretty comprehensive. That was published in 1954, so that was the experience we had from 1952–53, so it covers about a year. Three years later we published the follow up. So, even that first paper generated worldwide publicity and the following year I was invited to go the States to the May meeting of the American Psychiatric Association. Some very distinguished people went to that conference. Aldous Huxley was there among others of the day who were distinguished in their field. I started getting invitations, first of all in this country, to various mental hospitals to talk about how to set up LSD units, then later on to various conferences aboard. I had quite a good time!

When you started using LSD at Powick, how did you determine the dosage?

That was purely experimental. The main work was done in Switzerland on the effective dose. Fortunately the effective dose was between 50 and 150 micrograms (μg), well below the tolerance level, so you can give people quite safely up to 500μg and they're not really going to come to any harm, so that was reassuring. I mean, it's an incredibly safe drug. The dangers are of course the psychological effects it has on people. Chemically and physiologically it's entirely safe, and has very few effects on the organism that can be measured. In Stoll's paper Hofmann talked about his blood pressure was raised a bit, and his pulse was raised, but they settled down after an hour or two, but otherwise, nothing.

There must be quite a difference in the psychological impact of an LSD dose between 50 and 250μg.

Yes! Absolutely!

So how would you judge a dosage for a particular type of treatment? Or was that done randomly at first?

Not altogether. We recognised that psychotic patients were not suitable, and I think that is generally recognised now. But there were plenty of cases of neurosis, anxiety states and obsessional conditions. A few depressives, but depression was not a very good subject, it could be dangerous as they could get more depressed. It was largely I think on a trial and error basis. But people came forward and were very glad. Any new treatment that psychiatry had was bound to be a sure-fire goer in those days. We trained a group of nurses, who we managed to keep, who were designated just to the LSD unit itself; and we had volunteer car drivers who brought the patients in, and they became part of the team because we used to report to them that a patient might have had some hangover from the day's treatment when they took the patients home, and we gradually shifted the treatment from being on an inpatient basis to an outpatient one.

Can you describe the layout of the LSD unit at Powick?

It was a purpose built unit. There were five treatment rooms meaning we could treat up to five patients at one time, with three nurses and two doctors. Very occasionally we'd need to keep the patient in overnight so we could do that. There was also a nurse's station there where they dropped LSD, that sort of thing. We almost didn't use any props, the only one we had was this teddy bear and we also had a record player, most patients liked music.

What music was most popular?

Almost entirely folk music or anything that was traditional.

Who chose the music?

We asked the patient if they would like it, and what their favourite was. We had a pretty good selection of records.

When patients were near the end of their LSD experience were they allowed to come down naturally or were they given a drug to supress the effects?

Sometimes they were given either a barbiturate or occasionally a spot of Largactil. But generally speaking they came down naturally, but we gave them a barbiturate or something in case they had difficulty in sleeping. And we always encouraged them to telephone if they needed to, and some of they did.

How did the apparent sparseness of the treatment room and its contents fit in with later theories about the environment in which LSD should be taken— Leary and others' ideas about set and setting for instance?

There was nothing specifically about it to suggest a medical setting. It wasn't just clinical. We had a blackboard and a record player. We tried to make it as pleasant as we could and they could create anything they wanted.

Were your patients told they were being given LSD?

Oh yes.

And were they given any information about what LSD was and what effects they might expect?

Partially, there was not a lot we could tell them. We used to get the patients together in a group at the end of the day, not always but sometimes, so they could exchange experiences and ideas and they had a pretty good idea what it was all about.

Did you run group LSD sessions?

We never ran multiple patient LSD sessions, they were all run solely with individuals, we never ran group LSD sessions. I know people did but I can't think it was a success. I'll tell you who did though, Spencer, the General Consultant at Powick. He took over from me for a year or two after I left. He was sort of self-trained therapist, I mean he had some good ideas but I don't think his heart was in his practice.

Can you tell me when the first conference in Britain devoted to LSD took place?

At the RMPA in 1961; it's worth noting that the RMPA which was the forerunner of the Royal College of Psychiatrists had quarterly meetings, but their quarterly meetings were always a mixture of psychiatric papers on different subjects which were discussed. This was the first time that the whole of the quarterly meeting lasting three days that was devoted to one subject. It was also the first time when non-medical people were invited. This book, *Hallucinogenic Drugs and their Psychotherapeutic Use* (Crocket et al, 1961), is the Proceedings from that conference, is really the Bible [laughs], I mean it's really all here. We had some very serious people, their names have probably dropped out now, but for instance Stephen Black from the medical research council who had done a lot of work on deep trance hypnosis was there.

Yes, he was an interesting guy and took part in several TV documentaries on strange phenomena and in the mid-1960s, such as UFOS and the People Who See Them, which was one of the best documentaries on UFOs ever screened.

We also had Professor Maurice Carstairs who gave the Reith Lectures around that time, in Edinburgh. Cerletti from Sandoz, Richard Crockett, whom I worked with a bit, Betty Eisner from Los Angeles, who was a very good friend of mine, Michael Fordham who was a Jungian analyst—we had a lot of interesting discussions with the analysts at that time, Francis Huxley, another of the Huxley clan, Frank Lake of clinical theology fame, Christopher Mayhew—quite a galaxy of people.

Which particular conditions did you think LSD therapy worked best on?

That's a question people nearly always ask me. What I think is you don't really choose people for therapy by diagnosis. You treat them much more by the kind of feel you have for them, you think 'I could help this chap or this woman'. You have to have an engagement with the other person and then you discover if they have an anxiety state or a depression, or whatever. From the point of view of a scientific paper [laughs] you have to write down maybe anxiety states, maybe obsessional states or whatever. Worldwide I think almost every known condition has been treated, purely on the condition that these were the people we were working with. In Canada a long series of alcoholics were treated and they claimed success. I've never treated an alcoholic so I can't really say. I think LSD gives people hope, and I think it gives them access to a part of themselves they never thought existed.

Did any of your LSD therapy patients undergo what might be termed religious experiences?

Yes and no. Have you ever read Walter Pahnke's papers on the subject? He did the Good Friday experiment. It's very hard to tell where the boundary is between true religious experience and an experience of something that has a religious flavour or content to it. There is within ourselves a religious self, something innate in us.

How many times would a patient be treated with LSD therapy?

On average usually once a week, sometimes twice a week, not more often than that. Some therapists treated their patients every day—I think that was a mistake, it needs a few days to absorb the experience that you've had in any one day and it might take a whole week. Sometimes you need a gap of several weeks. There's no clear rule about that but that's the sort of average. Most patients I treated had some follow up with psychotherapeutic sessions after they had finished the LSD treatment, and I think that's pretty important to allow some sort of closure.

How long was LSD used in Britain in a psychotherapeutic context?

We started in '52 and I left the Powick LSD unit in '64 and it was time to start closing down then. Spencer went on to continue treating patients at Powick until, I think, about '69. But you see, street LSD use started in the early '60s, particularly in America. You've read Grof I expect? You'll remember that when he went to the States his original intention was to use LSD psychotherapeutically but when he got there found everyone else was taking LSD and so he never did so.

Do you think the negative publicity LSD began to attract in the early to mid-1960s was instrumental in its therapeutic use being stopped?

I think so. There were one or two high profile cases, which I appeared in court about. One was a wealthy American estate agent. He came to Britain, and spent more or less six months on an LSD high, and various other drugs, and then he went to visit a prostitute in Chelsea and they both took LSD. When he came to from the LSD he found she was dead and he had a heavy glass tumbler in his hand and he'd bashed her head in. A tragic case that received an enormous amount of publicity. I didn't actually give evidence, I was retained by defence for advice, really, on how to conduct the case. I think there was some justice in it, he got six years—he might easily have got life. There was also a lot of airy-fairy talk about people on LSD staring at the sun and becoming blind, and there were people who jumped out of windows. I think most of those turned out to be false.

Should the medical establishment have resisted the changes and carried on using LSD?

Well, they did! Not in Britain, but notably in Germany. I don't know but I think it might be possible they might still be using it there! The British psychotherapeutic establishment weren't *told* they couldn't stop using LSD, but the press were against it, it was made illegal and the British Medical Journal ran a campaign against its use.

The other thing was that, I think it was in '63, the patent that Sandoz held to manufacture LSD ran out, and so after that time anybody could make it and it was made extensively in places like Czechoslovakia. Prior to that Sandoz kept a very tight grip on where the LSD went to, but once the patent ran out they didn't apply for its renewal, so that was really the end of it.

LSD therapy continued in what was then Czechoslovakia, there was a man called Milos Vojtěchovský who went on using it probably until well into the '70s. I went to visit his clinic in 1970 which was about ten miles outside Prague and had a most interesting day there. He was running a small mental hospital, and he divided his patients into three: those that he believed needed mainly occupational therapy, rehabilitation work with a bit of psychotherapy; the second group were those he thought needed group therapy; and the third lot were those who needed LSD. A very interesting division! It was a small hospital of about one hundred beds, ideal. He was doing some very good work, and even though it was only two years after the Russian occupation— and the Russians would not allow any drugs—somehow he managed to persuade the Russian government that he was doing therapeutic work and he managed to persuade them that he could use LSD psychotherapeutically.

What was your opinion about LSD's non-medical, street use by, for want of a better word, 'hippies'?

On the whole it was a bad thing. It had come at a spiritual time of course, in the sixties, Flower Power coming in on the back of the Beat movement. There was a tremendous 'high' among young people and inevitably they sought drugs to intensify their experiences and that's what it was largely about. And with Timothy Leary saying 'Turn on the world' and even therapists saying everyone should take it, which is absolute nonsense. Then there were the therapists in the States, who shall remain nameless, who were taking LSD with their patients. Who keeps the boundaries? It was an era when every kind of experiment with human experience was being explored.

Did you introduce a Canadian called Al Hubbard to LSD, as Martin Lee claims in Acid Dreams?

No, I've never heard that before. Definitely no. I've heard of Hubbard and may probably have met him, but no.

Were you aware of the Secret Intelligence Service experiments with LSD in the 1950s and the Ministry of Defence trials with it in the 1960s, at Porton Down?

I was aware of them, yes, aware that *something* was happening but not the content or the details. They had no connection with the medical establishment and weren't going to talk to anybody. They had the notion, like they did in

WWI, that if you got the wind in the right direction... they often talked about drifting LSD vapour over the enemy.

Did you ever take LSD yourself, and if you did what was your opinion of it?

Yes I did. I took it for me, to see what I could learn about myself and to find out what the patients were experiencing. I don't know if I formed an opinion. What I did learn was that you should never take LSD alone, you could get into all sorts of difficulties if you do, and you need to have a trusted person with you. I had Sister Hopkin with me. I did it one Sunday. We were both off duty, and she was just there, it was very, very helpful. I have written it up but I don't intend ever to publish it, I'll keep it private. It wasn't just a whim, it was part of the work of getting to know LSD. One or two of the Registrars also asked if they could take LSD and they followed the same procedure. There is of course the question as to what extent LSD is addictive and I'm always maintained it is not truly addictive. You can get addicted to the *idea* of LSD though. In all my patients I only came across one, who said that a year after taking LSD he had an intense desire to take it again. He even thought about breaking into the LSD unit to get some!

As for LSD's use in the future, there aren't very many psychiatrists who feel that it's a useful drug. When I started using LSD in therapy over 40 years ago the split had already started between general psychiatry and psychotherapy, and that divide has gradually widened into psychotherapists and psychoanalysts and an increasing number of lay-psychotherapists, all doing very good work. And then you have the general psychiatrists who have become more and more a victim of the drug companies. I really believe you can be a psychiatrist these days without having much knowledge of the mind, if you hand out the right pill to a patient.

So there's a future yet for LSD in the treatment of malaises of the mind?

Oh yes, very definitely, yes.

Ronnie Sandison died on 18ᵗʰ June, 2010. His papers are now in the Wellcome Trust, London (as yet uncatalogued).

14

Francis Crick, DNA & LSD

Type "Francis Crick LSD" into Google, and the result will be links to around 30,000 websites. Many of these websites make, or help support, the claim that Francis Crick (one of the two men responsible for discovering the double helix structure of DNA), was either under the influence of LSD at the time of his revelation, and/or used the drug to help with his thought processes during his research.

This narrative has been circulated on the internet, and to a lesser degree in print, to such an extent that it has become an article of faith among many in the global psychedelic community. The story is further repeated endlessly on mailing lists and forums, often used to bolster claims that LSD can provide breakthroughs in analytical and creative thinking.

It's a great tale, one might even say a (t)ripping yarn, and one which goes a long way to legitimise the use and potential of LSD as a tool for creativity. And who better to have as *the* poster boy for LSD than a revered scientist, the discoverer of the structure of DNA? But the fact is that the story simply isn't true. It's an urban legend. The product of churnalism. The simplest method to determine what level of truth—if any—underpins the claim is to examine its sources, and the timeline of the story.

Prior to Crick's death in 2004 there had been no mention anywhere of him using LSD as part of the process of discovering the double helix. Until, just ten days after his death, that literary bastion of truth and moral fortitude the *Daily Mail*, published an article on 8th August 2004, headed *'Crick was high on LSD when he discovered the secret of life!'*[1]

Written by journalist Alun Rees, using information based on an interview conducted with a friend of the chemist Richard Kemp (one of the two chemists who manufactured LSD for the 1970s British LSD manufacturing and distribution conspiracy known as Operation Julie), the article is a mishmash of wishful thinking and idle speculation. It implies that Crick used LSD as part of his quest to discover the double helix structure of DNA and, furthermore, that Crick was involved in the genesis of Operation Julie.

If this story held even the slightest grain of truth, one would have thought the story would have been at least *rumoured* while Crick was still alive. But it wasn't. Rees had obtained the post-mortem journalistic 'scoop' from one Garrod Harker, allegedly a friend of Richard Kemp.

According to Harker, Kemp told him that he met Francis Crick at Cambridge University in the late 1960s. Crick allegedly told Kemp that some Cambridge academics used LSD in tiny amounts as a thinking tool, to liberate them from preconceptions and to encourage their genius to wander freely in search of new scientific ideas. Crick also allegedly revealed to Kemp he had perceived the double-helix shape while high on LSD.

'It was clear that Dick Kemp was highly impressed and probably bowled over by what Crick had told him. He told me that if a man like Crick, who had gone to the heart of human existence, had used LSD, then it was worth using. Crick was certainly Dick Kemp's inspiration.' claimed Harker in the *Daily Mail* interview. In the interests of journalistic accuracy, Rees then visited Crick at his home to confront the Nobel Prize winner with the story, only to be told by Crick—allegedly, of course—'Print a word of it and I'll sue' .

Presumably *Daily Mail* readers were expected to believe that the story couldn't be published before Crick's death because of his threat of legal action, and that threat is used in the article to strongly imply the story was genuine. It's a great journalistic technique; allege that a 'celebrity' has told you a secret but that this secret is so special that if you reveal it during their lifetime, they will take punitive legal action. It then makes sense to reveal the bombshell after their death, and use the alleged threat of legal action to explain why you kept quiet about it until now. It's a wonderful piece of circular logic and almost guarantees your scoop will be published because, whether true or not, no legal action can be taken against journalist or newspaper because the subject is dead.

Whatever the case, once printed *after* Crick's death, the story immediately leapt from the printed page onto the internet where it has spread and grown uncritically, becoming a kind of fact-currency for those wishing to justify their 'scientific' use of LSD.

One website[2] refines the rumour even further to claim that, 'Francis Crick who died in 2004 (88yrs old), admitted on his deathbed that he had been regularly taking small amounts of LSD when he arrived at the conclusion that DNA must exist as a double helix'.

Crick's alleged disclosure to Harker wasn't revealed while Crick was in the final process of dying, but by grafting the story onto a 'deathbed confession', value is automatically added because who on earth would make a story up if they only had a short time left to live? The 'deathbed confession' is a common motif in contemporary folklore (see, for instance, the numerous cases of 'deathbed confessions' in which former members of the armed forces have 'revealed' their knowledge about crashed UFOs and captured aliens, etc.), yet accounts of 'deathbed confessions'—especially those making dramatic, history changing claims—are rarely, if ever, true[3].

As an example of the extent to which Crick's urban legend has embedded itself deeply into popular psychedelic culture, Graham Hancock, a well-known and respected fringe archaeologist and psychedelic explorer, repeats it in his book *Supernatural*[4] and also elsewhere, such as this extract from an interview with *The Daily Grail*; 'It's not a widely known fact that Crick was under the influence of LSD when he discovered the double-helix structure of DNA and that this supreme achievement of scientific rationalism, for which he won the Nobel Prize, came to him in an altered, even mystical state of consciousness.'[5]

Note the use of the word 'fact'. Hancock does himself a disservice by uncritically accepting the story of Crick and LSD without any attempt to prove the story, or refer to any provenance for it. No doubt many readers of the book accepted the story as 'true' and will repeat it in conversations and suchlike, spreading the legend further.

More recently, the late Swedish historian of the psychedelic, Patrick Lundborg has incorporated the rumour in his otherwise remarkable book, *Psychedelia: An Ancient Culture, A Modern Way of Life*. Accepting the enhanced version of the tale hook, line and sinker, he writes, 'Crick, who testified on his death bed that LSD had helped him realise the double helix structure of DNA'[6]... and so it goes on.

If writers as well respected as Hancock and Lundborg accept and believe the Crick DNA story, then their followers are likely to believe it too. The tale, already in folkloric terms a 'friend of a friend' story, is then further and uncritically spread, written manure for the viral growth of an unchecked story. Once started, despite evidence to the contrary being available, an urban legend is an unstoppable force.

The devoted reader at this point might say, well, yeah, but there's got to be *something* in the story, surely? Maybe, a little[7]. It is well evidenced that Crick supported the sensible use of drugs such as marijuana, as he was one of the famous signatories to the full page advertisement in *The Times* of 24th July 1967, which called the laws against marijuana 'immoral in principle and unworkable in practice'[8] .

This ad was placed by the Society Of Mental Awareness (SOMA), a cannabis reform group that comprised several psychedelic luminaries and supporters, including the likes of R.D. Laing, Steve Abrams, and Francis Huxley. Indeed Crick was central to SOMA's aims, in that he finessed their formula for THC tincture, then still legal under prescription.

There is no doubt of his commitment to mind expanding drugs, but does that mean we should accept as gospel truth that one, un-evidenced, account of him using LSD in the discovery of the double helix nature of DNA?

Crick also hinted at some, possibly experiential, knowledge of LSD in a 1998 interview with Jeffrey Mishlove[9]:

> **CRICK:** *In the case of LSD, for example, you only need 150μg to have all these funny experiences, you see. It's minute. And that's because they fit into special places, these little molecules, these drugs which you take. They fit into special places in these other molecules. They've been tailored to do that.*

> **MISHLOVE:** *Do you have a sense of the process by which hallucinogenic drugs such as LSD, or psychedelic drugs, actually affect the brain? What is going on there?*

> **CRICK:** *Well, I don't have a detailed knowledge, no, I don't, and I'm not sure that anybody else really knows. They have a rough idea.*

> **MISHLOVE:** *We know that obviously there's a chemical influence.*

> **CRICK:** *Well, typically, different ones act in different ways. But a common thing is to see colours more vividly, for example, and often to see things move in a way when they're not actually moving, and things of that sort. So they boost up in some way the activities of what you might call the colour parts of the brain and the moving parts of the brain and so on. But the government isn't very keen on giving money for research on that sort of thing.*

But, Crick's support for the legalisation of marijuana in the late sixties, and a working knowledge of LSD, is a big step from him actually utilising the psychedelic in his work with DNA, well over a decade earlier. Rees' article, being based on a third hand source with no supporting documentary evidence, is unsound.

Additionally, the chronology necessary to enable Crick to have used LSD as an aid to discovering DNA is also fundamentally flawed.

LSD almost certainly (notwithstanding possible experimental military use, which began at around the same time) first arrived in Britain during November 1952, when Dr Ronald Sandison brought a quantity back from Sandoz Laboratories in Switzerland. Almost nothing was known about LSD in Britain at that time, and for several years the drug was only available to a few psychotherapists and the Secret Intelligence Services (MI5 and MI6). Therefore, the chances of Crick getting hold of LSD during the time he was working on DNA (i.e. up to 1953) are slim.

However, Crick was known to have used LSD later in his life. His biographer, having spoken to his widow, ascertained that although Crick claimed not to know Richard Kemp and David Solomon, he did know Henry Todd, who introduced him to LSD in 1967. (All three were major players in the Operation Julie conspiracy, which was initially based in Cambridge, where Crick lived until 1977.)

Crick was apparently: '...fascinated by its effects—by how he became confused about what familiar objects were for, and by the way it seemed to alter the passage of time'[10]. So, Crick certainly did take LSD several times, but this was many years *after* his discovery of DNA's double helix. No factual, or indeed anecdotal, evidence has yet appeared that indicates he was connected with the drug's manufacture or distribution.

Steve Abrams, one of the aforementioned SOMA cannabis law reformers and a key mover and shaker in Britain's counter-culture, also railed against the story written by Rees for the *Daily Mail*. In an extract from a previously unpublished interview I conducted, in which Abrams discusses Richard Kemp's role in the Operation Julie events, Abrams commented:

> *I would like to have got in touch with him* [Kemp]
> *about this ludicrous story about Francis and about*
> *discovering the structure of DNA while on an acid trip.*
> *It's so insulting. The journalist who wrote this, he was a*
> *crime reporter on Operation Julie, and Stewart Tendler*
> *put me in touch with him and told me to be very careful*
> *talking to him because he's a very nasty man and he was*
> *Crime Correspondent for the Daily Mail.*
>
> *He actually turned out to be rather nice. And he*
> *admitted he didn't know if the story was true, and it's*
> *obvious nonsense. I didn't believe that the guy called*
> *Gerrod Harker existed but he does exist, but the point*
> *is the way to find out was to check with Kemp. Kemp*
> *was supposedly told this story by Crick. Now Kemp*
> *asked me about Crick so I'm pretty sure Kemp never*
> *met Crick.*

Does this provide confusion or clarification? Of course the only person who *really* knows the truth is Crick, and he's dead. Perhaps we could allow that Kemp *did* talk to Harker about Francis Crick's later use of LSD and, as so often happens, the story became conflated with other rumours and a dash of journalistic imagination. Perhaps we must accept that whilst highly unlikely, it is still *just* about vaguely possible that Crick did use LSD during the discovery of the double helix structure of DNA. But all the available evidence argues against it and by mindlessly repeating the story as 'fact', the psychedelic community is guilty of perpetuating the rumour, undermining the genuine cases where psychedelics *have* been involved in making scientific breakthroughs. And there has been as least one major, undeniable case in which that has taken place; Carey Mullis' claim (detailed in his book *Dancing Naked in the Mind Field*) that he used LSD in his understanding and development of the Polymerase Chain Reaction[11].

All this might seem like a storm in a tea cup, stepping on the mellow of the psychedelic daydream. Who cares? Well, I do. The present psychedelic renaissance is afoot and going well. LSD tests with humans are now taking place again, and scientists are beginning to re-discover the enormous potential psychedelics have for creating and sustaining real change in individuals and thus societies. But the psychedelic renaissance has its critics and its enemies too, and if claims such as those made about Crick can be easily shot down in flames, what does that say about the credulity levels of those within the psychedelic community who would believe and promote them?

You can hopefully see what I am getting at. Yes, by all means let's shout from the rooftops when well-known people come out about their positive use of psychedelics. But let's also be prepared to confront rumour and falsehood, and denounce it as such to prevent it tainting the historical journey we are currently embarked on.

15

Adventures in a Yorkshire Landscape

The year was 1974. My big acid year. There was a plentiful supply of outstanding LSD and I and a small group of trusted psychonauts sallied forth into the mystic on a more or less weekly basis—basically just to see what would happen. We thought we were seasoned and adept trippers, able to handle any weirdness the drug could throw at us. But there were one or two events that baffled us and which shook us to our collective core

Flashback: My girlfriend Helen had been 'studying' the Tarot, in the somewhat lackadaisical way we dipped in and out of the occult in those days. A little knowledge is a dangerous thing but we were bold and thought it would be an interesting evening's entertainment to see what happened if we took acid in conjunction with doing a Tarot reading. What could possibly go wrong?

From the time we made that decision, the die was cast and was rolling its inexorable way into the future. A suitable Saturday evening in late summer was selected for the experiment, which we were already reframing as a 'ritual'. We convened at The Bungalow, a property owned by Andy's parents but solely used by their errant son for all manner of drug debauchery. A huddle of flares, cheesecloth, beads and denim, as befitted the times, we eschewed chairs in favour of the floor, assumed a cross-legged position, and began.

Had we known then what we knew a few hours later we would have treated the event like a *real* ritual, paid more intention to intent and consequence as well as performed the necessary banishings and other magical practices required prior to tampering with the fabric of the multiverse.

The LSD we intended to take was brown microdot, purchased for 50p (50p!) a hit a few weeks earlier at the infamous 1974 Windsor Free Festival and smuggled back in an undergarment. Helen and I had test flown the dots at the festival (a trip recounted in my book *Albion Dreaming*, where I am anonymised as 'Allan Staithes') and were aware of their potency. One each would be more than sufficient. One each was probably, in reality, too much.

Helen, Andy and I each took one of the dots, and Helen told us what she intended to do. The Major Arcana of the Rider-Waite tarot was shuffled by us all in turn and then Helen dealt the cards. Firstly she dealt us a card each, face down. This, when turned, would be a representation of our character, both generally and throughout the trip. Then she dealt a fourth card which, when turned, would denote the quality and characteristics of the trip itself. And then she dealt a final card, also face down, to be turned over in the jingle-jangle morning, which would give us the point of the trip.

We turned the 'character' cards over. I can't, now, recall exactly what they were. But excitement and anticipation combined with our naivety of the occult and tarot interpretation caused the cards to assume apt personal significance and generated some discussion as to how appropriate they were already. In retrospect we were opening ourselves to suggestibility. We *wanted* the cards to mean what we wished, hoped, or indeed feared.

This process took perhaps forty minutes or so. The acid hadn't yet hit. We were stranded starfish awaiting the imminent flood. Standing on the runway, waiting for take-off. Cattle uneasy, air of unrest. We lived the musical references in those days, because they were true and poeticised our acid experiences. A tingle here, a perceptual shift there, but nothing major. But we knew it was coming.

As the drug slowly elevated our minds we turned our quivering nerves to the card that was to denote the quality and characteristic of the trip. One of us flipped the card over. *Death.* It was the Death card in all its brutal, stark, skeletal symbolism. Subtleties and nuances of meaning in tarot symbolism meant nothing to us. This was, and meant, DEATH and it was HERE, NOW. In the eternity of that moment, the full force of the acid rolled over us like a tsunami. The walls melted, logic and proportion fled the scene and my stomach turned to ice. Icy fingers of panic shot from my adrenal gland and gripped my scrotum. I mouthed something to my fellow trippers and the expressions on their faces showed they were having exactly the same experience as I. I was scared out of my tiny adolescent mind and knew we had started something we couldn't stop.

Anxiety pulsed through us. We needed to change the vibe, and fast. Coats on, and the traditional early trip walk was embarked upon sooner than envisaged. We sallied forth from the bungalow into the swirling light of the thick pulsing dusk, walking quickly, trying to distract ourselves from the sense of foreboding that was stalking us. We scurried the few hundred yards into the tiny centre of Roberttown, a handful of shops and a couple of road junctions, heading for a friend's house where we might find sanctuary from Death.

As we neared the centre of the village, we could see a police car pulling up outside the phone box. A lad exploded out from it, grabbing at the police officer who was half out of his Panda car. The lad was visibly distraught, screaming, 'He can't be dead, he can't be dead' at the police officer. In the context of the acid, the tarot card and our surging panic, the word or concept of 'dead' was not what we wanted to hear, and any form of police activity was the last thing we wanted on our minds. What the fuck was going on? The 30 seconds or so during which this scenario was played out was like watching a scene from another century through the lens of a multi-coloured smoke-filled bottle. But we knew it was real and we, somehow, were a part of it. As we jabbered at each other, trying to work out what was happening, whether to stop or go back, whether to be or not to be, the lad got in the police car and it drove off.

Gathering our rapidly disintegrating resolve about us we pressed on. We knew that a quarter of a mile up the road we could go to Chris': Chris, one of our acid gurus, in his hippie hovel, with his warm personality, soft lights, open fire, chessboard, dope, and Grateful Dead albums. We knew if we could get there, all would be well. He would welcome us, calm us down and make everything alright.

He wasn't in.

Our salvation was gone. We daren't go back so we had to go forward, to the brow of a hill that overlooked Hartshead church and Hightown, a normally quiet area of country lanes and fields. We could sit and gaze over the soothing landscape, watch the skies and calm down. We got to the point of observation and were further confused. Instead of the quiet, nocturnal country landscape we expected to see before us, about a mile away, at the cross roads, we could see a patchwork of coloured, flashing, lights. We had no idea what or why they were, but they suggested a goal for us to attain and a diversion from an ever-mounting panic, so we set off into the dip toward them. Much nonsense was talked between us about what was going on and how well we were handling it considering it all: *Who are you kidding?* asked Death.

When we came out of the dip, about 400 metres from the lights, we could clearly see what they were. It was a—then state of the art—police Range Rover with a huge, extending, flashing light, an ambulance and two police cars, as well as group of people with torches and powerful lamps. *For fuck's sake!* We were driven on by morbid curiosity now, utterly convinced that the trip was out of our control, open to whatever was going to happen. Trying to look nonchalant (have you tried that recently in an Afghan coat and patched, flared jeans?) we walked slowly past the lights. The story unfolded; a motorbike had gone through the wire fence and at that moment, a body was being lifted out of the field. As we watched, aghast, as though we were watching a film, indeed were *in* a film, a car screeched to a halt and a woman got out, saw the body and let out a blood curdling animal howl of anguish that cut through all time ever and, most of all, the eternity of now. We froze to the spot.

We walked fast then for a long time and for many miles, gabbling to one other. What had we witnessed? What had we been part of? In our deluded, tripped out minds, by mixing acid with the tarot and drawing the Death card as the emblem of our trip, we had in some way 'caused' the events to happen. It was a long night before we returned to the bungalow as the sun began another day. Among the discarded tarot cards, one still lay face down, shimmering in our tripped dawn vision, freighted with potential meaning. We turned it.

It was the Fool. What else could it be? Once again our naivety helped confirm our belief that the Death card represented what was going to happen during the trip and the Fool card showed us we had been taught a lesson. We were absolved. Free in the new morning to start afresh, unburdened by the events of the previous evening. We read into it what we needed to. But we needed to unburden ourselves to someone and so, in the growing light of the new day, still tripping hard (remember pilgrims, this was *proper* acid almost certainly originating from Richard Kemp's Operation Julie lab in mid Wales), we set off to walk the six miles or so to Brighouse.

Our destination, another acid guru, this time one who was familiar with the dark side of things. Lindsey was asleep when we arrived and although his wife wasn't best pleased to see three young trippers disrupt the domesticity of her sunny Sunday morning, the man himself appeared and we were made welcome, spliffs and coffee helping us re-enter the quotidian world. A-glimmer with residual psychedelic shimmer we breathlessly told Lindsey what had happened and how as a result we had, during our walk to his house, devised an entire system of psychedelic magic that accounted for what we believed we had caused.

He listened, smiled that wry smile of his and laughed. You took strong acid and frivolously evoked forces you couldn't handle and basically got what you deserved, was his sage commentary on our lysergic madventure. Somewhat deflated, but relieved we wouldn't be pursued into eternity by dark forces, we accepted his pronunciation and thought we'd got off lightly. We banished by listening to the Small Faces *Happy Days Toytown* and went on our merry way home for a long sleep.

So, what did happen? A rational view might be that the whole experience was a complete drug addled coincidence, wishful thinking, chance and interpretation conspiring to lead us to believe that our trip appeared to predict a death when in reality, we were just stoned observers to a tragic event in the real world, stupidly believing we were in some way connected to it. Which was it? I really don't know, and my take on the events, still strong in my memory after 40 years, varies depending on whom I'm talking to and what I allow myself to believe at that moment in time. One thing I remain certain of is that if you take LSD, or any other psychedelic, and essentially start playing games with the multiverse you must accept that what happens to you will not necessarily be what you expected, or wanted.

Caveat susceptor!

16

Reservoir Drugs

When chemist Albert Hofmann's accidental alchemy created LSD in 1938 he unleashed on the world a drug so powerful that it had the power to permanently change lives and alter the individual's core beliefs about the nature of reality. Literally millions of minds were blown and the cultural landscape was never the same again.

One of the many cultural side-effects of LSD was its ability to generate some really great urban legends. For instance, one rumour has it that if you take LSD two (or is it seven?) times, you are legally insane! Another, stemming from a 1967 newspaper article, holds that LSD will make you stare at the sun until you go blind. This was swiftly proved to be a hoax, but the legend lives on for mothers and journalists to frighten the young and the paranoid. You want more? Well, everyone knows that dealers hand out LSD-laced tattoos saturated with LSD to children to get them hooked, don't they? Sure they do, dealers just love giving drugs away to people who will freak out and end up in hospital surrounded by police wanting to know their source! And of course taking LSD affects your genes and so it causes deformed babies (where? Have you met anyone deformed by their parents' LSD use?). Not to mention its propensity to drive babysitters to put babies in microwaves. And so on, each tale less evidenced and more lurid that the last, each heavily freighted with the barely subliminal message that LSD is bad medicine.

But of all the Fortean fables associated with acid the 'LSD in the water supply' urban legend is by far the most potent and long lived. And, unlike the rest of them, this one has at least some basis in reality. The legend comes in many forms, but the basic premise is that various individuals and groups (invariably framed by the media as political or psychedelic terrorists), have conspired to introduce LSD into the water supply, usually by dumping huge quantities in reservoirs. Society's fear is that the dramatic effect of LSD on the masses will result in a disoriented and incapacitated population who are rich pickings for invasion, mind control or simply as a vivid demonstration of the drug's power over 'straight' society by enemies of the state.

Over the past 50 years the legend has manifested often, appearing in newspapers, magazines, books, films and TV shows. The idea sounds vaguely plausible, but is it? Has it ever happened, and if not just how did the story grow into an urban legend?

All legends have their genesis in at least a grain of truth and in this case the origin of the LSD in the water tale appears to lie deep in the archives of the CIA and their fascination with the drug as a possible mind control weapon. The effects of LSD were first noticed in 1943 by its discoverer, Dr Albert Hofmann and within a few years the CIA had begun to experiment with it in their search for a truth drug.

The psychedelic water saga had its genesis at the height of the Cold War in 1953, when the intelligence agency approached Dr. Nick Bercel, a Los Angeles psychiatrist working with LSD in a psychotherapeutic context. After querying him as to the possible consequences if the Russians were to put LSD in the water supply of a large American city, the spooks demanded Bercel calculate how much LSD would be needed to dose Los Angeles' water supply with LSD.

Of course, this immediately begs the question why the CIA, who were at the time experimenting with and had considerable knowledge of LSD, couldn't work this out for themselves? But we'll let that question pass, for inconsistency and anomaly are essential ingredients in the alchemy of any urban legend.

Bercel dissolved some LSD in a glass of chlorinated water, which promptly neutralised the psychedelic, leading him to tell the CIA the notion was pointless and not worth pursuing. The spooks were unconvinced, allegedly designing another version of LSD that was not neutralised by chlorine. Yet although the experiment had failed, the *idea* that LSD could be used to mass-dose the population had been created and though scientific opinion was against it, the idea was just too powerful to give up and started to take on a life of its own.

The CIA became obsessed with the idea. One formerly secret document concluded that even if the notion of contaminating an entire city's water supply was out of the question, there were still other micro-possibilities. For instance, one CIA document noted: 'If the concept of contaminating a city's water supply seems, or in actual fact, is found to be far-fetched (this is by no means certain), there is still the possibility of contaminating, say, the water supply of a bomber base or, more easily still, that of a battleship.... Our current work contains the strong suggestion that LSD-25 will produce hysteria (unaccountable laughing, anxiety, terror).... It requires little imagination to realize what the consequences might be if a battleship's crew were so affected.'

The CIA's Technical Services Staff (TSS) was also very interested in the possible manipulation of a city by introducing LSD into the water supply. In John Marks' classic spook chronicle *The Search for the Manchurian Candidate* he recalls a member of the TSS saying, 'We thought about the possibility of putting some in a city water supply and having the citizens wander around in a more or less happy state, not terribly interested in defending themselves'.

The idea received another boost in 1958 when the chief officer of the US Army's Chemical Corps, Major General William Creasy, declared that psychedelic compounds were an ideal way of dealing with the enemy. Creasy logically argued that spiking a city's water supply with LSD was a much simpler, humane and cost effective method of taking control of a populace than the effect on life and limb of simply bombing it into submission. And, of course, dosing the entire population had the added advantage for capitalism that buildings and infrastructure remained intact. When the electric citizens came down from their trip they could be ordered straight back to work for their new leaders, already part programmed and timid and submissive from the terrifying ordeal they had been through.

Creasy told *This Week* magazine in May 1959, 'I do not contend that driving people crazy even for a few hours is a pleasant prospect. But warfare is never pleasant... would you rather be temporarily deranged... by a chemical agent, or burned alive...?' Creasy's suggestion was never taken up, but Timothy Leary, soon to become the poster boy for LSD evangelism, took the idea and gave it a twist. In a 1962 article published in the Journal of Atomic Sciences, he suggested the US government should plan ahead for such an eventuality by dosing their own water supplies, thus preparing citizens for psychedelic attack by the Communists!

Another early source of the legend is the British Ministry of Defence's (MoD) investigation of LSD. In the early 1960s, the newly created MoD was testing LSD on troops at Porton Down in Wiltshire. One of their ambitions was to develop an LSD delivery system so the drug could be used as a battlefield incapacitant, destroying the fighting spirit of any opponent and rendering their strategy and attack in disarray. There is no direct evidence to suggest the MOD looked at putting LSD in water supplies, although they briefly discussed dispersing it on the battlefield in vapour form. The MOD soon abandoned the idea when they realised the effects of LSD on large numbers of people was not predictable and therefore not controllable.

Neither the CIA nor the MOD's speculations about dosing water supplies appear to have progressed much further than the brainstorming stage. But word of the speculation had spread and rumour seeped out into the general population, acting as a base from which the scare story of LSD in the water supply grew. The idea of LSD as a mind-controlling water contaminant having now entered the Petrie dish of modern media culture, it was only a matter of time before the public picked up on it. And the first known reference to the mass use of LSD by elements outside of an Intelligence Agency or military context occurred in a British magazine.

Prior to 1966, there had been virtually no media interest in LSD in Britain. Although use of the drug was widespread among the young and hip it was as yet still a truly underground scene. This situation changed quickly and forever on 19th March 1966 when quintessential swinging London magazine, *London Life*, ran an interview with Desmond O'Brien, co-founder (with Michael Hollingshead) of Chelsea's World Psychedelic Centre.

Titled 'The Drug That Could Become a Social Peril', the article opened with O'Brien rather unwisely introducing himself as 'Mr. LSD' and claiming that anyone could take control of London in under eight hours by putting LSD in the water system. *London Life* speculated further by quoting Dr. Donald Johnson, former MP for Carlisle, who confidently asserted: 'It is quite feasible that LSD could be used to take over a city or even a country. I agree if it were put into reservoirs, it would disable people sufficiently for an enemy to take control.'

This brief, but ill-advised, mention of LSD as a psychedelic contaminant thus entered into the media's consciousness and began to spread, becoming a counter-culture virus and a media bête-noire on both sides of the Atlantic within months.

In America, the media-led moral panic about LSD hit fever pitch in the latter half of the sixties and there was a genuine fear among the political establishment that unchecked use of the drug could overthrow the cherished American way of life. Psychedelic activists, of both the serious and the merry prankster variety abounded. They were re-cast by media and law enforcement agencies as terrorists, hell bent on indiscriminately bending minds with the devil-drug no one really understood. Suddenly, LSD seemed to be everywhere; at parties, on campus, at suburban barbeques, even in the workplace, slowly and insidiously changing people's consciousness, telling them that things were not as they appeared. 'What if', pontificated Mom and Pop, 'what if these freaks manage to get us all to take it? We'll all become like *them*.' There goes the neighbourhood!

The November 1966 edition of *Vue*, ran one of the many scare stories published about LSD that year, 'Why They Had to Outlaw LSD'. In a round-up of the drug's effects writer W.H. Carr, clearly having taken a huge dose of disinformation, noted, 'A few ounces of it, dumped in the water supply of a major city, could shake up millions' . This paranoia, now firmly entrenched in the minds of Mr & Mrs America wasn't lost on some elements of the counter-culture, who decided to use it to their own advantage in the escalating war between hip and straight society.

In June 1967, during a federal investigation into organised crime, the motives of the Neo-American Church (founded by Art Kleps, a former associate of Tim Leary), were called into question. Dr. James L. Goddard, commissioner of the U.S. Food and Drug Administration, gave damning testimony in Washington before the House subcommittee. He quoted Neo-American Church publications that stated they believed in the psychedelic assassination of politicians, and the placing of LSD in city water supplies should the Church be suppressed. Goddard also read from a document that said that if the Church was attacked in any way, it would fight back with psychedelic weapons such as 'clouds of dust sprayed over cities and LSD in the water supply'.

Scary stuff and just what the straight suburban masses feared. But Goddard had failed to realise that the Neo-American Church were acid surrealists, psychedelic pranksters for whom the *idea* of acid in the water supply was almost as powerful as the real thing. They had no intention of carrying out their plan but knew it would freak the straights out.

Abbie Hoffman, another self-confessed acid prankster and 'Yippie,' probably generated the most notorious instance of the LSD in the water legend. Besides being an acid-head, Hoffman was also very active in left wing politics, a somewhat dour movement to which he brought humour and surreality. During the run up to the Chicago Democratic National Convention in 1968, Hoffman was in daily contact with the media, trying to get them to take him seriously, but at the same time using acid prankster techniques to get headlines.

Hoffman recalls, 'There was a point when we announced to the press that if they fucked with us we were going to put LSD in the drinking water'. The reaction to this threat was dramatic and the story was heavily covered on TV and in the papers, with thousands of National Guardsmen being posted to guard the reservoirs against hippies. This particular version of the legend took on an interesting twist when Hoffman said, '…we're negotiating with the Deputy Mayor behind the scenes and I said, 'Why can't we work this out? To show my good faith, I'll tell you that you can take all your soldiers away, because it's chemically impossible to put LSD in the water supply—LSD simply doesn't dissolve that readily.'

Time magazine wryly noted how easily Chicago's political administration had fallen for the scam, hook, line and sinker, 'Mayor Richard Daley and his police and military aides appeared to accept at face value all of the fiery statements made by the demonstration leaders. Chicago's newspapers repeatedly listed diabolical threats aimed at the city, ranging from burning Chicago down by flooding the sewers with gasoline, to dumping LSD in the water supply, to having 10,000 nude bodies float on Lake Michigan.'

The Deputy Mayor was now caught between a rock and a hard place. 'I know it can't happen', he agreed, immediately contradicting himself by saying, 'but we can't take any chances anyway'. The acid in the water myth had now gone beyond reality and common sense and could not be stopped, even in the knowledge that it was not even chemically viable to dose large numbers of people in this way. As LSD evangelist Tim Leary once said, 'LSD is the drug with the most unusual emotional and psychological effects when compared to any other drug. Because just the *idea* of the drug is enough to cause terror among those who have never even taken it!'.

Hoffman also recommended that the Deputy Mayor check with the chemistry department at the university to double-check whether it was possible to dose a reservoir with LSD. The politician replied that he had already asked the scientists on his staff who had told him it could not be done. Nevertheless, such was the paranoia surrounding LSD that the Deputy Mayor was concerned that Hoffman might be using 'better scientists' and thus on such shaky reasoning were the National Guard despatched to prevent hippies pouring LSD into the water system.

Abbie's brother Jack commented: 'He had people convinced, actually convinced, he was going to drop LSD in the Chicago reservoir and get the whole city tripping. Can you imagine believing that? It would have taken dump trucks full of LSD to have any impact, but Abbie was so convincing he had them eating out of his hand.'

Sadly even some of the more serious elements of the hippie community began to fall for their own psychedelic confidence trick, further fuelling the 'acid in the water' legend. Political activist Mary Sue Planck recalls 'Well, I had heard people talking about putting LSD in the water in Washington DC, and in other places too. Anytime let's say a politician was coming to town to speak somewhere people would fantasize about going down there and dumping a few hundred hits, or a few thousand hits...'

Hippie exploitation books and films were all the rage in the late 1960s and the LSD in the water legend was a godsend to them. 1968's *Wild in the Streets* was a satire featuring a rock star who is elected as President when the voting age is lowered to 15. In what must have been a very real fear for many Americans at the time, he sets up concentration camps for everyone over 35 and yes, you guessed it, dumps LSD into the Washington D.C. water supply! Deanne Louis Romana's *The Town that Took a Trip* had the strap line, 'In Eden everybody's thirsty and the water supply is full of LSD!'.

Robert Siffert's 1969 novel *The Polluters* dealt with the subject in some depth. "We decided.' The boy ran on, 'that the only thing to do was to get this society back to reality was to shock it into a sense of awareness of the now...We've expanded their minds...We got together with others who knew the score... We got the chemistry students the engineering drop-outs... we picked out the biggest centres of the establishment in the country. We found a way to get into the public waterworks in each city...' he grinned at Stan. 'Acid!' 'Acid?' asked Stan. 'LSD, man, the greatest boon to mankind!'"

LSD was now so infamous and feared that the entertainment media had to invent something even stronger.

In the 1969 episode, Is This Trip Necessary, the popular spoof secret agent series Get Smart saw evil scientist Jarvis Pim (Vincent Price) threatening to spike Washington DC's water supply with a psychedelic even stronger than LSD!

But if straight culture had fallen for the myth it seemed that the counter-culture had done so too. In 1973, Michael Hollingshead, the maverick Englishman who had turned Tim Leary on to LSD in 1961, published his autobiography. It seemed that the usually perceptive Hollingshead had fallen hook, line and sinker for the LSD in the water legend. What had started out as right wing paranoia from Major William Creasy had been adopted as a possible truth by Hollingshead and the psychedelic luminaries, Timothy Leary, George Litwin, Gunther Weil and Richard Alpert, who jointly signed this statement.

> *If an enemy does drop LSD in the water supply and if you*
> *are accurately informed and prepared, then you have*
> *two choices. If you have the time and inclination you*
> *should sit back and enjoy the most exciting education*
> *experience of your life (you might be forever grateful*
> *to the saboteur).*

As is the way of urban legends, the story waxed and waned. The 1970s saw rumour go underground for a while as LSD use became less of a novelty. Then, in 1978, after years of surveillance and infiltration, the police finally cracked the UK LSD manufacturing and distribution ring known in Operation Julie. There was a media free-for-all and every acid myth known to man was trotted out to scare the public. During the sentencing of the primary conspirators in early 1978, the *Daily Mirror* rushed into print with front-page headlines trumpeting, 'We'll Blow a Million Minds!'. 'An entire city stoned on a nightmare drug — that was the crazy ambition of the masterminds behind the world's biggest LSD factory. They planned to blow a million minds simultaneously by pouring pure LSD in to the reservoirs serving Birmingham'. Despite the headline filling most of the front page, other than those few sentences, nothing more was heard of the dastardly plot which was, of course, non-existent.

Dick Tracy, in his highly critical piece on Operation Julie for the *New Musical Express*, quoted the *Mirror*, adding 'The water supply story can be traced back in the media to at least the mid-'60s and probably before. I have had personal experience of this while working in the information caravan at one of the large Isle of Wight festivals, when I heard an almost identical story being dictated over the phone by a *Mirror* reporter. It wasn't true then, either'.

From fiction to fact and back again, the acid in the water supply legend found a home in Ken Chowder's 1985 novel *Jadis*, 'It was absurd how easy it was to invade the lives of others: put mercury in the oranges, cyanide in the Tylenol, LSD in the reservoirs; shoot the pope, shoot the president, shoot Sadat, shoot down the Korean plane, invade Grenada; all too easy.'

Except, as we are seeing, it's not 'all too easy' to put LSD in the reservoirs. The idea is great, many people talked about doing it, even more feared the possibility, but there is no evidence anyone ever tried to make the actual act a reality. But the fear was certainly real.

'Homer Loves Flanders', a 1994 episode of The Simpsons saw Shelbyville dosing rival town Springfield's water supply with LSD. This leads Homer's wife Marge to drinking the tap water and commenting, 'Oooh, the walls are melting'. Even in a show like The Simpsons, which has more drug references than any other TV show, the myth of LSD in the water was still so potent that executives from the Fox Network tried to prevent this show from airing.

Probably the most recent example of the LSD in the water myth was cleverly embedded in the script of Torchwood, a Dr Who TV spin-off series. In the episode called 'Everything Changes' (broadcast in 2006) Captain Jack Harkness queries what evidence it would take before people accept the presence of the Cybermen. The character playing Gwen Cooper retorts, 'My boyfriend says it's like a sort of terrorism. Like they put drugs in the water supply. Psychotropic drugs, causing mass hallucinations and stuff.'

So, much rumour and speculation about LSD in the water supply, but could there really be any truth behind the claims? Well, of course it *could* happen, people *could* put LSD in a water supply such as a reservoir but would it have any effect? I consulted a retired LSD chemist, who commented:

> *I did a quick calculation which might help. Assuming that the drinker drank 1/2 pint of water, and needed 100µg, then you would need 1kg of pure LSD for every million gallons in the reservoir. That's not counting any decay from sunlight, heat or chlorine in the system.*

As an example the Elan Valley reservoir system in Wales, built to provide the city of Birmingham with its water supply, holds 100,000 megalitres or 21,996,924,830 gallons. Using the LSD chemist's calculations it would require astronomical quantities of acid (22,000kg), an amount somewhat unrealistic and unfeasible to manufacture, to even begin to effectively contaminate the water supply for Birmingham.

The problems multiply further. Only a tiny amount of water in a reservoir is actually drunk neat—the majority is boiled or used in cooking or other domestic processes such as washing up, lavatory flushing, gardening etc, all of which would destroy the psychoactive component of the LSD. So the idea, while theoretically possible if a wide range of variables could be stabilised, is really a non-starter. Why then has it had such a hard to kill existence, constantly re-appearing in slightly different forms each year?

The answer is that fear lies at the heart of this particular urban legend. Fear of LSD, fear of losing one's mind. Fear that a subculture who wishes to overthrow the existing order might employ LSD to disrupt commerce and 'ordinary' life. The idea that psychedelic terrorists would tamper with the water supply adds an extra frisson of terror to this urban legend. Water is fundamental to us as individuals, we can't avoid drinking it in some form and we trust implicitly that what comes out of the tap is safe.

So, next time you hear some raddled old hippie banging on about how the psychedelic revolution could happen if the entire water system could be dosed with acid raise a glass of tap water to him and laugh. You are safe. Or are you…?

17

Music is Alive, Magic is Afoot

In 1967 the Incredible String Band were still just an inside tip for the psychedelic cognoscenti (including most of the Stones and Paul McCartney), but 1968 was the year in which they started to reach a much wider public. 'The Hangman's Beautiful Daughter', the album which helped them make that transition had been recorded during the acid tinged winter of 1967...

The Hangman's Beautiful Daughter: catalogue no EUKS 7258 to its matrix (EUK 258 if you are a mono purist), but a sonic entity of unfathomable complexity and numinosity to those who know and love it. Of all the Incredible String Band albums, *Hangman's* confers on the listener musical and lyrical gifts their other albums hint at but only occasionally deliver. If any album ever made you want to devote your life to the psychedelic experience, renounce temporal and social obligations and head for the wildwood dressed in skins this, surely, was the one.

Maybe it was the times, maybe the chemicals. Maybe it was just the right *people* at the right time, tuned in and turned on, waiting and eager to receive, a transmission from *something*. It's arguable, of course, but this Head believes the late sixties British acid zeitgeist was never as crisply ensnared as on *Hangman's*, which is one of *the* great psychedelic listening experiences. Here's why, and why it still echoes down the years…

Hangman's was the album which catapulted the Incredible String Band, essentially Lowland Scots Mike Heron and Robin Williamson, from little known quirky post-Dylan drug-dabbling folk-fanciers to psychedelic stardom, in sales, live performances and critical appraisal. Prior to the album's release in March 1968, the Incredible String Band had hardly performed in England other than a few London gigs and small provincial venues. But the hip cognoscenti recognised their potential and they had already supported Pink Floyd and Fairport Convention at the Saville Theatre in October 1967 and played a double bill with Shirley & Dolly Collins at the Queen Elizabeth Hall later that month.

Let's start with the title. In an era of album titles alluding to the acid experience such as *Piper at the Gates of Dawn* and *Are You Experienced?*, *The Hangman's Beautiful Daughter* represented acid ambiguity at its best. On the cusp of the album's release, journalist Karl Dallas queried the title and had his head messed with by the duo's surreal, stoned logic, recalling: *'It was an interview filled with sudden, reflective silences in which I sometimes felt that my questions were like rocks being thrown into a deep, clear pool, disturbing its calm.'*

> **Robin:** *In a way you could say the title thought of us. What does it mean? You can explain it at several levels.*

> **Mike:** *The hangman is death and his beautiful daughter is what comes after. Or you might say that the hangman is the past twenty years of our life and the beautiful daughter is now, what we are able to do after all these years. Or you can make up your own meaning. Your interpretation is probably just as good as ours.*

Pretty much like the acid experience itself!

Hangman's is regarded by many as *the* British acid album, though Williamson, ever evasive about his use of LSD, claims to have eschewed psychedelics, at least at the time of its release: '...by that time I'd probably stopped taking drugs, it was very much what was going on at the time but I'd pretty much lost interest in drugs by then.' It certainly *was* what was going on and the String Band appeared to be living a seriously psychedelic lifestyle—the timeless life, as the biological protagonist in *A Very Cellular Song* points out.

Hangman's is certainly not to every psychonaut's taste though. It is not an album which you just play, listen and relax to, as with many so-called psychedelic albums. Oh no. It is not, for instance, 'easy listening' psychedelic music such as post-Syd Pink Floyd (lauded as a psychedelic band but really driven by beer and dope), or music whose complexities you can immerse yourself in, such as, say, the Grateful Dead's intricate, telepathic, cosmic jams, or Shpongle's constantly mutating sonic geometry. No, nothing like that at all. *Hangman's*, as with the most meaningful psychedelic experiences, requires some meaningful input from *you*. It requires active and deep listening. You have to be *there,* with every word, every note, every image. You must—a strong word, perhaps—but you *must* make the effort, otherwise the sheer strangeness of the album, first encountered on psychedelics, may well destroy you! But, given the right dosage, attitude and an open and enquiring mind, it is a psychedelic portal to the kaleidoscopic musical Narnia imagined by Heron and Williamson.

One pilgrim at the Church of Hangman's noted, 'The first time I heard this I thought, "What a load of hippie twaddle!" but the second time I heard it, I fell in love with it and have remained so ever since.' It's *that* sort of album.

The psychedelic tone and content of *Hangman's* had been hinted at on the String Band's previous, second, album, *5000 Spirits or the Layers of the Onion*. The title alone suggested newly acquired psychedelic knowledge of the multiverse and its possibilities. The cover, an intoxicating riot of colour depicting a multi-coloured hermaphrodite, dripping with mythological symbols, rising to the heavens from an acid-head's vision of earthly fecundity, was created by Dutch artists Simon and Merjike, collectively known as The Fool, and visually reinforced the change in choice of drugs.

The music too had changed. *Spirits* was a huge leap musically from their eponymous first album which was just trad folk with a hash twist. Yet strange as they were, essentially the songs on *Spirits* were short (no longer than five and a half minutes), folk based, dope and acid tinged existential cosmic nursery rhymes, by turn playful and intriguing. Those unfamiliar with *Hangman's* and wary of taking the plunge, high or straight, should first test the waters with *5000 Spirits* and see how they fare!

Hangman's consist of ten songs, lasting 47:08 minutes. But time, as the Zen teacher Dogen perceptively said, is 'Three arms and eight elbows', i.e. meaningless. Under the influence of psychedelics though, 47.08 minutes could be several millennia of heaven, hell or a combination of both.

Come with me now, let's go back to 1968 and see what it might have been like. Imagine you're illuminated, about 90 minutes into your chosen psychedelic (it would, of course, have been high quality LSD at the time of *Hangman's* release, probably in sugar lump form). Earlier that afternoon you've finally taken the plunge and spent 39s/11d (that's £1.99 to you dear reader) at your local record boutique on an album you've heard so much about but have never dared experience. You've put on your loose and comfy tripping clothes and have called round to see a couple of friends, suggesting they might like to try your recently acquired and well dosed sugar lumps. They gratefully accept.

After the initial rush of the acid, you suggest to your tripping partners that they might like a challenge. How about this new album that everyone's been raving about. It's supposed to be far out. Yeah, yeah, ok, whatever, just hurry up and put *something* on.

So on hands and knees you shuffle your way across the carpet to the record player, the now rubbery, distant digits at the ends of your hands (don't look at your palms!) picking the album up for examination. Lights and colours shimmer and refract from surfaces all around you, flickering and strobing in the periphery of your vision. This is strong stuff and no mistake. You pause for a moment (was it *really* just a moment, or half an hour, bringing another String Band lyric to mind, 'I was your slave, now you are mine, I am time...'); transfixed. What in the shop had looked to be a simple, if strange album cover now assumes the appearance of a sacred artefact, and illuminated manuscript.

Robin Williamson once described *Hangman's* as a 'winter album', and the original front cover (the covers were reversed in subsequent vinyl editions) finds Robin and Mike, sat on a snowy drystone wall near Balmore, near Edinburgh, against a backdrop of an icy cerulean sky. Folkies no longer, our heroes are now clad as psychedelic monks in functional smock and cloak, more Man at LSD than Carnaby Street fashion victim. They look the part, living personifications of Salvador Dali's dictum 'I don't take drugs, I am drugs'. Except they did! And they are looking straight at you!

The rear cover photo catches them communing in a bare copse with Mike's new girlfriend Rose Simpson, Robin's on/off beau Licorice, his dog Leaf, two friends (Roger Marshall—with chain—and Nicky Walton), and a gaggle of perplexed-looking children (author Mary Stewart's) in wacky hats. The image strongly evoked the communal ethic emerging in the sixties counter-culture.

You stare in wonder. You wish they were your friends. You wish you looked and lived like they did (the early String Band lived the life, in communes and communal living settings in Scotland and Wales). It was as though the sleeve designer had, by some visual alchemy, distilled the very essence of the acid lifestyle into imagery. You almost feel you don't need to even bother to listen to the album; every cell in your body has it all writ down. You're very high indeed now and it would very likely be possible to attain enlightenment by acid osmosis alone, just by grokking the album sleeve.

Pan only knows how long this series of thoughts has diverted you, so you re-focus, slide the shiny black disc from the sleeve and onto the turntable ... *Click, crackle, crrrrrshhh...* the needle bounces onto the vinyl and you barely make it back to the settee before the ceremony begins. The quality of sound in the room has suddenly changed, your listening apparatus has, Tardis-like, become an aural cathedral, your ears conduits for the thrilling magnificence and glory of sound as the first song from this psychedelic hymnal begins. In those far off times, listening to music on acid was often as much about divining what the musicians were trying to tell you lyrically about life, the multiverse and everything as it was about the beat, the melody and the rhythm. You listen carefully, expectantly...

Koeeoaddi There kicks off this evening's psychedelic sermon. *'The natural cards revolve, ever changing'*. What *do* they mean? Is it Taoist philosophy, acid adage, or merely words forged from experience, twisted echoes of Williamson's Edinburgh childhood fluidly wrought in music? Just when you've wrestled that problem to the ground, the chorus kicks in:

> *Earth water fire and air met together in a garden fair*
> *Put in a basket bound with skin*
> *If you answer this riddle you'll never begin...*

Easy. They're talking about being us, being human, physical beings. Obviously. But wait, if you answer the ostensibly easy riddle you haven't begun, have you? Begun what? It all seemed so simple. Back to square one. This sort of enigma, on psychedelics, can seriously mess with your mind. The answer's obvious, yet according to Mike and Robin it's not. Or perhaps it *is* a knot, a philosophical one, a koan, one you can sing along with but one which will haunt you for the rest of your life as you try to balance answer with implication. And again, just as you are getting to grips with the possibilities that track stops and everything changes once again as your ears are assailed by *The Minotaur's Song*.

It's not what you were expecting. But after *Koeeoaddi There* what *were* you expecting? Is it Gilbert & Sullivan on acid, or the Bonzo's on acid *parodying* Gilbert & Sullivan on acid? Or is it just a load of twaddle, the Emperor's New Sound and should you take it off quickly and put some Hendrix on before the others laugh at you? As the nonsensical lyrics and skewed music hall tune grind along you realise there can be no hiding place. These guys know what they are doing. Either take it off now and fail, or rise to the challenge of being high and listening to what Heron and Williamson think about the great mystery we find ourselves in, day by day, second by second. As an original discriminating buffalo man this is, after all, why you bought the album in the first place, remember!

Witch's Hat—you knew it—they've seen them in the same places, as you, 'in quiet places where the moss grows green'. An unearthly tune with a shivery, wintry feel, 'the wind is cold, the year is old, the trees whisper together'. Delicious sounds drawing your mind and body out into the green cathedral where everything is alive, everything possible. And if only, if only you knew where you could get some black cherries at this time of night, what rings you could wear!

Only three tracks in and already you are already musically and lyrically somewhere you would never have believed existed. 'They're a bit like Donovan' someone had said to you a few weeks back. Really? Not even close or in the same universe! And where else in 1968 would you find gimbri jostling with chahanai and oud, water harp and mandolin, sitar and Hammond organ along with the usual guitars? This was world music before world music was even a twinkle in Andy Kershaw's eye!

So far, so unusual. And then, the pulse of an organ and *A Very Cellular Song* begins. To quote David Crosby, 'Now, we will get weird!'. Mike Heron has often alluded to the fact that this song had close connections with the LSD experience—as if we hadn't worked that one out—and told me in 1994: 'All it was, was a trip, and that was the music I was listening to, that interspersed with Radio 4, bits of plays, people talking to each other, and I happened to be listening to the Pindar family before I started.'

To this day the opening acapella chorus of;

> *Lay down my dear brother*
> *Won't you lay and take your rest*
> *Won't you lay your head upon your saviour's breast*
> *For I love you, but Jesus loves you the best, and I bid you goodnight,*
> *goodnight, goodnight...*

...thrills me. This part of *A Very Cellular Song* was stolen from the Bahamanian Pindar Family and was also frequently by the Grateful Dead at the end of concerts. And from that simple introduction you are led into a kaleidoscopic acid vision of being very, very, high among the essence of the natural world. It's quite a ride and as the examination of the ameoba's life and times slithers and squelches to an end, the song's coda, a joyful eastern chant, taken from a traditional Sikh spiritual song called *On That Day* assures you that, just like Aldous Huxley told you, everything will be *all right*. Altogether now:

> *May the long time sun shine on you*
> *All love surround you*
> *And the pure light within you*
> *Guide your way on*

Words to live by! Part of you wants the song to continue forever. But another part is glad it's over and for a minute you hope the entire album is finished so you can take stock of what has been downloaded into your being.

Then, nothing. A resounding silence. Except it's not a silence, it's the endless music of what's happening. Outside, the wind rattles and soughs. Cars occasionally hiss past your window. Somewhere in the distance mice are playing football. Side one has ended.

You make the long journey again across the vast tundra of the carpet to change sides, wishing you'd pre-rolled a spliff to calm things down but accept that asking the others to do that now is pointless. They are staring into the middle distance not sure quite what's happening to them and when, if even, it will ever end and what, for fuck's sake, has actually started. Of course, from the warm comfort of retrospect, you know that side one was just the warm up, even *Cellular Song*, just an entrée to eternity.

The String Band were among the vanguard of early post Beatniks and hippies who had seen through the flimsy nonsense of 'straight' living. Many who had turned onto LSD were leaving for the Far East or eschewing the soul-corroding drabness of city living to expand their consciousness, and experiment with new ways of living, in the country. *Mercy I Cry City* opens side two and is quite clear in its feelings for life in the big city: 'you cover up your emptiness with brick and stone and rush, oh I can see and touch you but you don't owe reality much'.

I won't spoil the next four tracks with description. Buy the album or listen to it again to discover their lasting treasures. Save but to say that *Waltz of the New Moon*, *The Water Song*, *Three Is a Green Crown* and *Swift as the Wind* are out there, far out there, weird, imbued with a lyrical and music strangeness that create a psychedelic synthesis that can only be experienced, not described. Real, personal, acid visions.

The final track, the plaintive, drowsy, *Nightfall*, with flickering sitar, brings *Hangman's* to a close, yearning for sleep to end the experience, bringing in dreams, 'As time's echoes reflect on your water.' Some people never listened to *Hangman's* again after one acid-fuelled listen. Their lives are diminished. For others, right from the album's release, it represented the golden road to unlimited devotion, becoming a psychedelic musical touchstone against which all other musical experiences melt right away.

Contemporary reviews of *Hangman's* show the almost universal acclaim which met this strange album—and also show that critics could, when they wanted, write some pretty good descriptive prose about music. The *Sunday Times'* Derek Jewell was well impressed, making *Hangman's* Record of the Month in March 68: 'Quasi-poetry and phoney mysticism now cling to the skirts of popular music, but the Incredibles are not pseudo. Their work is convincing, beautiful, idiosyncratic, yielding more with each playing.' The Observer's Robin Denselow: 'Together with the Beatles' Sgt. Pepper it seems... to be the most important disc to have been produced in Britain for several years.'

Melody Maker ran a preview, opening with: 'When poet Pete Brown, lyric-writer for the Cream, heard... Hangman's, he said: "That's what the Rolling Stones have been trying to do."' He was right, and on *Satanic Majesties Request* you can hear several *Hangman*-isms. But the Stones' media-hyped association with the dark forces was ersatz, transparent acid-lite psych-pop, when compared to the far deeper source that the String Band were tapping into on *Hangman's*.

Several reviewers tapped straight into the musical and lyrical core of the album, immediately picking up on the pantheistic, animistic nature of the lyrics and the experiences from which they had been drawn.

Robin Denselow again: 'Taken as a whole, the songs are a plea for wonder at existence, a sometimes mystical, sometimes pantheistic involvement in an alive universe. In many ways it's a Wordsworthian romanticism, pro-nature, pro-imagination and anti-urban... The expression of awe at being alive and the sense of organic connecting between all things comes, at times, near to religious statement.' Word!

Praise indeed from the establishment. More excellent reviews followed in the wake of the March 1968 concert at the Royal Festival Hall. In the *Financial Times'* Anthony Thorncroft penned a perceptive piece about both concert and band: 'The ISB are the nearest thing to godliness among the art school set: judging by the Establishment figures scattered among the audience they are about to be taken up by a more hard-bitten public.' (You can just imagine the likes of Marc and Syd, among others, in the String Band's early audiences, furtively scribbling notes under their Afghan coats!) '...It is doubtful whether the delicate flavour of the Incredibles will make the transition. They compose their own mystical songs around melodies which ebb and flow with butterfly brittleness, and lyrics which link poetry and nonsense in an unholy marriage. The principal sources are Eastern and medieval music and, after a first hearing of disbelief, those prepared to accept the Incredibles' magical world can get on terms with the most unique talent to come out of the current song-writing revival.'

Americans were no less enthused; Richard Goldstein (*New York Magazine*) hit the nail on the head, describing Robin's voice as having a 'reedy whisper that sounds like water seeping out of ancient rocks', exhorting his readers to go out and buy Hangman's so they could be the 'first (on your block) to worship at the universal church of magic'. Let's have some more Goldstein, he's nearly as good as the album! 'Each song is a tone-poem etched in filigree; delicate yet sturdy. Each lyric is an utterly disarming cross between a hymn and a nursery rhyme.'

I couldn't find a bad review, and the ones that weren't full of superlatives owed more to the reviewer's lack of imagination and skill with language rather than any dislike of the album. Everybody knew, to some degree or another that, in the words of Buffy St Marie, '*Music is alive, magick is afoot*'. And so it was. Switched-on Heads across Britain were rushing home and turning on to *Hangman's*, their minds permanently scarred, often scared, by its austere, cold beauty to such an extent that it compels obsessive writing such as this, decades after the album's release. The power of music eh?

Critical acclaim was such that *Hangman's* was nominated for a Grammy award in the USA in 1969, *Cash Box's* Grammy nominee list revealing *The Hangman's Beautiful Daughter* to be in the 'Best Folk Performance' section along with Judy Collins' *Both Sides Now* and Dylan's *John Wesley Harding*. Strange days indeed.

For the 2010 CD re-issue of the album, Robin Williamson was coaxed into writing a short essay which absolutely defines the essence of *Hangman's* and is worth buying the CD for even if you never venture into the music itself!

> *For me it is impossible to speak of the days and years in which these recordings were made in any language other than the language of incantation....*

> *The fire in a fiddle tune is from a bone-fire flame.*
> *Birdsong bears the music of the whistle. The beat of the*
> *heart is the pulse of melody. Time is the keeper. The*
> *drone of bees, whales and coyotes and wolves their*
> *singing. The sun shouts on in Golden. The moon lulls.*
> *And while we live and breathe—what else but celebrate.*
> *All so.*
>
> *Music is a power which comes from the eternal.*
> *Sometimes humans get to play it. Sometimes they don't*
> *get in the way too much. And the music gets through.*

Me? I loved *Hangman's* from the day I first heard it, somewhat belatedly in 1974, and I love it dearly to this day. It continues to have a profound effect on me and is an integral part of my musical DNA, an album without which I would be far from who I am. I always find it challenging, rewarding, refreshing, and essential. If you have not heard *Hangman's*, straight or high, I envy you your maiden voyage into those uncharted waters. If you are familiar with *Hangman's* but haven't listened to it for a while I suggest you turn on, tune in and prime yourself with a long walk, preferably in wild and elemental, weather, slip it onto the musical regurgitation system of your choice (please let it be a good sound system, for your own benefit) and connect with, well, you tell me.

But remember: 'The opposite is also true'.

> *May the long-time sun shine on you*
> *All love surround you*
> *And the pure light within you*
> *Guide your way on*

18

An Acid Alchemist Speaks

'Something to blow your mind away,

something that I made today'

– An Interview with Casey Hardison –

Most LSD and other psychedelic drugs are brought into being by underground chemists. Some of these acid alchemists have become legendary. Augustus Owsley Stanley, for instance, is a household name within the psychedelic community and has his own entry in the Oxford dictionary where 'Owsley' is a noun to describe high quality LSD originating in his labs. Others such as Nick Sand in the USA, and Richard Kemp and Andy Munro in the UK have also achieved notoriety. In 2004 another psychedelic outlaw came into the public eye when US citizen Casey William Hardison was sentenced to 20 years in prison for LSD, DMT, and 2C-B manufacture in Britain. Casey mounted a spirited defence and a subsequent appeal based on sound legal and moral principles, but was unsuccessful. Throughout his time in prison Casey managed to keep up communication with his friends on the outside and was eventually released on 29th May, 2013, and was deported to the US.

Andy Roberts: *When did you first take LSD, and what was your opinion of the experience?*

Casey Hardison: By the night I first took LSD, I had spent 8 years clean and sober in Alcoholics and Narcotics Anonymous where I had recovered from a seemingly helpless state of mind, chock full of manifestations of internalised shame. The night I ingested LSD I knew the co-founder of AA, Bill Wilson, had taken it and had had an enlightening experience. Controversy remains over just how much the spiritual awakening Bill had, had found its way into the 12 Steps of Alcoholics Anonymous. I certainly had experienced the spiritual awakening of the AA mantra: Unity Service and Recover. But that fateful snowy night, having recovered, I awoke again and again to unity and to so many marvellous new realms of imagination and insight. No words can convey how valuable the experience was to my evolution as a compassionate and mindful human: it was the motivation for my desire to make LSD and be of service.

What gave you the idea and motivation to synthesise LSD or any other psychedelic?

In the middle of this first ineffable LSD experience I had buried myself in the pea gravel down by the Coeur d'Alene lakeshore in northern Idaho. I was floating there in reverie, my heartmind ablaze: one, everywhere and everything. I heard a gong-like chime. It was 3 o'clock and it was time to go to school. Excitedly, I knew I would study this stuff, this experience and the conversations constellated around it. In my first biology and botany classes I began to know that I would one day make this problem child, this wonderdrug, this sacred medicine.

Many people believe those who create LSD and other psychedelics to be, basically, mind alchemists. Do you think the mind-set and intent of the individual chemist can affect the quality of experience imparted by the drug?

Thank you for the sobriquet, drug wizard and mind-alchemist. I'll take them both. And with no authority at all, except for my own subjective experience and memetic programming, I would like to think that my mind-set effected the vibrations of the environment encoded in the crystal as it precipitated out of solution. And one may hope, as I did, that this would lead to an enlightening experience by all who would partake.

Prior to embarking on making a batch of LSD or any other psychedelic did you ever carry out any specific, non-chemical process, preparation, such as meditation or other practices? What was your mind-set during the actual chemical process? Did you have any non-chemical, possibly what might be called ritual, practices? Was there any specific music you listened to during the chemical process of making psychedelics, if so what; and why?

In general, I would clean the lab, bake the glassware dry, weigh and tare it, set up all the equipment and lay out new bench protector mats. I also had a fairly consistent ritual of smoking 5-MeO-DMT beforehand in conjunction with a mantra-style meditation. As I flowed through my bench practice, I attempted to keep a mind-set of compassion rooted in praise, gratitude and love for others and myself. I often played uplifting and enlightening music: more frequently than not I would play Krisna Das 'One Track Heart' at least once and I let crystal precipitate to Shim Shai's 'I Sense Your Presence'. Each of these are super high vibrations of devotion to our highest selves and I hoped their message would carry through to the communicant.

Various underground LSD chemists have claimed to have played around with the synthesis process, i.e. the recipe for making acid. Do you think there are improvements still to be made in this regard and if so, would you comment further?

I am sure improvements will be made. I would love to see the genetic transfer of the ergot alkaloid enzymes to other species that can be grown in submerged culture in a lab. If this were to happen the genie would be forever out of the bottle and the alkaloids would be available to every interested person. This *Claviceps* species bottleneck is the single greatest weakness in the clandestine manufacture of LSD. Next, I'd like to see improvements in the methods of isolating and cleaving ergot alkaloids to lysergic acid. I'm not sure where the state of the art is for the actual final synthesis of LSD from lysergic acid, but my use of the peptide coupler PyBOP, after Dr. Dave Nichols, was definitely an improvement on the Edgewood Arsenal $POCl_3$ condensation.

You were arrested in 2004 and subsequently sentenced to 20 years in prison after representing yourself in court. Why did you do that, and do you think you got a greater or lesser sentence than if you'd had formal legal representation?

I made the decision to represent myself in court when I realized that my barrister, Rudi Fortson, spoke with a forked tongue and would be "personally embarrassed" to represent me on human rights grounds. Barristers swear an oath to and speak for the Queen. There was no possibility of putting forth my Cognitive Liberty and Equal Rights arguments through the mouth of a man who still desires "silk" from the Queen. Rudi received his piece of silk and is now a "Queen's Counsel" for that is what QC means. I was left with no real choice. And, no I don't think they throttled me on my representation. They sentenced me for having the temerity to flout their laws and think myself innocent.

Why do you think you received such a large and disproportionate sentence for making psychedelic drugs when set against much more lenient sentences given in the same year to murderers, rapists, paedophiles and others for whom there is evidence they have harmed other human beings?

As Dr. David Luke wrote me in prison: "they're more afraid of the unconscious contents of man's mind than murderers, rapists and paedophiles". I tend to agree. It definitely wasn't my failure to pay tax, it was that I paid no heed to their "authority".

The judge in your court case was of the opinion that your sole aim in making psychedelics was profit. What is your opinion of that statement?

Anthony Niblett was obtuse on this point. He knew that wasn't true but had to make it sound worse than it was so he could justify the injustice he was performing. There is no possible way he thought my defence a ruse or my actions anything other than in line with my commitment to making a difference in the world. He even commended me several times on my presentation of my defence, stopping once to ask "are you sure you're not legally trained?". I wasn't, but I was a fast learner.

Consideration of set and setting are vital for any psychedelic experience. Do you prefer taking psychedelics inside, or out in the natural world, and why?

Well, I've had some pretty blistering experiences inside, whether it be a prison cell or a Grateful Dead concert. But I think I prefer psychedelic experiences outside, in nature, with one or a few friends or al(l)one. When I'm in nature—and by that I mean an environment free of man-made objects save what I brought myself—another rhythm develops, and my senses resonate inside and out. The insights produced in those moments tend to have more species level importance to me. Often they are about my organism, its limits and possibilities. Moreover, the sounds carry me away. They are the original icaros.

What did you think of your time in a UK prison?

I had a blast! Not all of the time, mind you, but I made light of a strained situation. It was certainly much easier than the States and, though I couldn't leave, I was present to the inescapable fact that I was still living better than two-thirds or more of the planet: I had food, clothing, shelter, a few good friends and a fairly clean and disease free environment. I had hot and cold running water, a kettle to boil water, a flushing ceramic toilet with a lid and an onsite medical clinic. It was however a monotonous regime but this kept time ticking over at a pretty good clip. There was a lot less violence, gang activity and the like than I expected, hearing about the US system. Most of the time I played chess, read newspapers, studied physics and law, etc. Of course, there was plenty of time for bull-shitting about whatever. All in all, I survived and it wasn't that bad. I turned it into my sanctuary, my Augustinian cave, my retreat: many people pay good money for such experiences. I got mine free.

Were you able to continue your psychedelic use in prison? If so what can you tell us?

I most certainly was. Their doors stopped little to nothing getting in. I had people send me LSD, 2C-B, DMT, 5-MeO-DMT, mephedrone, kratom, and the list goes on. None of these were solicited; they just arrived in the mail. I was able to dose dozens of inmates as well and attempt to wake them up from the penumbral dreamtime they were living in.

Some people have claimed that during a psychedelic experience they have had contact with/been contacted by what might be termed intelligences or entities. Have you had any such experiences? If so can you give an example?

I have no certainty this has ever happened to me. I have, however, made shit up to this effect. I tend to think that the molecules themselves are entities. And, they have given me great insight into the vastness of my intelligence. Sure, I've seen the typical machine elves laughing at me and thought ayahuasca was an alien being that resides in my brainstem, but I was high at the time.

Do you think these experiences represent objective/real experiences involving entities external to the mind/body, whether their origin is earthly, extra-terrestrial, inter-dimensional, aspects of our mind/psyche or a mixture of any of these and more?

No. I think that these experiences are personifications of the DNA instincts innate to us. They appear to be generated and sensed by our own brains. Jung would call them manifestations of the archetypes. Plato had his perfect forms. I tend to keep it simple and not tool off about possible alien intelligences. In short, I do not know. If there are aliens, I can't wait to try their drugs. As Neil said: "He brought out something for the trip … he said it was old but it's good".

Should we act on the information imparted by these 'entities' or just observe/ listen and remain agnostic about them and the information they impart?

This question presupposes that these entities exist and that they are doing the imparting. This may not be the case. I think we should translate our own insights into action, especially those that arise from upward or ascendant thinking. If it's going to create more negative emotion then don't do it. If it brings an uplift of positive emotion and feeling then do it. Often people think something and forget they are the authors of that thought. Sometimes, on psychedelics, one can remember a reality they sentenced themselves to decades ago, no pun on sentence. As the author, I am free to rewrite my reality. So please, consider taking responsibility for making that information up and then act on it that awareness. You'll be pleased with the results. I promise.

What, if any, significant quality of being do you think psychedelics can bestow/impart to those prepared to be receptive?

The most significant quality of being that can be imparted by the psychedelic experience in those prepared to be receptive is being grateful for being here at all. The joy and wonder this brings can throw one into a child-like innocence, it can also bestow compassion for others and their individual paths. And if you're not careful gratitude can lead one into a life of service to humanity and a desire to care for the earth. In that it can remind us that we are not here to subdue and have dominion over the earth but that we can be her eyes, her ears, her consciousness. And if we act on what we see and hear, what we feel and the thoughts we think, we will make this a better place than when we got here.

What's your opinion as to whether psychedelic experiences should be carefully planned, almost ritualised, as Tim Leary strongly suggested, or should they be more of the Kesey school of spontaneity arising from availability and purchase? Or both?

I seriously shy away from the world of "should". Do as thou wilt. I would suggest however, that newbies takes their tripping with some seriousness. Many times in the past when I found myself in difficult emotional or psychological turmoil in my mundane existence, I have sought counsel in the psychedelics with great intention. In these times the ritualised nature of the experience became a great meditation on ideas I might never have had. In other spaces, I would take acid nearly every time it was mentioned, a phial or sheet appeared, etc. Spontaneity has led me to some of the most productive of results I might have been intentional about. This year of the Grateful Dead 50th Anniversary shows I have eaten a lot of acid and not one of those times were of an intentional spiritual nature beyond dancing and having a good time, but who defines what is a spiritual experience? Dancing on acid with the Dead sure feels spiritual to me.

How relevant to the psychedelic experience, especially for those who have integrated psychedelics into a regular practice over many years, is keeping mind and body in excellent condition?

I think this is fairly relevant for myself. I like to be in good health. Indeed, I have never experienced psychedelics in ill health. I have always had a fairly good level of fitness and having kept an active yogic practice and meditation. In March, at peak health and whilst snowboarding, I broke my tibia and fibula mid shaft and the recovery has been very painful, especially in the muscles torn through with shrapnel. I couldn't stand the fogginess of the opiates so I basically roughed it. As I rediscovered at the GD50 shows, LSD is a fabulous analgesic. Dancing on acid has been some of the finest physical therapy I could perform.

Poor health and upsets about it can be magnified in the psychedelic mind states. I would like to think that those in ill health may be able to find some solace, some therapeutic efficacy in the psychedelic space, maybe even a new impetus and drive to recover.

In the more arcane corners of the internet there are accounts of how much of the LSD in the US and possibly elsewhere was manufactured and moved round by 'the family', people loosely connected with the Grateful Dead. Is that the case, or is it a drug legend, and can you comment about it if is true?

There is no way to know for certain. It sure is easy for someone to claim: "It's family acid, bro", but this does not make it so. In my opinion, there is emerging a whole new genre of acid chemists entirely disassociated from the Grateful Dead family. It may be that some of the bottlenecks in the production and distribution of large amounts of LSD are controlled by a few thoughtful old-timers out there that have been working on solutions for decades, making sure there would always be ergot precursors and whatnot. Maybe they're part of the Dead "Family", maybe they're just part of the acid dealing families on Dead tour, maybe they're entirely unrelated to the Dead and making their own paths to the problem child. If we can translate and publish the lysergamide synthesis pathways via other organisms easier to maintain and reproduce, we will have transcended the greatest bottleneck, where to get the ergot alkaloids. I would hope this would result in many more acid chemists from all walks of life, thinking globally and brewing local. In that vein, I am more of the persuasion that the genie should be out of the bottle and not in the hands of any one "family".

Similar internet fables tell of the 'thumbprint', those who wish to be LSD couriers being obliged to dip their thumb in LSD crystals and take it, in order to demonstrate their, devotion and purity I suppose, to the cause. True or fable? If true, have you ever done a thumbprint and if so could you comment on the reasons why, the experience itself and how you felt afterwards?

I'm not sure about the fable nor have I partaken of the courier's purity and devotion ceremony. After all, the chef is not the waiter. And, if you don't trust the brothers around you, then what the fuck are they doing around you? The thumbprint experience, however, trumps Terence's heroic mushroom dose in my humble opinion. One may safely assume that a descent thumbprint of LSD, even in fine powder, would be at least a milligram or ten hits but as there are so many variables a cautious trajectory may be called for. At other times, a finger-swipe has been called for. Not for the faint hearted or the paranoid, I say.

Thumb or finger printing is like any other intentional high-dose LSD experience. The world is whizzing by at a blistering warp pace and yet perfect stillness abounds. Of course this is just words employed to describe my experience. The map is not the territory. It's best to remember that it's subjective and that we each may respond differently to LSD. If you have doubts, leave it out. If you feel confident, drop in!

If the above is not the case, what's the largest amount of LSD you have taken, why and in what circumstances/for what purpose?

I licked my stir rod whilst precipitating LSD once. That hit my head the hardest. I have no idea why I did it but I saw a chunk of fluff and licked it up.

You have, for better or worse, attained celebrity/fame for being one of the great psychedelic chemists. Very few really have come to the public's attention but of the ones that are known, which one do you rate as the uber-chemist and why?

I have modeled myself in the vein of Sasha Shulgin and Darrell Lemaire. These two were pioneers in the making of many differing psychedelic compounds and I wanted to learn the basics of tryptamine and phenethylamine chemistry from them. The two had long been friends. Darrell had an old-school mining background and approached each synthesis from a few steps back to avoid detection by law enforcement which might be monitoring the supply of the precursors he acquired. Sasha, with his DEA license, didn't have these concerns. This gave me an expanded eye on synthesis pathways. Darrell had given me a number of pieces of laboratory apparatus that he had made. Each of these pieces belied an old school industrial ingenuity. Somewhere between Darrell's and Sasha's approach I constellate myself.

A few obscure, but reliable psychedelic websites and mailing lists have mentioned an LSD chemist known as The Lorax. Are you at liberty to impart any information about him, his motives, why he chose that specific name etc.?

No, I am not.

The LSD experience can be extremely intense and difficult, even for the experienced tripper. MDMA is also classed as a psychedelic but is qualitatively very different. What are your thoughts on MDMA as a psychedelic? And what do you think of the combination of LSD and MDMA when taken together?

I find the MDMA experience very distinct from LSD. Words would fail to describe the differences. I accept MDMA as a psychedelic, in the mind manifesting sense, but "true hallucinations" would be quite rare for both MDMA and LSD. I enjoy taking them together, "candy-flip" style. I prefer the LSD first and the MDMA on the way out. All seems puffier and floatier this way. Plus the MDMA can facilitate great conversations as the party winds down.

What is your opinion as to whether LSD and other psychedelics should be freely available, on demand, to anyone who wants them?

I am uncertain about the principle of free availability. I'm all for the chemists getting a living wage. It's not like the government is going to be handing them out free and transparent. I would suggest that if an adult wants to have a psychedelic, then they should be able to inform themselves freely, and choose freely amongst the highest quality psychedelic brands. At this point I would think a purchase would ensue. If a chemist wants to make quality wares and people want to acquire them from that chemist per their terms, what business is it of mine? The State may want to regulate quality control, labelling and age restrictions. I see no problem in this sort of reasonable regulation.

If you believe regulation of these transformative substances would be the way forward to making them more widely available, what would your suggestion/s be?

I think we ought to have annual conversations about particular drugs of the 20 most popular and say this year we're going to make LSD lawful to consume, possess, supply, produce, etc., but, only after a transparent conversation with the public. Next year we'll try 2C-B. As for specific regulations, these will have to be determined on a case-by-case basis. I would like to think that we have enough smarts to figure out a reasonable and proportionate regulatory structure that distinguishes between peaceful and not peaceful drug use, between harm to oneself and harm to others. They do it with alcohol and tobacco.

As you know, in recent years a variety of conspiracy theories and revisionist histories about the origin and purpose of LSD have sprung up, especially in the US—Jan Irvin, Mark Stahlman etc. Do you give credence to any of these and does it matter whether LSD was created intentionally by Hofmann for the Rosicrucians or whoever?

I have no idea what the truth may be, there are so many factors involved beyond the control of anyone or any series of actors. And, in the end, it will matter not one iota. No matter how hard any elite organization may have tried, they could not control for unintended consequences of letting the psychedelic genie out of the bottle; and now there are so many purveyors, proselytizers and partakers of psychedelics that, to quote Nick Saunders, "all the king's men cannot ever put the psychedelic genie back again". As for giving Yawn Irvin credence, in my opinion, the guy reads so much into such little information I'm surprised there are enough gullible people to swallow it all. When I made LSD there certainly weren't any agencies involved to command my action. I was doing it for the love of myself, the love of humanity and the love of the molecules.

There's also a theory that the CIA introduced LSD to the counter-culture in order to disrupt and dilute its political and social power? Any comments as to whether this might have been the case and if so, again, does it matter or was the psychedelic revolution successful?

I can see how this may very well be the case but again we are dealing with unintended consequences here. How could they know that nearly every facet of modern Western culture would appear affected by the psychedelic mind state? Hell, even Target is displaying bras with the flower of life all over the display. Whodathunkit? As for the psychedelic (r)evolution, no it has not yet been fully successful. When we each all start acting for the good of each other, the planet and such, it will be successful.

Which, if any, psychedelic elder do you regard as your mentor, whether via literature or personal knowledge, and why?

I have no real mentors, I love and admire so many. I take bits and pieces from them all. If I were to choose only one it would have to be Sasha Shulgin, he was in it for sheer curiosity and to explore manipulations of his mind. He also had a deep passion for liberty and the constitution. The same could be said of Jonathan Ott. So I guess that somewhere between these two, I constellate myself.

In recent years there seems to have been something of a psychedelic renaissance with increased availability and increase in quality of LSD, MDMA and other psychedelics. Serious scientific studies are also taking place and the media's stance against psychedelics is also, to an extent, softening and more open. What's your advice to any individual who wants to help in any way to raise people's awareness of the scientifically proven benefits of psychedelic drugs?

Speak about it wherever people will listen, and be truthful that there are risks to exploring one's mind. There may be demonological thinking to confront, aspects of one's psyche one would like to remain hidden yet may be exposed. Talk about the transformations you might have experienced: how you've come to fear death less, handle uncertainty with more calm, let go of doubt about your intrinsic lovability, etc.

Do you use any non-chemical methods to attain a psychedelic high? If so which ones and what can you tell us about them?

It is not possible to use non-chemical methods. Everything you do has its basis in chemistry. I've used so many: breathing, sex, yoga, drumming, dancing, dreaming, etc.

In Britain we have a long running radio show called Desert Island Discs on which people are imagined to be marooned by themselves on a desert island and can only take a few items, which they name and discuss on the show. May I be somewhat light hearted and re-frame this as Desert Island Trips and ask you: Which three fiction or non-fiction books—either about psychedelics or otherwise—would you take with you?

Robert Anton Wilson's *Prometheus Rising*
James Austin's *Zen and the Brain*
Enlightenment by MSI

Which fiction or documentary film—either about psychedelics or otherwise— would you take with you?

Flight from Death

Which three CDs would you take with you that, in your opinion, capture in sound the psychedelic experience?

Amused to Death by Roger Waters
Closing of Winterland by Grateful Dead
Pink Floyd's Dark Side of the Moon.

Thank you Casey!

Note: *This email-based interview took place over a couple of months as Casey answered questions amongst his daily activities, often editing and refining them as he went. I feel he put as much of himself into his responses as* *he did when manufacturing psychedelic drugs, and I thank him from my heart for doing so (on both counts!). In a Facebook exchange during December 2015 I dedicated The Incredible String Band's The Juggler's Song to him, not least for the line 'Something that I made today, something to blow your mind away'. In his email response Casey wrote: 'Thank you Andy, if I'd known, I would've played it in the lab!'*

http://youtu.be/VRRqh6ltXDE

19

Misty Mountain Drop

This is a piece of fiction I wrote to encompass various matters of interest to me around Earth Mysteries, psychedelic mushrooms, shamanism and the cyclical nature of time. It also contains numerous small quotes from (and references to) songs and bands. There will be a prize for anyone who manages to spot them all!

Above, an icy blue dream of a late December dawn, shot through with spectral herringbone clouds fading into a sky offering limitless promise to all beneath its dominion. Below, the speck of a small silver VW camper rolling west along a mazy road that wound through mountains to the north, and a long moor stretching south to the sea. Suspended in between, the raggedy contrails of military jets scorching glyphs into the sky, spelling the future for those with the wit to understand.

It was that sort of day. This is where they were. This is where they wanted to be. The van sped on.

Recent heavy snow had vanished from all but the highest summits and deepest north-facing hollows. Shortening days of limpid skies and lengthening star-drizzled nights now set-dressed the land with a heavy ice rime, revealing galaxies of shimmering diamonds as rays from the newly risen sun glanced across the scattered, shattered rocks.

The van sped on.

Ravens wheeled and tumbled playfully in its slipstream; winged black absences tailing the van as it journeyed the meandering, undulating mountain road. The ravens knew. They'd been waiting.

'What a landscape', Dan mused aloud, leaning back in the passenger seat, entranced by the dawn's revelations, yesterday's daydream believer in what tomorrow might bring, sound-tracked by the tunes on the CD player, 'Ravens. Wow.' An omen perhaps, he thought.

Chilly chilly winds blowing, lovely spring coming soon...

'We won, we're here, we're chosen. I claim our prize.' Jem's voice from the driver's seat, rising sing-song over the next line, broke his reverie. 'We did indeed win, we are indeed here. We were chosen and the prize will soon be ours'; he intoned back, mock-ritual style. They had played out this exchange in numerous permutations since they left home at silly o'clock, several hours and six counties ago, spiral light of Venus beckoning from the horizon as they'd left Albion and entered Cymru.

The banter was old now but no less true, and much nearer fruition. They *had* won. They *were* here. Almost. The pair fell to discussing the implications of their prize as the van entered a band of thick forest on either side of the road. They chattered on, oblivious, as the rising sun strobed through the trees.

He, late twenties. Tall, thin with an outdoor vigour about him. She, similarly aged, gamine, alert, sharp. Lecturers from the East Midlands by trade. Hippies by persuasion. Smiles and laughter peppered their conversation. Even after several years together every day was a joy. They were in love. Obviously.

As the van cleared the thick avenue of trees, a building suddenly appeared on the left.

'Stop!'

'What? Here?'

'Yeah, pull into that car park. There's the mound, across the road.'

Following my fortune, now the Holy Grail is found...

Jem clicked the CD off as she scrunched the VW to a halt on the gravel outside the pub, narrowly missing a couple of young men unloading what appeared to be scaffolding from a Transit van.

The car park was overflowing. Gleaming top of the range 4x4s butted up against beat-up Land Rovers stuffed with bruised flight cases and tangled tripods, their model names fresh from a macho ad man's sad wet dream. Scattered groups of smart young things huddled smokily in designer outdoor gear, talking loudly against the wind and themselves. A gaggle of svelte young women clutching clipboards flitted between the clusters of people, a handshake here, a smiling nod there. Air kisses de rigeur. Media folk. Being introduced, brought together, networked. Even through the windows of the camper and above the noise of the wind it was visibly and audibly clear to Dan and Jem that great excitement was afoot.

Long before the sound of the engine fan had died, a clipboard clutcher was tapping at Jem's window. 'Can I see your pass please?' Pressing the window button with one hand and fumbling with the other for the plastic file containing the information they'd been sent, Jem managed to proffer the laminated pass through the half-open window. 'Ahh, so *you're* the prize winners, I *thought* your, er, your *vehicle* looked a bit out of place, but then I thought maybe you were TV researchers, they can be a *bit*, well, you know, as well....' The sound of her words faded into the rising gale but the hint of disdain still stained her face. Respond or not, thought Jem? No point. We won, we're here.

'Anyhoo, you *do* know it's not until tomorrow, don't you?', asked Ms Clipboard, waspishly, the irritating vocal uplift at the end of each sentence, turning the redundant question into a statement, annoying Jem, who just wanted to get parked. 'Yeah, yeah, we thought we'd get here early to take in the atmosphere and maybe get a walk up Hrafn.'

'Ok, no worries. Here's your window pass. Stick it *here*. Don't hassle the crew and make sure you're over *there*, 9:30am prompt, so the Time Team researcher can get you a good spot for the mound being opened. By the way, you *do* know you'll be interviewed by the press, don't you?' Dan nodded, leaning over and relieving her of the pass as she flashed an insincere smile, twirling off across the car park in the strengthening wind, to join a flock of her own kind.

The old coaching inn's peeling sign was partially obscured by thick ivy and a mildewed banner advertising *Sky Sports Here!* But the name, *Y Brenin Llwyd* was still just about visible. Peering through the encroaching ivy and Virginia creeper was the cracked and splintered image of an ashen-faced king, his head cloaked in a silvery, lightning-rent nimbus, looking down balefully at the creative shambles of a 21st century outside broadcast unit. With its tiny arched windows, the squat building looked to Jem as though it might have once been a chapel, or at least had ecclesiastical DNA somewhere in its architectural past.

'So much for Welsh heritage', she muttered. 'Crass way to treat such a fantastic old building.' Dan hmm'd, nodding agreement, distracted as he thumbed through their heavily annotated copy of *Mysterious Wales*.

'Put the String Band back on, I liked that one, Jem.'

Dark was the night, praise God the open door, I ain't got no home in this world anymore....

'Here it is. Page 167. Listen, this is what the Bords' say about it: *Hrafn Twmp. Discovered during forest clearance during the Napoleonic Wars little is known about this mound, as the landowner and tight-knit local community has consistently refused to allow excavation. Local finds of feasting detritus and various artefacts indicate a late Neolithic origin with continuous occupation of the area to the present day. The surrounding mountains are dense with megaliths, many as yet uncatalogued, and the remoteness of the area suggests there is much to be discovered.'*

He read from the book for the umpteenth time as the track ended, crazy kazoo augmented percussion dwindling to a silence, broken almost immediately by another knock at the window. A woman's face loomed, smiling through the condensation, contorting in a manner that suggested its owner believed facial expression alone could operate window mechanisms. Jem took the easier option and slid the window down to reveal another clipboard holder, this one with added notebook and a small device she recognised as a voice recorder.

'Hi, Amy Tomlin from the *Observer Magazine*. Any chance I could grab a few words with you?' She nodded in the direction of clipboard girl who was now jabbering into her mobile phone. 'Felicity told me you'd arrived early so it seemed like a good opportunity to have a natter.'

Dan looked at Jem. Pulled a face; *Felicity!* 'What do you reckon?' Jem shrugged and smiled, 'Could be fun, and your mum would just *love* it.'

'Ok, give us a minute to get in the back'. The journalist stepped to one side as the couple exited their respective doors, Dan sliding open the side door, all three stepping up into the rear of the van.

Dan gesticulated at the bench seats separated by a table. 'Grab a seat. Want a brew? Ignore the mess, we weren't expecting visitors'. Jem moved into the galley to prepare the obligatory cup of tea even before Amy had chance to respond.

'Yeah, a brew would be super. This is all pretty cool actually. Been thinking about getting a mobile home.' Dan snorted, wincing at the same time, 'Camper van, please! Mobile homes are those huge shiny things with a bog, shower, and what have you'.

'But what do you do when you, er, you know...'

'Think bears, think Pope...'

'Eeurgh, ahh, I see. Right. Ahh.'

Tea was already being poured as Amy, her face still puzzling over the toilet arrangements, finished setting up her voice recorder and positioned her notepad on her knee.

'Ok. Straight to the point. You know this event is by invitation only and special invitation at that. So, how have *you*, effectively a pair of, well, *civilians* for want of a better word, come to be at what could be one of the major British archaeological discoveries of the 21st century?'

'That's an easy one, we won a competition', Dan almost smirked with satisfaction.

'So you're not archaeologists?'

'No. You *know* that.'

'Go on...'

'You want the whole story?'

'If you don't mind.'

'Ok, I was born on...'

'Very funny', Jem interjected crossly. 'Don't be a smart arse Dan; just give the girl a straight answer!' Dan's sarcasm was his way of flirting—trying to flirt—and it was already annoying her.

'Sorry, couldn't resist. Well, Jem and I have always had an interest in archaeology. Not the boring stuff, mind. All that scraping away at bits of earth, only for whatever is found to be covered up for posterity? Mondo tedioso! No, *Time Team* has its plus points but it also has a lot to answer for.'

'So...?'

'No, we're more into how archaeology can learn from folklore and how contemporary belief can be traced in the landscape. Does that makes sense?'

'Sort of. Now we're getting somewhere. You're folklorists then?'

'No, that's too limiting a term. Broadly speaking, and if you *must* have a definition, I suppose, we're psychogeographers.' A pause. 'If that makes *any* sense at all.'

Amy raised a quizzical eyebrow.

Great, thought Jem, before giving voice to her concerns. 'I can see the headline now, *Psychopaths Win First Prize at Archeo-event of the Century.*'

The reporter's puzzlement turned to laughter. Dan spluttered his tea and even Jem smiled at her own witticism. Sometimes Dan's pretentiousness could be really off putting, embarrassing even, if you didn't know him. Maybe even if you did. And the way he was now on the cusp of openly flirting with the reporter, albeit in his own stunted fashion, was definitely pissing her off.

'Ok, to put it as simply as possible, how about we're interested in how the environment affects the emotions and behaviour of individuals from a folkloric and archaeological perspective?'

'Right, getting it now.' Amy looked up from her notes, smiling and nodding, as if to say 'Why didn't you just tell me that in the first place?'.

Jem registered the exchange and smiled inwardly. Good, she thought, the journalist thinks he's as much of a tit as I do sometimes. Still, he knows his stuff and now—if ever—was the time to flaunt it.

'Tell me about the competition'

'You know *Archaeology Today*?'

Amy nodded.

'Well, they ran a competition called *Actual or Natural*—see what they did with the words there—and we won it," Dan said.

'Sounds interesting, tell me more'.

'Yeah, they printed loads of photos of landscape features taken from odd angles, and you had to say where they were, and whether they were actual archaeological features or natural topographical ones. We spent two weeks solid going through books, maps and...'

'And just guessing,' interjected Jem, smiling. 'And looking at Google Earth. But we nailed it, and here we are.'

'Good for you. And the prize was...?'

Dan looked smug, shuffled back in his seat and took a hit of tea. He knew she must already know, but had no problem in talking about it again.

'The prize... the prize was to be with Dr Anne Ross as she opens the mound, the twmp, that one across the road'. Dan gesticulated through the misted windows. 'To be one of the first human beings in well over 3,000 years to see what lies at the centre of this amazing ritual landscape. Our eyes seeing what our ancestors put there to, well, no one really knows, do they? To put it bluntly I'm so excited I nearly piss myself when I think about it!'

'Dan!' sharp words from Jem, admonishing as much by glare as tone.

'Sorry but it's true, and you know it girl.'

Amy turned to Jem.

'So it's safe for me to say you've been in a state of considerable excitement since you found out you'd won?'

'He has. Well I have too. Who wouldn't be?'

'You used the term 'ritual landscape'. Do you think my readers might be familiar with that?' A knowing smile accompanied the question. Amy was adept at getting her interviewees to spill the beans in their own words. Direct quotes made writing up the story much simpler and gave that extra touch of authenticity. Jem braced herself for another one of Dan's definitions.

'Ok, how about the concept of areas of land set aside from 'normal' use but extensively populated with monuments and sites that had an interdependent ritual or ceremonial purpose. Standing stones, mounds, that sort of thing. Usually dating from the Neolithic through to the early Bronze Age. Settlements tend to be few and far between in these landscapes and the thinking is that they were, as the name suggests, created purely for ritual purposes, and often connected with seasonal or archeo-astronomical observances.'

'That last bit again, in easy-speak please?'

'Er, I suppose, er, rituals connected with the equinoxes and solstices, stones lined up on significant lunar and solar—maybe even stellar—events'.

'Right, got you; I think I can use that as a direct quote, though without the 'ers' perhaps! So, do you know much about the dig itself and what might be under the mound?'

Dan and Jem quickly exchanged querying glances. Who was going to speak? *Were* they going to speak? Silence, for the time it took for the unspoken decision to be made. It couldn't matter now, thought Dan, the mound will be open tomorrow and nothing we say now can give the game away. She probably won't grasp what we're telling her and by the time it gets into print it will all be over and we'll know.

'A bit. We've been doing some digging', his voice, more serious now, broke a hush which seemed to last hours, but was no more than a few seconds.

Amy leaned forward, interested, a smile playing on her face, 'I thought you weren't archaeologists?'

'We're not' laughed Jem,'He doesn't mean that sort of digging.'

'No, digging around in the archives, speaking to locals and stuff.'

'Surely that's been done already?'

'It might have been, I don't know, but either the information there doesn't interest them, or they haven't found it. Most likely the former. Archaeologists are a funny lot. They like hard, tangible *facts*.' Dan made the " sign for quote marks with the index and middle finger of each hand as, slightly disdainfully, he said the word. 'Folklore is just stories to them, doesn't really interest them much.'

'Right, so…'

'What we found… was…' Dan sipped his rapidly cooling tea and gazed past Amy, through the window and out beyond the bustling scene toward the mound. 'We found…'

Here we go, thought Jem, 'This could be half an hour of a job'. She slid into the kitchen area and started to put another brew on, Amy nodding 'yes' to her quizzical look.

'Hob Nobs, Amy? You might need 'em!'

'It was Jem who found it really'. Ha, she thought, at least I'm getting the credit. 'She noticed some stones marked on the map that had names such as Cerrig Llwyd and that sort of thing. Boundary stones are often given these sorts of names, but boundary stones can also have folkloric or archaeological significance and purpose. And any stone bearing a name, natural or placed, invariably has a history or a purpose. Often both. Anyway, we spent a few long weekends up here over the summer; saw what it was like on the ground. Walked miles, probably more than the original archaeological survey did prior to the dig. Talked to some locals. They were friendly enough, and told us rambling variations on an old folktale about a hidden treasure they had 'always' known to be here.'

'Hidden treasure, eh?' Amy's eyes widened with interest.

'Well, yeah, but no, but... it's not that simple. Treasure in folklore isn't always what we think it is or want it to be. Not always... physical. I don't really want to say too much more. Bear with me...'

Amy fell silent, intrigued.

'Anyway, this was all bubbling away in our heads when we arrived for our second visit, last October. We called into Llantawt at the bottom of the valley and saw a poster for a folk club here at the Grey King. It was on that evening, so we spent| the afternoon visiting a couple of the stone rows that are aligned on the mound, had a bit of tea and trotted off to the pub. We expected it to be all woolly jumpers and cupped ears, thick-set hairies with their own tankards. As it was, that was just the women!'

Dan laughed loudly at his own joke, ignoring the mental tumbleweed rolling across Amy and Jen's expressions. Neither cracked so much as a smile.

'Okay, sorry. It certainly wasn't anything like that. Much younger crowd, most under 30 and mainly, we found in the course of conversation, people who'd settled in the surrounding mountains during the fall-out from Thatcher's Britain. A smattering of New Age travellers. Though the *Daily Mail*—maybe even *your* paper—would probably term them Junkie Dole Scum. Fair bit of dope smoking going on—we didn't complain, did we Jem?—and loads of funky freak folk interpretations of classic Dylan and Band tunes, even a Holy Modal Rounders' song or two. It was brilliant.'

'Dan, the point being...?' Jem banged the tea pot on the table in front of him in a sharp get-on-with-the-story kind of way.

Amy was feverishly scribbling as Dan poured the tea, waiting for her to catch up. The Hob Nobs were seeing some serious action as all three refuelled.

'I know, it all sounds a bit waffly,' he gave Jem a sharp stare, 'but the point will become apparent soon. Stick with Mr Boring and his Jackanory for a while, eh?'

'No, you tell it beautifully, Dan,' Amy murmured, smiling far too coyly for Jem's liking, 'You should have been a story teller.'

Puhleese, thought Jem, don't encourage him.

'So, anyway, toward the end of the night, this old bloke, farming type, shuffles in. You know the type, all old overcoat with string belt accessory and folded over wellies. Very shepherd at C&A. Think Compo with a crook and flat cap. No one paid him a blind bit of notice. Anyway, he waited 'til the applause died down from a particularly good rendition of *Random Canyon*, then took the floor. The whole place fell completely silent and I thought the old bugger was going to get booed off before he'd even started. Not a bit of it. From the smiles and nudges I could see through the blue haze it was pretty obvious the hoary old codger was well known. Off he went. Launched into this weird acapella folk lament the likes of I've not heard anywhere before or since. You know Williamson's *Invocation*?'

Blank look

'Didn't think so. Pity. If you did this would make a bit more sense. Well, it was *like* that, but a hundred times eerier. Simultaneously high and low in pitch, slightly phased as if two people were singing out of time with each other, and with a low, cello-like drone underpinning it. All from this one guy. And unless he was secretly twanging his belt string, or worse, I couldn't *see* any instrument.'

'What was the song?'

'We'd never heard it before, and we know our stuff when it comes to old folk songs.'

Jem nodded. 'Tell Amy what it was about, then.'

'If you can remember it I'd really love to know more.' Amy was agog now, wondering where the story was leading, thinking how she could write it up for her feature with this extra slant. What would she call it? 'With the Weird Wanderers', perhaps? It would be good, she knew it.

'Remember it?' Dan's voice overrode her musings. 'Every cell in our bodies has it all written down; it's etched on our souls. Never mind the competition. It's that song which has *really* brought us back here today. The passion and awe in the old lad's voice was just beyond religious, beyond sacred. It just came from somewhere else. Do you want to see the words? We took notes on a beer mat and then reconstructed the lyric afterwards. I'm afraid we can't let you use them in the article, though. Maybe the last line. What do you think, Jem?'

Jem was rooting through a ring binder bulging with plastic pockets, eventually producing one single sheet of typed A4 paper. She passed it to Amy, humming a mournful tune as she did so.

'That's the tune? Weird. It reminds me of... of... you know, I'm sure I *know* it, I do, but I can't quite place it. I know, it reminds me of... ahhh. Bugger, it's there but just out of reach. Really quite strange, this.'

'Yeah', laughed Jem. 'It does remind you of something, but it reminds you more of a feeling and a place than a song, don't you think. But it's a feeling you've never previously had, about a place you feel as though you know but can't quite remember?'

'Yeah,' Amy's voice trailed off as she took the piece of paper from Jem and started reading it.

'Wait 'til you read the words,' Dan almost whispered, loathe to interrupt Jem's humming.

Silence once again. Distant muffled sounds of technicians setting up lighting rigs and workmen erecting fences drifted in and out of the van. It was as though a blanket of snow had suddenly fallen, hushing the world, and completely changing the acoustics of the van. The air became thick. Hairy even. Dan began to hum the elusive tune, Jem added a harmony she never knew was there and Amy's lips mouthed the words as she read, her face quizzical at first, followed quickly by a look of amazed realisation and, as she handed the sheet back to Jem, a sad, mournful far-away look in eyes from which tears slowly ran.

She repeated the last line aloud.

Once they went so high, they never came down again

Jem repeated it again, this time, to her surprise, singing it perfectly to the tune, holding the word *high* just long enough to make the words following tumble quickly, but naturally, to an end. Perfection hung in the aftermath of the refrain, steam from the hot tea creating an incense-like ambience in the camper.

'It's, well, you know, *beautiful*, it's *awesome*, if you know what I mean? Fuck, I'm a journalist and I can't properly articulate how it makes me feel. Do you know? Really?'

'We do,' Dan and Jem said in unison, grinning.

'It gives me the feeling, like I'm being slowly taken out of this world, drawn, er, *sideways* into another, more *real* version of it to, to... a place I can't remember, for a time I won't forget.' Amy blinked the tears away and shook her head vigorously, trying to salvage the vestiges of an objectivity she knew she should be using. 'Goodness, why am I *talking* like this? And, more to the point, why am I *crying*?'

Dan smiled at the obvious emotion the song had evoked in her.

'Yep, does it every time. We only look at it occasionally, it leaves us drained.'

'But what does it mean?'

'Not a clue, really. I suspect at least part of its meaning is the effect it has. But we both feel it's intimately connected to this landscape, the sites on the mountain, and what lies under that mound.'

'Did you speak to the old guy about it?

'He was for offski straight after his turn—he always does that according to the guy behind the bar—but I managed to collar him. Bought him a pint of the gloomy-looking local cider that resembled something from Attenborough's *Blue Planet*. Tried to get some sense out of him. Not a chance. Just a song for the times, was all he'd say, just a song for the times. Wouldn't tell us where he learnt it other than "here", or what it meant other than "this". He was friendly enough—in between slugs of the druid fluid—but the song just wasn't up for discussion. You got the impression that for him it just *was.*'

'Did any of the others there know anything?'

'No, well, that's the even odder bit. Apparently Old Father Time rocks up to the club about four times a year and whines out some hoary old lament about the skill set needed to right inverted ruminants and the problems inherent in locating milk maids on a misty morning. All good, traditional stuff. The locals lapped it up. But they'd never heard *this* one before. It freaked them out too. Apparently he lives on the lower slopes of Hrafn by himself with a few of his woolly friends for company. His family have always been there, like *forever*. Just like in the best ghost stories!'

'Sounds like a bit of a cliché to me, a bit *woo* as some of our younger readers might term it.'

'Woo but true! How about *that* for a strapline! The fact is that all clichés are rooted in truth and authenticity and this guy was as authentic as the sheep shit on your shoes,' Dan pointed, smiling.

'Eeugh! Interesting as the song is, I'm not sure what it's telling us about the opening of that mound over there.'

'No? You're just not getting it then, are you.' Dan's tone now peevish and snappy.

'Ahh, us journalists, we're like the archaeologists, we like perfectly packaged facts. No vague stuff. You've got me now. I can hardly try to get across in words what the melody and lyrics of that song made me feel. Readers would think I'd gone nuts.' She checked her mini recorder was still on, nodding assent to Dan, 'Go on then'.

'So, anyway, after piecing together the lyrics of Mr Man's song we began to put two and two together. Using large scale maps of the place, you know 6 inch to the mile, fuck that metric stuff, we managed to plot all the locations in the song, found them on the map. They were all on a dead straight line. It was weird.'

'A ley line? Wow!'

'No, not a bloody ley line.' Dan almost sighed the words. 'They don't... ach, never mind. An alignment, eh, let's just call it that, shall we, an alignment?' Jem was secretly pleased he'd dropped all attempt at flirting now he'd realised the journo was a bit of a thicko when it came to *their* subject. She knew he didn't like thick women.

'Surely someone else had done this already. Surely an alignment of ancient stones would attract someone's attention?'

'We've been through this already. You'd have thought so, but no. Perhaps because the alignment wasn't inter-visible, I don't know. But the features that mark it are in a straight line. Just shows what's still left to be discovered with a bit of effort.'

'So what *is* to be discovered? Ahh, I *see*, the *mound*... does this mean...'

Dan interrupted her, not wanting her to draw her own conclusions. Time was passing and he needed to be out there.

'There's the rub. We just don't know, do we? Yet.'

He lowered his head to get a better view of the moor rising across the road from the pub. 'Up there, starting at the mound, every stone in the *same order* they were in the song. Breakthrough! We were getting the gist of what the old bloke had said about the song coming from 'here'. It was *about* here. It's a trail, a track, a route, call it whatever you want. Not necessarily *just* a *physical* track either.'

'Could all this be, you know, just a *coincidence*?'

'Hardly. As the man says, there are no coincidences but sometimes the pattern is more obvious. You know what I mean?'

Blank look.

'Ach, it's from a song. Most things are.'

'Old boundary markers then? Come on Dan, you know I've got to try and package this stuff for the Mr & Mrs Sunday Supplement Reader.'

'Not boundaries on the ground. Not just that. But you might be on the right lines.' Dan smirked. If she didn't get it he certainly wasn't going to help her. In fact he was slightly anxious now, wondering whether he'd given too much away, things she could tell Robinson and co. just in time for him to squawk it out on live TV just as the mound was being opened, their thunder well and truly stolen.

'So you'd sum up how then?' Relief, she wasn't pursuing that line of questioning.

'We know that tomorrow morning, on the Winter Solstice, Tony R and his timid team are going to open that mound. They'll find whatever they find but we don't—do we Jem—think it will have any real significance if they haven't completed the proper observances first.'

'Observances?'

'They obviously don't know and you don't need to. You've got your story. Suffice to say if they haven't travelled the path in the song, at the right time, in the right state of mind, all they find will be pretty pointless. Sure, yeah, they'll find whatever's *physically* there, but that's only the half of it. It's hidden treasure in more ways than one.'

'And you're going to find it?'

Dan sometimes wished he knew when to shut up. It was almost 9.45am and they should have been out and away by now. Enough.

'Is that enough' he snapped, 'We really need to be...'

'Dan, don't be so rude.'

'Yeah well, we need to be off, there's less than six hours or so of good light left you know.'

'Ok, ok', laughed Amy, 'I get the picture.' She scooped up her stuff into a bag. 'It's cool. Listen, you've been great. I've got everything I need for a great feature in next week's magazine. It'll make great post-Christmas reading. Just bung your address on this post-it and I'll be sure you get a copy.' Jem quickly scribbled their details and with that, Amy slid open the door, revealing behind the condensation on the windows, and to Dan's immediate and obvious disgust, a flashy new Range Rover with familiar door livery, pulling into the car park to disgorge a popular media figure.

'It's...' gasped the journalist, quickly smoothing her skirt and straightening her cag.

'Yes, we know, Mr Popular Archaeology 2012. Tony Fucking Robinson. Ha! He's even smaller in real life. No doubt he's been tasked with the job of boiling down the exposition of a genuine mystery into bite-sized chunks for TV-watching Guardian readers who like their archaeology fact-lite and children-friendly. For fuck's sake!'

'I didn't think he'd be here until the reveal tomorrow.' Amy smiled an apologetic goodbye. 'Must grab a word. Sorry guys, got to go... thanks again, you were great.' And off she skipped towards the TV presenter, headlines in her eyes, Dan's final, cynical, comments not even registering.

'Right, that's got rid of her. Day's getting on. Hope she gets what she wants from the Time Midget.'

'You knew he'd be here Dan. You know we'll have to be interactive and chatty with him tomorrow, so just suck it up. Some people would give their eye teeth to be interviewed by him.'

It was quiet in the van again, the external ebb and flow of weather and media preparation once again muted. The high winds had now dropped and Dan was eager to get out on the mountain as soon as possible to test his theories. He knew that as winners of the competition, tiny Tony would canvass them as to what they thought the significance of the mound was, and he wanted to be able to pontificate at length and to give experiential depth to the physical archaeology. Who knows, he might just get asked on subsequent *Time Teams* as a talking head. The voice of the informed amateur, perhaps? He mused on and developed this fame daydream riff for a few minutes, his hopes and aspirations far beyond any possible reality. Jem's voice pulled him back into the van.

'What's the plan then?' she asked for the third time. Dan stared at the clock in the dashboard, making mental calculations as to what was possible in the remaining daylight hours. Across the road the moor stretched out and up in the bright sunlight, colour and angle morphing rapidly from moor to mountain, the horizontal seemingly becoming vertical within a mile or so, drawing the eye up toward the distant summit of Mynydd Hrfran.

'Ok, let's rustle up some breakfast. Fifteen minutes and we should be on our way. Should be easily back down by just after dusk, might even get a few hours in the pub, schmooze with the media, that sort of thing. Plenty of time for a good night's sleep so we can grab front row seats for the excavation in the morning.'

Jem reached for the rucsacs.

'If you think we've got time, I'm up for it. One of my special omelette breakfasts before we go?'

Dan winked, licking his lips in anticipation.

'Yeah. Leave the sac, you sort the goodies and I'll do the gear.'

They fell into a well-practised routine, Dan filling the sacs with the usual stuff, while Jem chopped mushrooms and onions, grated cheese and broke eggs for the omelette. The oiled and waiting pan issuing forth plumes of blue smoke like a temple thurible.

Her culinary alchemy complete, within minutes they were tucking into one of Jem's finest spicy mushroom omelettes, deep in conversation about the impending excavation.

'What do you reckon will be under the mound?'

'We've been through this before—you know I haven't a clue and, like I told Amy and from what I've read in the archaeology literature and websites, neither do they. But if we're right, and if we do this properly today, well, who knows what it will mean for us.'

Jem cleaned the plates away, Dan shouldering his rucsac before she'd had time to wipe the surfaces.

'Ok, let's pack up and piss off. Into the mystery, eh?'

They crossed the road, tightening straps and adjusting walking poles as they went. The mountain track began across the road from the pub, directly opposite the mound, climbing steadily through dense bracken and scattered alder and mountain ash.

The day was brighter than ever now. Clear blue skies, all cloud vanished and the wind barely a soft breath. This, thought Dan, is going to be interesting and, hopefully, not a little awesome. Jem indicated east with her walking pole, grimacing. A long line of low, jet black cloud could be seen but it was about 50 miles away. Whatever it was carrying was being deposited on luckless dwellers somewhere in the Welsh Marches. Not their problem.

Following the shepherd's songline as it made its mazy way up the mountain. Dan and Jem stopped at every stone, every mound, touching each of them with ritual intent, saying or thinking a few words of private meaning. The pub changed size as they rose, diminishing to a meaningless dot after a thousand feet or so. It was a beautiful day. They felt good, laughing, swapping in-jokes and commenting on the natural wonders as they presented themselves, from the micro-intricacies of a frozen spider's web stretched across chromatic yellow gorse to the macro-splendour of how the summit ridge stood stark against the cerulean skyscape.

Dan could feel it now and he knew Jem could too. A rising anticipatory warm glow, pulsing with the rhythm of their exertions. Lines from Bjork's *Big Time Sensuality* spoken and acknowledged.

Very soon they were out of sight of the road, pub and mound, entering a dip through which ran a wide stream. There was no bridge.

'Wide enough to jump', Dan called, as he forded the stream in one leap, laughing at his dexterity in the circumstances. Jem tried to emulate him but splashed to the other side giggling, losing her balance as she did so, falling, twisting to the ground, the pure blue above her starting to pixilate pulse and swirl with colour and shape absent just seconds earlier. The induction phase was always subtly surprising and revelatory she thought, opening her mouth to tell Dan.

'This is awe…' She froze, mid-word, colour draining from her face as she mouthed L-O-O-K, left hand jabbing maniacally up the slope, back across the stream, glassy eyes bulging with terror. Dan, more in control, quickly looked to where Jem was gesticulating, her words still unable to make the transition from stimuli to speech.

A high, thin, piercing, silvery whistle shredded the air, screaming around them like cosmic hirundines, its sonic matrix interspersed with short, harsh vocal barks. Iced fear shot through Dan's veins as the prickle of goose-bumps chilled and tightened skin on arms, legs, scrotum even, spreading across and through his scalp and into his mind. He fought hard to control his blurring vision, narrowing his eyes until the bright sun became a slate grey hue holding the landscape still as he looked up, to see a giant figure pointing down at them.

Things were happening fast. Jem stumbled to her feet babbling about being watched, clinging to Dan's arm as he panted deep breaths, trying to get a grip on what he was seeing. The angle of the slope set the figure off starkly, black against the sky, with the suggestion of a dark face under a cap, one arm still extended, pointing down towards them, the other holding a staff and all the time this mad, almost stammering bark punctuated by a shrieking whistle.

Then it clicked. 'Fuck, yes! Jesus Christ. That was scary.' His rapidly disintegrating composure began to recover. Terror chills turned to clammy skin. Realisation triumphed over chaos. Perspective and psychedelics had combined to fool her, fool him. It was only a shepherd, directing his dog which must be roaming somewhere amongst the sheep up the valley to the north.

'Hey, hey, Jem, it's ok, it's just a shepherd. Nothing to worry about.' But he *was* worrying now. The explanation was good but something was wrong, the *shepherd* wasn't moving. It was perfectly still. Too still, too tall, too black. This was wrong and unwanted, too early for a hallucination, surely? And they hadn't taken *that* much. Had they?

Look away, deep breaths, look away, deep breaths. The exertion of toiling up the hill; concentrating on the pattern of the stones; the onset of the 'shrooms—it was all warping Dan's perceptions and falsely informing his expectations. Got to stay calm, he told himself.

Dan tried to get a grip as waves of recently metabolised psilocybin swept through him. He wasn't sure now how long this had lasted and tried desperately to think himself out of it. Instead he found he was just staring intently at a lichen covered rock, its vivid yellow crotal skin writhing and pulsing, undulating as faces and patterns formed and dissolved, coloured pinheads of light exploding outwards.

It would be so easy to just let go and become engrossed, he thought. And at any other time... but the sound of Jem's wails forced him to look back up to the heights again. Shit, it was still there, still pointing. Ignoring it wasn't working. Waves of terror were again flooding over him now as his senses stretched to make sense of something that shouldn't be.

Then, just as quickly as before, laughter. Laughing out loud, shaking with the release of tension, tears forming in his eyes as he dropped to the ground dragging a whimpering and confused Jem with him.

'What are you laughing for?' she pleaded, 'what's happening? I don't like this anymore. It's not like when we take them at home. Should we go back?'

The sky changed again, steel grey back to sky blue; the landscape softened and accepted them once again. Dan jabbed towards the black sentinel.

'It's a rock, some rocks ... rocks ... only rocks ... just fuckin' rocks!'

Holding her shoulders firmly from behind, he pointed her in the right direction, tilted her head and indicated how the jumble of rocks against the sky looked—looked to *them* at least—like a figure, and how the more they looked the more they could *make* it a figure. Dan now shook with laughter instead of fear. It was almost possible to relax again into the mushroom pulse now.

But that noise. Again. All around, physically punctuating the dense air with staccato flashes of colour. Dan wheeled around, just about able to separate sound from vision and pointed again, this time across the other side of the valley. 'Look that *is* a shepherd calling his dog. His voice is just bouncing across the valley and us being a bit addled connected it to the rock man. Wow, this stuff is strong!'

And it was. Pete, their trusty dealer, had promised that taking the mushrooms outside in the day would be an experience of a different magnitude to their usual domestic nocturnal psychedelic journeys. Dan's theory was that the people who created this ritual landscape used some form of psychedelics to enhance their communion with the presences who dwelt in the landscape, the *genius loci*. So called 'magic mushrooms'—*Psilocybin semicilenta*, had he bothered to mention this to the journalist—grew abundantly on the lower slopes of Hrafn and thus it was logical to think Mesolithic and Neolithic peoples had surely used them in their shamanic rites.

It was obvious, or at least it was to Dan and Jem. They were familiar with Andy Letcher's book *Shroom* in which he had argued there was no historical evidence to suggest prehistoric man used *P. semilanceata*. But so what? Absence of evidence didn't mean evidence of absence. You only had to look at hunter-gatherers and so-called primitive tribes in existence throughout the world today. *They* all used some form of psychoactive organic substance.

Logic, if not common sense, dictated to Dan that the ancestors here had used something of that nature too. And it had to be 'shrooms. Had to be.

Long nights tripping with Jem, rapping about and researching the mound, the sites on the moor and mountain, all topped off with the mystery shepherd's multi-layered song—which in itself was a psychedelic experience—had utterly convinced him that the secret of the mound lay in the ingestion of the appropriate psychedelic, followed by the correct circumnavigation of the sites in the song.

Sure, it was a mish-mash of speculation and untried experience, and friends had told him as much. But he was certain, and winning the competition to be at the opening of the mound was the icing on the cake. A sign. Maybe even a portent. Whatever it was, Dan knew everything was coming together for the Winter Solstice and fate, or more correctly, as he put it, the wyrd, meant he was going to put his speculations into action. As he joked to Jem and anyone else who'd listen, 'What could possibly go wrong?'

They resumed their pilgrimage, rising out of the dip onto the high heather moorland plateau, the jagged summit still a couple of miles ahead of them. The map, when he finally adjusted his eyes to the confusion of contour and colour, showed a track running up to the plateau from the valley to the north.

Amazingly, where the track crested the plateau's edge, there was a circle of vehicles, battered but brightly coloured vans and coaches parked up next to a laager of yurts, tipis and tarpaulin benders. Flags streamed lazily in the breeze and a rhythmic pulse of music wafted from the encampment. A few dogs roamed outside the perimeter and a group of figures could be seen standing round a fire, shuffling to the beat, one weird beard thrumming on a hand drum, contributing to the rhythm.

'Let's have a look', grinned Dan.

'I'd rather not, what if they're dangerous? We're not exactly in the right state of mind if they get arsey with us, are we?'

'Nah, they're hard-core hippies, road people, who else would be up here? We'll be ok. We can tell 'em about the rock man! They'll understand.'

The first rush from the 'shrooms seemed to have receded somewhat after the chaos brought on by the rock sentinel, and an electric calm now descended on the pair. But they were in no doubt as to how high they were, minds elevated and perceptions finely tuned, the now slowly lengthening shadows of the afternoon. The light was splitting into colours neither had names for. Mid-afternoon reddening sky on black mountains with flickering sun rays in rainbow shards, flashing the way across the high moor to the travellers' camp. This was a good day, thought Dan, and it could only get better.

'You ok?' He asked Jem, touching her lightly on the cheek. An all too rare but immensely welcome gesture, she thought. Especially now.

'Yeah, bit wobbly. This stuff is always a bit of a shock and today is more of a shock than usual! But yeah, coping ok. Just keep close to me; I might need to hold on!'

As they neared the encampment a tall, heavily bearded man strode out to meet them in a long, and long since past it, overcoat. He moved toward them, staff in one hand, black-feathered wide-brimmed hat on his head. Dan thought he looked like a modern-day biblical prophet from a *Mad Max* film set. Jem briefly considered he wouldn't have been out of place drinking Special Brew on a park bench. They met, stopped, and nodded greetings. The conversation was as brief as it was enigmatic.

'Are you on your way up?'

'Yes, following the stones'.

He laughed, piercing green eyes shooting from Dan to Jem and back again.

'Know what you're doing'

Question, statement or directive, Dan couldn't be sure.

'What, you know what we're doing?'

'No. What are you doing?'

'Going up, like we said?'

'Then what?'

The simple obviousness of that question stunned Dan.

'Er, coming down again?'

'What, like Humpty Dumpty? The Grand Old Duke of York? We've all been *up*. But not up there. It's what you do when you come *down* that matters.'

The rest of the group of travellers were now ranged closely behind their emissary. Standing. Still. Silent. Only the hand drummer moved, tapping out a varying beat to which Dan's heart involuntarily marched.

'I, I don't know. I... we were hoping that by following the old ways we would, could... I just wanted to say hello, we must be going.' Dan *knew* that was a line from a song but couldn't remember which or, for that matter, why he'd used it.

'You remember it all from before, do you lad?'

Two ravens suddenly shot overhead as if from a bow, leaving long, shimmering trails behind them in the reddening sky.

'You should take heed of them. Birds are arrows of the wise. Are you a hero?'

'What do you mean?'

'Ah, that's the half remarkable question, lad. You'll understand it better in the sweet bye and bye.' Dan's mind flashed back to the last thing they'd listened to before leaving the security of the camper. How the *fuck*?

The man turned, his friends turning with him, walking back to their campfire without a backward glance. Only the dogs remained, growling low and staring directly at Dan and Jem.

'What the fuck was all that about?' Jem looked puzzled and not a bit scared. The 'shrooms were rising again and she felt the need to move if only to take her mind off them.

'Don't know. Never mind. He was talking in riddles but I'm fucked if I know what he meant. But the strangeness all adds to the day!' Dan was perturbed, rattled even, by the exchange but kept his thoughts to himself, trying to shrug it off as they rose the final thousand feet or so to the mountain top, the named stones further apart now, but no less important, and each one still ritualistically acknowledged.

It was a struggle now against their mounting physical exhaustion and the increasing onslaught of the mushrooms. But by coaxing each other, promising and anticipating the vistas and who knows what else that would await them, they reached the summit cairn, a huge pile of rocks that Dan sensed was pretty much the same dimensions as the mound by the pub. Promising, very promising.

'Dan, you realise we have no chance of getting back down until morning now?' Dan knew. He'd known it all the way up really, but wasn't going to tell Jem until it became obvious. They had enough bivvy stuff, and anyway, spending the night on the summit was surely part of the ritual. Of that he was sure.

His mind slipped to memories of the legend of another mountain, Cader Idris, far to the south. Legend had it that those who spent a night on its summit were forever changed, leaving either a poet or a madman in the morning. Was that a vestige of a similar tradition to the one he believed he'd discovered based on the mound and the ritual track up Hrafn? Jem's pleas that she was fading out brought him back to his now kaleidoscopic senses.

They just had enough time and sense to slump to the ground behind a large boulder, donning some extra warm clothes out of the sacs before the mushrooms reached their peak and cut them loose from what was left of consensus reality. Bodies entwined, holding hands tightly and with eyes closed they merged into a spinning vortex of thought and image, overlaid, interlaced and freighted with elusive half-hinted meanings, outcomes and consequences.

He was everything. She was everything. Fractals of existence, each within the other, both separate yet without boundary. A chant, borne on the wind, entered Dan's mind and he could see Jem was hearing it too. More, she was chanting along with it, the voice in his head coming now from her mouth. The voice phasing in and out of key and timbre until it was the voice of the shepherd in the pub.

I am a stag: of seven tines,
I am a flood: across a plain,
I am a wind: on a deep lake,
I am a tear: the Sun lets fall,
I am a hawk: above the cliff,
I am a thorn: beneath the nail,
I am a wonder: among flowers,
I am a wizard: who but I
Sets the cool head aflame with smoke?

I am a spear: that roars for blood,
I am a salmon: in a pool,
I am a lure: from paradise,
I am a hill: where poets walk,
I am a boar: ruthless and red,
I am a breaker: threatening doom,
I am a tide: that drags to death,
I am an infant: who but I
Peeps from the unhewn dolmen arch?

I am the womb: of every holt,
I am the blaze: on every hill,
I am the queen: of every hive,
I am the shield: for every head,
I am the tomb: of every hope.

Round and round went the chant until the words became just one condensed *feeling*, a pressure that threatened to burst their heads into flame. Ravens, obsidian totem birds, iridescence trailing from their wings, swooped low through the word blizzard, echoing the chant, rising and falling in shape; now midge size, now albatross proportioned. Dan watched as Jem raised and spread her hands, her aspect darkening as she took flight, arms now wings, legs moulded as tail feathers, head beaked and gimlet-eyed she soared with the *hrfan*, human form and consciousness becoming bird shape, bird world, bird time. *Bird*, he thought, the word had lost all connection with its meaning in the outer word. No words had meaning anymore. Sensation on his face now. Water? Rain? He flashed on a lyric from an old Jefferson Airplane song.

> *You call it rain*
> *But the human name*
> *Doesn't mean shit to a tree*

And with that he too let go and instinctively followed Jem, attaining avian consciousness and *seeing* the world as did these winged servants of the air. The Jem raven clipped his wings with hers and spoke. *Kronk.* She spoke again, but now mind-speaking all the questions he had been trying to avoid. What little human thought he retained allowed him to realise that reasoning was pointless. What *was* reasoning anyway? Instead, he dived and hoped she would follow. They dived down toward the crags below, swooping and fluttering against the lichened rocks, her following, their aerial jinks and twists becoming more tortuous yet neither one making any gain on the other.

This was pure bird play and the other ravens joined in, spiralling round them, turning on their backs to offer claw and beak for contact and comfort. *Kronk*-ing bird lore that Dan felt and learned without effort, being shown what it was *really* like to experience the multiverse as a creature unmediated by consciousness.

They flew now as part of the black conspiracy, down over the mountain, over the travellers' camp, over the many stones they had so tortuously processed past only a few hours before. Any thought each had was instantly the other's, both remembered, forgotten and anticipated, as bird and human bird exchanged centuries of delight and wisdom in a wing beat.

As they passed over the rock sentinel, their companions screeched with laughter, shaming Dan and Jem's last vestiges of humanity. Now over the *Brenin Llwyd* they could see the lights of the excavation and the detritus of the futile media circus beneath them. Spiralling low over the mound the ravens *thokked* and *kronked* but neither Dan nor Jem could take meaning from this. Some things begged realisation in the sweet bye and bye.

Clear dark skies became opaque, as a weather front blew in from the east and hit them hard. Rain lashed and wind split the feathered flock, pushing them apart and back up the mountain. Dan grasped that they were raven no more but had merged into the sheet of rain, he and Jem now droplets of moisture being smeared into the landscape by the howling tempest. Blown back toward the summit, their core of awareness was formed and reformed, again and again, dashed repeatedly against the rock crags of the mountain's summit mound, broken apart and blown back into the storm before they finally mingled together as water run-off on the rock's mottled lichen.

The sensation now was one of finality, calm, gentle flowing, flowing from rock into the earth and down into the streams which fed the Afon Hrfan.

Then, nothing.

Jem opened her eyes. It was almost pitch black. Above her the patterned stars shimmered against the silvery skein of the Milky Way and to the east a line of ravens flew silently across the distant pre-dawn horizon. Primary perception resolved into first thought. 'We survived.'

Dan was laid at her side and also coming out of the night's phantasmagoria, fumbling for his watch. 'Fuck, that was something. What time is it? We're late.' His watch glowed 7.30 am.

Jem noticed they were both covered in particulate; myriad bits, small scraps of lichen, moss, grit, gorse and heather clung to them. Dan pulled a raven feather from Jem's hair, laughing, until she pointed out he too also had one in his. *The ravens*. It was coming back to him. No time to talk now.

'If we've time, we can change back at the car, but in the meantime lets walk down like this, let's take as much of the experience back with us as we can. We can even wash in the river, ditch the old clothes and be truly re-born, baptized of the mountain. You know the old nature mystic, Thomas Traherne, what he said?'

'No.'

'Well you should.'

Dan sang.

You never enjoy the world aright
Till the sea itself floweth
In your vein till you are clothed
With the heavens and crowned with the stars

'Steady on Dan, you're babbling. It's like the mushies are coming on again. I can't cope with anymore.'

It's ok, ok. It's just the residue ebbing and flowing and I've got so much to say about what we went through.'

'Yeah, but let's not get too weird about it, eh? It's been too weird as it is.'

'Too weird? You can never have too weird my dear.'

'I'll take your word for that. Ok, at least with this shit all over us we'll fit right in with the hippies if they're still there.'

Their bodies were stiff, unused to movement, but Dan chivvied hard. They had to be at the dig site by 9:30am. Plenty of opportunity to discuss what had happened either on the way down or, after the mound opening. Jem dug out the food and fluids and they refuelled as they walked, stiffly at first, from the mountain summit and down the path ascended the previous day. Overhead, two ravens wheeled against the dimming stars. *Kronk, kronk.* Jem looked up and then smiled at Dan, with a look of mutual recognition and acknowledgement. There would be much to talk about but for the first mile they picked their way down in dark silence, the only sounds being the click of walking pole on rock and whispered curses as muscles were coaxed into action.

As they neared the plateau Dan broke the silence.

'Coming down's the best bit.'

'What, from the hill or from the 'shrooms?'

'Both. We're new, fresh and yet old as the hills. As the man says, I will never grow so old again. Money can't buy that sort of experience y'know.'

'What? Mycology can buy what money can't, is that what you're saying?' She laughed. 'Wait 'til we tell Pete.'

'Tell Pete? What you gonna tell him? That we took 'shrooms, merged with everything and returned reborn? Nah, it just sounds like hippie shit, and irresponsible hippie shit at that! No, only we know what went on, because we were there, and we don't really know the half of it, yet. We experienced the world unmediated by culture or creed, and all through the agency of the mushroom mind. Now we're ready for whatever might be unveiled at the dig this morning. A couple of hours to go and we should easily be down.'

Jem mused on all this. Something wasn't quite right. The timing seemed ok—just as she remembered who they were and what they were doing. But still ... Dan was on a roll now so she just plodded on and listened.

'Try telling that to the Head of Department, more like! I can just see it on the headlines now! Lecturers in 'Shroom Shock'. No, I told you, these experiences are special, individual, sacred even. Even talking about it afterwards starts to devalue its meaning, so let's shut the fuck up and walk, eh.' Jem found she couldn't shut up though and the banter continued for a while, she trying to make some sense of it all, trying to take it all back to the world below, to the real world of... what was real though? Another song crept into his head, she thought. *Back to life, back to reality. That* was weird. She heard what he thought! God those 'shrooms were strong. All the time he was playing it down, joking and joshing, poking fun, trying to take the edge off the enormity of what they'd been through together, his way of playing down what still might be to come as consequence.

Down they went, down through the growing early morning light. Each in silent reverie, looking at the world through clearer eyes. Dan's mind raced as much as Jem's mouth. What had happened? Why did he feel like *this*, a 'this' he couldn't even begin to explain to Jem. But maybe she was feeling it too? 'Beginner's mind' Suzuki called it, his mind off on its travels again, after the Zen term for seeing the world for the first time, all the time, the names of phenomenon superfluous to the experience of them. Blake's 'heaven in a grain of sand' re-branded as heaven in six grams of 'shrooms, thought Jem, and he felt her thought. All the clichés made unutterably real. Who could we tell, indeed *how* can you tell of such things?

They dropped down onto the plateau. Ahead of them the travellers' camp now looked drab, a desultory fire surrounded by what looked like pretty much the same group of individuals. Had they even moved since yesterday afternoon? Cans littered the ground, glinting in the rising sun.

Dan waved and shouted, 'hey, good party?'. The huddle of raggedy humans stayed huddled round the fire, hunched against the now bitter wind that whipped Dan's words away into the rocks. No answer. He yelled again. Rangy stringless dogs, lurcher cross maybe? he thought, set up a howl of unholy communion, but the figures remained with their backs to him. Perhaps I can only be heard by dogs he thought, amused, thinking 'fuck you, then' before turning and hurrying down the track after Jem.

Behind him, from the encampment, he could just about hear music and quickly recognised it, shuffling funk beat, Latin percussion, *'gone, gone, gone'*. Ha, Traffic, another of his favourite bands. This was just too good to be true. Everything perfect, everything making sense as they came down. Yeah he mused, we've been real gone. He could barely contain his excitement or anticipation about what they would find when they got to the mound opening. Whatever it was, they were more than ready for it, of that he was doubly certain.

Jem was far ahead now, barely visible in the swirling mist and increasing snow that had sprung from nowhere. He needed to catch up but he felt a pang of regret that the travellers failed to acknowledge the psychedelic explorers as they returned triumphant. The concept of hubris drifted briefly across his thought-scape but he swiftly dismissed it.

He reached Jem as they reached the edge of the cwm, pressing up behind her and nuzzling the warm neck inside her scarf. They halted for a few minutes, surveying the scene in the valley below. It was as though a white wall was coming toward them, the air boiling with flecks of white, grey and silver in all possible shades. A heavy stillness came over them both and Jem began to turn toward him as the full force of the snowstorm hit. Within seconds it was all they could do to cling to each other to remain upright. Where last night it had been a mental, spiritual and existential storm now it was a physical one. Gravity rather than direction dictated their steps. Down was the only concept of travel available to them. No cold now, no sensation other than the blanket of white solitude. Sometimes it felt to Jem as though they weren't even moving, weren't even there, as if they could just be locked forever in this white dream world.

They reached the last steep slope before the road. Two hundred feet or so above the mound now, looking down. A completely different scene to that of yesterday in that there *was* no scene. Dan held his watch close to his face. 11:00am. That's couldn't be right. He held it in front of Jem's eyes, her panic reflecting his. She held her watch up—11.00 am. Tears formed in her eyes. They'd missed the mound opening, missed what they'd worked for and won. Worst of all they had missed the revelations and possible initiation Dan was sure would be theirs after the initiation they had put themselves through.

Something wasn't right. It didn't *feel* right. And as that feeling began to rip into them, through a lull in the storm, the dismayed and confused pair became witness to the tableau being played out a few hundred feet below.

The mound had been partially opened, sliced like a cake with almost a quarter of it removed, the centre covered with a tarp. They must have started late. Thank fuck for that! From what they could see the archaeologists were minutes away from revealing whatever lay in the mound's centre. A crowd was gathered, TV lights shining. But there were other, more disturbing things taking place nearby. Across the road in the pub car park was a Mountain Rescue land rover and an ambulance. Covered stretchers were being moved from one vehicle to the other, the TV crew that should have been covering the mound opening were now focussed on the ambulance, clamouring for information.

'Someone's had an accident. Looks as though it's delayed the dig,' said Jem

'Obviously. Looks as though they haven't fully opened the mound yet, we might be just in time. Someone else's misfortune could be our good luck. Come on. Hurry!'

Dan and Jem almost ran down the final few hundred yards. The icy treacherousness of the slope demanded they move cautiously and it still took them the best part of five minutes. Concentration, the angle of the slope and then the vehicles meant they lost sight of what was happening at the dig. Soon they were on level ground, moving as quickly and politely as they could through the throng gathered near the ambulance. No one paid them any notice as they fairly sprinted toward the mound.

Now they could see. The tarp obviously covered a 'something' in the centre of the mound. The camera crew had moved from the ambulance and were setting as Tony Robinson ushered Dr Anne Ross into position for the reveal interview. The wind was whipping up again strongly now and thick snow was blowing in at a 45-degree angle. They might just make it. No one asked for their passes as they slid through the crowd and the incident tape used to cordon the dig off. They stopped behind Dr Ross and Robinson. They'd be next up for interview, they'd been told.

'Great. He'll interview her then we'll see what they found. We'll get an interview then, and I can tell them the background to it all, what you found. We'll show them that amateurs can know as much as professionals.'

'So, Dr Ross, we're here at Twmp Hrafn. You've already been shown what our viewers will see. What can you tell us?'

'Where to start Tony? The weather is setting in and I suspect we only have a few minutes to talk. This is a remarkable site. Most remarkable. From what I saw a few minutes ago there's no doubt that this is a site from which people departed this world to the world of the ancestors. Not a burial site as such but a site of sacrifice. One bound to the land and to which people had to perform various observances before they could be accepted to the world of the dead.'

'How do we know? Surely this is all just conjecture?', Robinson smirked.

'Perhaps, but perhaps not dear boy. There is a strong local tradition, a legend, in these parts that led us to suspect what was going on. Field work confirmed it but we kept it a secret so as not to disappoint the viewers.'

Dan looked on incredulously. She ... *they* knew all along. They knew more than us, he thought.

'Everything points to a kind of ritual, the vestiges of which can still be seen in parts of other parts of the world as well as in our folk tales, in which two people are chosen, or offer themselves, for sacrifice to ensure the gods are propitiated. As I said, some of this comes from anthropology, some from folklore tradition, some of it we're guessing at—but isn't speculation what drives archaeology, Tony?'

Robinson nodded, the hood of his Berghaus flapping and rattling in the now storm-force blizzard. Anne Ross, however, appeared impervious to the weather, and waited impatiently for the diminutive TV star to pay attention to her again.

'My best guess is that on the eve of the Winter Solstice there was a great feast. We've previously found the remains of feasting all around the mound and the foodstuffs have been dated to the mid-winter period. Probably some form of Beating the Bounds type ritual takes place, with the two chosen celebrants marking out the ritual path from mound to sacred summit and back again. If I were to go right out on a limb, drawing on what we know from indigenous peoples, no doubt an intoxicant was also employed as part of the ritual. Henbane, Belladonna or some form of hallucinogenic fungi, perhaps. Wales is certainly the country for it and there's a tradition of use to this day. But to the point—come dawn on the solstice, the two would return to the mound and be ritually sacrificed, their souls given to the land and to the season.'

'Fascinating stuff, Dr Ross, really. Now would you like to tell what we found here less than an hour ago? As far as I'm concerned it at least partly vindicates the theory you've just expounded. Then we have a couple of competition winners, amateur archaeologists whose opinion we are keen to get about this momentous discovery'.

Robinson motioned against the wind to some jobsworths who were holding the tarp down, an increasingly difficult job now the snow was falling heavily and the gale was screeching through the mass of people and cameras. 'Ready. When I give the word,' he shouted

In the near distance Dan heard Dr Ross's final words before the reveal.

'We found, we found a perfectly preserved sacrificial slab and the rough-hewn statues of two figures.'

'Now'

The tarp was pulled back and there it was, a huge flat quartz veined slab with channels cut into it. To its rear were two standing stones, roughly carved to give the impression they were male and female.

Realisation, bereft of understanding, formed, melted and reformed like ice crystals in the matrix of Dan's rapidly disintegrating consciousness. Each time the pulse was weaker but the realisation no less strong. He turned to Jem, trying to force speech, even as she turned to him with the same intent. No sound came as their gaze met, but in that moment he/she/they saw and understood.

Behind them the camera crew were shouting as a dense snow flurry whipped down the valley, now a wall of snow, tearing into the assembled gathering. People fled as snow enveloped all, wind scattering equipment and clothing. Only Dan and Jem remained. Jem's face showing each facet of her beauty contained holograph-like in tiny, individual snow crystals. She also now knew. Dan could have gazed at this forever, maybe this was forever ... but forever never knows and now, finally, he did. He held her hand as they walked, leaving no trace in the snow, the remaining few feet to the menhirs.

Then, suddenly there was no more 'she' or 'he'. Only the land and the seasons and the elements and the endless cycle of the present moment in which all things must have their being. Two ravens swooped low through the white tempest *kronk*-ing at the scene below them. Then they too were gone.

Gone, gone, gone.

20

Better Living Through Chemistry?

Operation Julie and the mystery of Hydrazine Hydrate
with Andy Munro

Between 25th and 27th March 1977, the largest drugs raids in British history took place. Involving several hundred police officers acting in a carefully co-ordinated manner, the raids revealed to the public the existence of a complex and labyrinthine LSD manufacture and distribution network. Millions of doses of extremely potent, high quality, LSD were made in separate locations by its two chemists, Andy Munro (London) and Richard Kemp (Wales), and their much sought after and lauded product was disseminated internationally from the early 1970s onwards, helping to fuel the growing worldwide psychedelic movement. The authorities suspected an organised group of LSD chemists and couriers existed, but they had no idea as to its size or scope. It was not until 1975 that Detective Dick Lee, stumbled upon a scrap—literally—of evidence which led to the formation of the multi-force investigative team (Operation Julie) which within three years would see the arrest, conviction and imprisonment of the major players in the world's largest LSD manufacture and distribution web.

Much has been written about Operation Julie, albeit not as yet by any of the key participants. The main narratives that exist have been written by police officers and journalists, and this has led to some confusion and myth making as to the origins of Operation Julie. In Dick Lee's book, Operation Julie, he cites the discovery, in April 1975, of the words 'hydrazine hydrate', on scraps of torn up paper, as the 'first tangible evidence of the existence of an acid team'. The pieces of paper were found in Richard Kemp's Range Rover, impounded by Dyfed-Powys police following a fatal road accident in which Kemp had been involved. Kemp was a person of interest to the police at this stage, but not yet suspected of LSD manufacture. Lee's discovery of 'hydrazine hydrate', scrawled on the discarded paper changed the situation and led him to believe this chemical compound was an 'essential ingredient in the manufacture of LSD'. The events that followed have become enshrined in the history of Britain's psychedelic history.

Yet there is mystery around the words 'hydrazine hydrate', and the role that specific chemical compound played in the manufacture of Kemp and Munro's LSD. Since beginning his 13 year prison sentence in 1977, Richard Kemp has refused to comment on any aspect of his time as an LSD chemist. This is unfortunate as Kemp could help clear up the mystery of 'hydrazine hydrate' as well as ensuring a comprehensive account of his involvement and motives was a matter of record. However, Andy Munro, the chemist who operated the LSD manufacturing laboratory in London has been kind enough to comment on and hopefully clear up the myth surrounding Dick Lee's serendipitous find in Kemp's Range Rover on that April day in 1975. The following account is written by Andy Munro and is his recollections of events and conversations:

Introduction

The purpose of this document is to correct certain fallacies which have become accepted belief regarding the methods used by the 'Operation Julie' chemists to manufacture LSD. Specifically, the idea that Hydrazine hydrate was used as a coupling agent in the final step of the process. It was not. It was believed—and still is as far as I can tell—that Kemp and Munro used different methods, and that Kemp used Hydrazine hydrate. He did, but not for the reason which the police and forensic scientists stated. The simple truth is that both chemists used the same coupling agent, because Munro was told by Kemp that this agent (CDI0; see later) was the best.

I must stress that this document is for information only and is not intended as an instruction manual for the manufacture of LSD. Many of the chemicals used are extremely dangerous, toxic and/or explosive.

The Coupling Reaction

Whilst the starting point for LSD manufacture can be almost any ergot alkaloid, the first objective is to produce lysergic acid. This is somewhat more stable—and less toxic—than the ergot alkaloids themselves, but is still somewhat unpredictable in its reactions with other chemicals. Normally, to make a diethylamide from an organic acid one could easily react the acid with diethylamine. However, in this case the reaction does not take place unless an intermediary chemical is made, by reacting lysergic acid with a 'coupling agent'. The coupling agent binds to the lysergic acid and is then displaced by the diethylamine to produce the required diethylamide. It is a simple fact that Hydrazine hydrate is unsuitable for this purpose. The story is that Albert Hofmann used it, but only did so once and then only on a micro scale. He soon turned to other agents. The list can be found on the internet and in Michael Valentine Smith's book, *Psychedelic Chemistry*. Smith is obviously no chemist but he has done a good job in collecting all the data.

One of the main problems in selecting a coupling agent is that lysergic acid is unstable, can't be heated too much or exposed to light. Many of the coupling agents which are suitable are themselves unstable—specifically they react strongly with water. So there is this additional problem that everything must be kept *dry*, and therefore any solvent used must be able to be prepared *totally* free from water.

Kemp learnt early on (from the French chemists he worked with in 1970 or, more likely, the consultant professor from Harvard, see Tendler and May's *The Brotherhood of Eternal Love*), that the best coupling agent to use was N,N-carbonyldiimidazole (which I will call CDI). This reagent is mentioned in an article (in German) in a little known journal called *Collection of Czechoslovakian Chemical Communications*, published in 1962. It is an easily handled solid, but it is destroyed by any trace of water; moreover the solvent used is DMF (dimethylformamide) which has a high boiling point (150°C), and the solvent must be removed to get at the LSD. So the evaporation of the solvent has to be done under vacuum, another set up to complicate the process.

I do not propose to go into the nuts and bolts of the whole procedure. It involves ether (extremely explosive) and huge extraction funnels, as well as the need to be done in a dark, dry environment. You can see the potential for failure, never mind death!

What about Hydrazine hydrate? That will be dealt with in the following section, which is an account of conversations that took place between Kemp and Munro, written from the point of view of Munro, as Kemp no longer wishes to comment on his involvement with the Operation Julie events. The following history is by Andy Munro:

A Chemist's Tale

During the period of detention in police custody, I had a couple of meetings with the police forensic scientists, notably a man called Neville Dunnett. The other man present spoke less and I have since forgotten his name. Dunnett told me that he believed Kemp used Hydrazine hydrate as the coupling agent, although Kemp had refused to meet Dunnett or to discuss his methods. I told them that they were mistaken, and that Hydrazine hydrate was useless. They insisted that it was Hofmann's method. We then discussed my method, which was CDI etc.

Later, in HMP Bristol, I mentioned all this to Kemp and we spoke about Hydrazine hydrate, since it was on all the policeman's lips. I told Kemp that the only useful reference to Hydrazine hydrate that I had found was in an obscure Hungarian Patent where it was used as a 'protecting group' to slow down the degradation of ergotamine during the production of lysergic acid— the first step in the process. Kemp agreed that was what he had used it for. I said that I didn't bother because the gain in yield was only 5% maximum, and it was just one more dangerous chemical to worry about. Kemp was a perfectionist and wanted that extra 5%. I told him of Dunnett's belief that he (Kemp) had used Hydrazine hydrate as a coupling agent. Kemp laughed.

After being sentenced we were allocated to different prisons. I went to Gartree, Kemp to Wakefield. Christine Bott, Kemp's partner went to Durham, where the woman's prison is situated within the men's prison. Because of their relationship, every few months Kemp was taken to Durham to visit Christine. He spent a couple of nights in the men's prison, had his visits, and then went back to his own jail.

Not long after I had moved to Gartree there was a riot there and three of the four wings were destroyed and the majority of prisoners had to move to other jails. I was sent to Durham. I was there many months and it was a truly horrible prison, with a tiny exercise yard which consisted of a series of concentric paths. In the old days, I was told, each prisoner could only walk in single file round one path, with no talking, and each path moved in opposite rotation to the one inside and outside of it. When I was there this rule had been relaxed and one day on exercise I saw Dick Kemp! He was up to see

Christine Bott and we started talking and he told me an interesting story.

When my lab was raided there was an amount of lysergic acid, rather dirty and un-purified, maybe 50 gms. It seemed that Dunnett and his mate decided they would make some acid(!), and use hydrazine hydrate as the coupling agent. However, try as they might, and they made several attempts, they could not get the process to work! So they visited Kemp in jail, told him of their problem and asked him to tell them how he did it. Kemp flatly refused to tell them anything.

We both had a good laugh over this, because we both knew they were wasting their time—and their stock of lysergic acid. You cannot use hydrazine hydrate to make LSD! Maybe on a small, micro scale, but for any bulk production it is not worth it. Lots of other agents have been used—see M. V. Smith—but all have their problems.

I did not see Kemp again until after our release, when I visited him and Christine at their house in Devon. I don't recall any further conversations about Hydrazine hydrate.

Conclusion

These notes should have convinced the reader that the words 'hydrazine hydrate' do not have a deserved link to LSD production. Mr. Lee's finding of the torn pieces of paper, with these words on them was a lucky break, though an undeserved one. Definitely a case of 'ignorance is bliss', it set him on the right track, for the wrong reasons. Just why Kemp had written those words on a piece of paper is also a mystery and I never heard him give a good explanation for it. The words 'hydrazine hydrate' are now part of Operation Julie folklore and I doubt if my account will change anyone's belief about the matter, but I wanted to write the truth, as one who knows, before it further solidified into myth.

21

Scale Green Birdman

This wasn't written by me, it was written by the one human being in the multiverse who I consider to be my soul brother, Graeme Hartley. I have shared the psychedelic experience with Graeme for over 40 years, since 1974, and can think of no finer companion for the many adventures we have had. Graeme and I share a common cultural history, geographical background, musical tastes, a liking for chocolate and a somewhat surreal sense of humour, among other bonds. And, well, we just like each other a lot! As others of our acquaintance either fell or faltered we kept the faith, pursuing the path, sometimes not seeing each other for several years, sometimes seeing each other several times a year, sometimes more, invariably high within a few hours of meeting.

Getting out into nature, into the Great Mystery, is one of the finest uses for any psychedelic. Graeme and I have had many such adventures; on moor, hill, valley, woods, parks and beaches. Graeme likes to pen a saga and this one was written about a powerful experience we shared in the Lake District's Grizedale Forest Sculpture Park, when we went to look at a number of interesting sculptures deep in the forest as part of a more specific quest to find David Kemp's legendary sculpture, Scale Green Birdman, one of the earliest sculptures— the fifth in fact—in an area which has since seen hundreds of sculptures come and go, some lasting just weeks, others decades and still in situ. But 'Sculpture' does not come even close to describing what Scale Green Birdman[1] actually was or what it meant.

So although Graeme wrote this poem, I was an intrinsic part of the experience and every word resonates with the memory of that incredible day. Scale Green Birdman was well concealed, deep in the high forest, far from any road and it took hours to locate, a true pilgrimage to a piece of art which said and gave so much to all who encountered it. Following a huge storm which left it exposed, easy to find and visible to all, Birdman was dismantled and no trace now exists. But to *experience* it you had to put the time and effort into finding it. When it took place is of little consequence and our memories now don't hold the date. A baking hot day, in another time's forgotten space, in the 20th century. Who knows? Who cares?

A Trip to the Birdman

by Graeme Hartley

So we're off on a mission
to explore inner space.
Up to Coniston lake
where -
after leaving at seven
to arrive at eleven -
we'll take a
little…black…pill
that might open up heaven.

To Grizedale sculpture park
where artists leave their mark,
hidden in daylight or coniferous dark.
On a leaf-dappled trail
their sculptures stand sentry,
inviting our entry
to guide us with art is their intention,
to tease us and lead us
to our destination.

As we 'come-up' on our trip toward the sublime,
we enter the forest of spruce, fir and pine
and as sight, sounds and senses scramble and muddle
and colours and shapes bleed into each other,
we come upon a huddle
of four figures.
A gathering of stone-sensibilty
but warm with a sense of humanity.
Passing by we shake our heads
and take time
to take a drink and to think;
'how did everything get so pink?'

Then as we run along the path we're to follow
the ground that we tread is not solid, but hollow
and our feet beat and echo
and our hearts pump and pound
and we laugh like wild children
atop nature's ground.

Then suddenly, so quickly,
the forest is gone
and there in its place something beautiful shone;
a stretch of still water that shouldn't be near,
so we stop and we wonder just how we got here.
Then we look at the sky in the place that's not there
and ask 'what are these birds that slice through the air?'
What species they are we've no knowledge or notion,
we can do nothing but guess they're from some other ocean.
Their wings leave bright trails that shadow their motion,
and as they swoop and they call in accents unknown
we're transfixed and transcendent
our minds truly blown.
And we sit for…a minute…an hour……a year.
Then Helen takes charge and leads us on from the mere.

On to a footpath of heather and gorse,
the trip's coming in waves now
and I love it; of course.

My body is trembling with cool Acid shivers,
there's no doubt about it
this stuff sure delivers.
Agg and I take a moment
to stand there and stare
and get into a spat about Kevin Ayers.
Then for a second, an aeon
we don't see eye to eye.
Until I'm distracted by the clouds in the sky.
I say; 'They're coming too close. They're might suck me in',
but Agg shrugs his shoulders and walks on with a grin.
On into the dreamery, the shape-shifting scenery
of greens and greys and purples and rust,
heaving and weaving as we kick up the dust
that catches the sunlight and hangs like
jewels in the air.
Then Helen is pointing
'Over there! Over there!'

On the edge of a scarp
overlooking the valley,
the Scale Green Birdman
stands alone and untended.
It's ramshackle frame, roughshod and appended
with totems and tokens, windmills and wings.
It's like a scene from a Western,
it's so fucking dramatic.
For a moment, I'm breathless
like a chronic asthmatic
I'm amazed, I'm in awe
I'm blissed-out,
I'm flipped out
tripped and ecstatic
but all I can say is;
'it's so cinematic!'

We push open the door
that hangs loose on its jamb,
and that's when it hits us

the full Acid BANG!
The interior is filled
with a lifetime of things:
birdseggsandfeatherssandelectricalswitches
stainedglassandleatherhangingloosewithbrokestitches
dialsandphialsandwoodendecay.
And I want to live there; to stay there and play
I want to be mystic; to learn of his way
I want to be wise; want my third eye to see
and for a few precious moments
I'm the Birdman; he's me.
A madman, a sage, a shaman, a seer,
at one with the prospect
integral to 'here'.

After an hour, a year, it's hard to gauge time,
we gather ourselves and move on down the line.
Still carving and pumping
the microdot surf.
We say goodbye to the Birdman
and the now sacred turf.
Back in the car as we search for some sounds,
we find a show so surreal it simply astounds.
The hills that surround us affect the reception
and the radio stations have lost their direction.
Sliding and gliding they merge into each other,
they phase and they fade and they slide and they slip;
the craziest soundtrack for coming-down off our trip.
Chris Isaac melts into the Wimbledon final,
a found-sound as weird as Duchamp's urinal.
And sat in the back
I'm happy and thinking
'this mash-up's amazing. Can I get it on vinyl?'

22

Getting the Fear

LSD in the horror fiction of Ramsey Campbell

> *To a certain extent, the experiences that I later*
> *had under LSD and so forth were things I had*
> *already done verbally in my fiction...*

Ramsey Campbell is arguably Britain's finest writer of horror fiction. Often favourably compared to (and liked by), US author Stephen King, Campbell draws from a deeper, more unsettling well of reality disturbance. As folklorist and supernatural fiction blogger Kai Roberts notes: 'Whilst Campbell is more popularly known as an undeniably gifted writer of outright "horror," his background is in the weird tradition and many of his best tales reflect this. *The Voice of the Beach* was an attempt to go back to the roots of his most formative influence H.P. Lovecraft and produce a work of cosmic horror to equal Blackwood's *The Willows*. Combined with his own LSD experiences, Campbell succeeds in creating something in the same spirit and yet utterly unique.' It's rare for fiction authors to tease out the dark side of the LSD experience; yet Campbell does this effortlessly, enabling chemical unease to chip away at his protagonists, landscapes to literally take on a life of their own, and the so-called 'love and peace' drug to become a portal through which crawling chaos can manifest.

Andy Roberts: *Ramsey, several of your horror fiction stories and novels either specifically mention LSD or appear to be informed by psychedelic experiences. Can you enlighten me further as to their influence in your life?*

Ramsey Campbell: I don't take drugs in order to write. I believe in depending on as little as possible to do that. But you won't be surprised to learn that the chief indulgences of someone who looked like the cover artist of Tekeli-li 3 appears to think I still look like, have been the milder drugs.

I'm intrigued!

I don't mean cocaine, which I sampled in the early eighties before seeing it nearly destroy a friend of mine. What makes cocaine so insidious is that by the time you've used it sufficiently to achieve the effects you are paying for, it's on your back. Cannabis and LSD are other matters, though not necessarily less problematic. Overindulgence in cannabis can lead to habituation- psychological addiction- which brings its own species of hangover, a dulling of one's senses and responses the day after, no use to a writer or, I should think, to anyone else. I did find I was still able to write, but it demanded more effort than usual to produce comparable work. Since it apparently takes several days for the metabolites of cannabis to work their way through one's system, perhaps once a week is the safe maximum. After all, the Sunday joint is an English tradition. Careless use of LSD—well, we'll return to that.

You've clearly given the pros and cons of drug use and writing a great deal of thought. Can you give me some examples of stories or novels that were psychedelically inspired?

I'm in confessional mood now, so let me identify the pieces I wrote under chemical influence. The first was a review of a Lovecraft issue of the underground comic Skull. I read it between tokes of a joint, and I don't believe I'd finished reading the first story when it occurred to me that there could hardly be a more appropriate state in which to write a review on an underground publication. So far as I can judge, the drug's only effect was to encourage me to vary my sentence structures more, but the experience amused me enough to try it once again, for another project which seemed sufficiently unconventional: "Among the pictures are these", an account of some very odd sketches which I'd drawn at the age of fourteen and which I rediscovered over ten years later. In this case the grass was an aid to precision, as I think the few people who have seen the sketches will agree.

Did you ever try and write when actually under the influence of LSD?

The only piece I ever wrote under the influence of LSD was the preface to a collection of early writings by HP Lovecraft which originally appeared in the Pawtuxet Valley Gleaner. More exactly, I set about writing the piece to distract myself from waiting for the onset of the drug. When I observed signs of the onset—sounds becoming isolated by an intensified silence, a restlessness of the words I'd written so far—I completed the next sentence and called it a day. Readers may care to discover if they can locate the aforementioned sentence and indeed the book!

Did any of your readers or critics comment about your psychedelic drug references or influences?

Donald Wandrei's broad hint in his blurb for *Demons by Daylight* that some of my stories are about drugs ("let those who long for *The Enchanted Fruit* beware of the consequences of eating thereof") or Stephen King's comment in *Danse Macabre* that "in a Campbell novel or story, one seems to view the world through the thin and shifting perceptual haze of an LSD trip that is just ending—or just beginning".

Praise indeed from Stephen King!

Yes, but Wandrei's comment, unlike Steve's, was made about tales I wrote *before* I'd had any experience of drugs other than tobacco or alcohol. Moreover, the protagonist of "Potential", the grey-suited figure in the edge of a would-be psychedelic event, halfway between hopeful and nervous of being offered drugs, was of course me. I'd

always valued unusual perceptions- childhood fevers had been fun-
and shortly after completing the last tale in *Demons by Daylight* I was
freed my first toke.

Did you use cannabis a lot?

I was hooked! No, not really. Months, maybe a year, passed before
I started smoking grass with anything like regularity. But there was
a year in the early seventies when I would roll a joint of high-grade
Jamaican before listening to music, or watching a film, or going out
for a walk. At least this didn't rob me of ideas, but it sapped me of
the energy to develop them. As to whether I would have had the ideas
without the cannabis, who can say? Certainly the description of the
park at night in *The Doll Who Ate His Mother* is derived pretty near
entirely from walks I took under the influence, and the final paragraph
of *The Height of the Scream* came to me in similar circumstances,
as did the lines about the spider in human form in "The Guide", and
several images which led me to write "In the Trees". I could go on. By
now I was using drugs to compel myself to relax, particularly between
novels, because the gap left by completing a novel makes me want to
begin work immediately on something else.

*What led to the progression from cannabis to LSD then? Acid is hardly
a drug of relaxation!*

Unless you're Anthony Perkins (to quote what he allegedly told
British customs officers), you don't take LSD to relax. I first took the
plunge, having read as much about the substance and its effects as
I could find, in late 1975: stared at the scrap of blotting paper, told
myself I'd take it in a minute or two, swallowed it an hour or more
later, went out with Jenny (who was probably more nervous about
my imminent condition than I was) for a walk in the park, watched
the army afternoon shadows of foliage appear to be about to undergo
some transformation, was persuaded by Jenny to go home in case
being in a public place caused problems, sat in the newly extended
kitchen of our house and concluded that nothing more would happen,
that my metabolism wasn't receptive to the drug... then the different
colours of the new bare plaster intensified and began to flow like oil

on water, forming Oriental patterns, and a cloud sailing outside the window became transformed into the glass of the pane and reached for me.

Was the psychedelic experience worthwhile from a creative point of view?

If an acid trip consisted purely of such visions, I might be still inviting them. My experience, however, is that one has to put up with a good deal that is confusing to the point of irritation, and even banal. In that first instance it was panic which caused me to struggle to reduce the intensity of the visions, an act which led to hours of unsatisfactory forgettable stuff. That night I discovered something which is seldom advertised about LSD; even when the trip seems to be over it's virtually impossible to sleep. I snoozed for a couple of hours before dawn, and dreamed I was being intimated into an American Indian ritual. For the next two days my consciousness kept feeling poised to shift into an unfamiliar me, not least while I was interviewing Roger Moore for the BBC about his new South African film. (During that period I was also introduced to the anthologist Hugh Lamb, who assures me that my state didn't show.)

It seems like that first LSD experience was wasn't as satisfying or paradigm shattering as you might have expected. How long was it before you used the drug again?

Nine months passed, and *The Doll Who Ate His Mother* was written, before I tried LSD again. This time I went alone to a nature reserve near Liverpool, but the experience was just as frustrating. I remember looking at the profusion of flowers on the landward dunes and dismissing it as a "psychedelic Disneyland". Feeling aimless, I returned to Liverpool and visited the Catholic cathedral, where I saw winged forms emerging from the wall of a chapel; then I walked through miles of streets where every face looked grey and pinched, to meet Jenny from work.

*He oughtn't to take acid while Cathy was near. Her
anxiety for him only made him feel threatened by a
bad trip. If she had been here, her obsession with
the atmosphere of the house would have infected
them all   – from The Face That Must Die (1979)*

*It's interesting that you appear to have experienced many of the classic
characteristics and qualities of the psychedelic experience, yet seemed
dissatisfied with them. Did you persevere in your psychedelic quest?*

I still felt awesome visions were possible if I could may achieve them.
Perhaps if I had then discovered the gentler, more controllable, but
otherwise similar experiences to be had from psilocybin—"words born
of spores upon the twining psilocybin", as the poet has it—I would
have come to a different end. During the next year or so I took four
more trips. Once I saw my shadow on a path and thought it was my
late grandmother's (I was wearing a corduroy overcoat like hers), and
there was quite a lot of such disconcerting stuff. But I also watched the
arch above the altar of a Norman church crack and disintegrate, before
gathering itself into muscular stone and rearing up again to support the
roof. From a Lakeland fell, I saw the fields and slopes gently rearrange
themselves around me, and I felt I was seeing the English landscape
for the first time, as indeed I was, nor have I lost that sense of it. Later,
on the peak, I watched distant mountains shudder and waken in the
mist, like gods. On the way down my vision became microscopic,
and I saw deep into the heather. En route to the hotel I was able to see
elaborate fossils in the pavement, and the pines above the hotel were
transformed into a primeval forest, dark and mysterious.

*Again, these sound like 'classic' psychedelic distortions of 'reality' in
that LSD can awaken and transform landscapes in a way that gives
them a depth and complexity hitherto unseen but never again forgotten.
But I sense some uneasiness in your psychedelic explorations?*

*The only way you can see new things here is taking
acid. I'm tripping now…. He'd heard things about
LSD, "Aren't you afraid of starting to trip when
you don't mean to?" "Flashbacks you mean? I*

never have them. I shouldn't like that." She gazed
at his skepticism. "There's no need to be afraid
of drugs," she said. "All sorts of people used to
trip. Witches used to. Look, it tells you about it in
here"... Perhaps she had been right; they might
take LSD together, when it was time. It might help
them to become one – from *The Face at Pine*
Dunes (1987)

The intensity of those hours should have been enough. A day or two later
it was certainly sufficient to precipitate a migraine which shattered my
vision and left me blind for perhaps half an hour. Nevertheless, back
at home I continued to smoke cannabis most evenings, even when I
noticed the cable to a hi-fi speaker looked unpleasantly convoluted
and scrawny. That ought to have warned me what I was risking, but it
wasn't until one Friday night that I had to acknowledge something was
very wrong. I was halfway through a joint when I felt too nervous to
sit still. I went to the front door and tried gazing at the terrace opposite,
but in the oily orange the houses looked alien, not remotely reassuring.
I went back upstairs to splash cold water on my face, and saw myself
in the bathroom mirror. My mouth was disappearing. The left side had
already gone.

That in itself sounds like something from a H.P. Lovecraft tale. The
unease, the shifting of perception and alienation when not on an LSD
high doesn't bode well. I had similar reactions after my first LSD
experience.

When his first marriage was ending, Evelyn Waugh wrote to Harold
Acton, "I did not know it was possible to be so miserable and live."
For "miserable" substitute "terrified" and you have my then state.
I was afraid to admit it to Jenny, even when she remarked that the
smell of me had changed; since a fly was buzzing round the house I
thought I was decaying. After perhaps an hour, I owned up, having
meanwhile tried to convince myself that she didn't know anything
was wrong. The worst of it was, that since I wasn't sure what had
precipitated the flashback, I didn't know if it would ever end. I spent
the next several hours struggling to see only the familiar, which made
everything ominously, and in some cases hideously, changeable.

Jenny helped me grow intermittently calm, as did several pints of Tetley's, by no means my favourite beer but the only alcohol in the house. Debussey's string quartet, and in particular Beethoven's Opus 135, were beneficial. Around four in the morning my fear of closing my eyes lessened enough to let me go to bed. I slept.

Your negative post-trip experiences are familiar to me and to others unfortunate enough to see the dark side of LSD. Did this state of affairs improve?

The following day I was still afraid—of looking in the mirror, or at paintings, or trees, or car headlights at night, and much else—and I grew more afraid as the weeks passed. I tried sleeping pills, Librium, an Ananda Marga meditation class; ultimately I consulted an acupuncturist and told him what I'd done to myself. Not very long after he started the treatments I was able to lie in bed without being assaulted with waves of light behind my eyelids, and so my recovery began, aided by a daily diet of Mozart's early symphonies conducted by Nevile Marriner. Readers of *The Parasite* may recognise elements I borrowed for that book.

You were fortunate you didn't develop mental health issues as a result of these experiences and how they carried into your quotidian existence. Yet it seems as though, unsettling and disturbing your psychedelic experiences were, you were able to take some useful elements from them and integrate them in your plots and descriptions.

> *As I turned towards the bungalows the glitter of the sea clung to my eyes. After-images crowded among the debris. They were moving; I strained to make out their shape. What did they resemble? Symbols—hieroglyphs? Limbs writhing rapidly, as if in a ritual dance? They made the debris appear to shift, to crumble. The herd of faceless dunes seemed to edge forward; an image leaned towards me out of the sky. I closed my eyes, to calm their antics* – from *The Voice of the Beach* (1987)

That is ultimately the point. If no experience I undergo is too awful for me to write about it, then no experience need be wasted. My psychedelic dabbling left me with a store of material I haven't yet exhausted. Much of the Lakeland episode formed the basis of "Above the World"; and "The Pattern" and "The Voice of the Beach" (among others) wouldn't have been written without psychedelic memories to draw on. Of course the stories were attempts to give form to them, though I even tried to convey the formlessness of most of my trips in a chapter of *The Face That Must Die*. My friend, author Poppy Z. Brite, has written that some of these aspects of my tales helped turn her on to drugs when she was sixteen- I won't deny I feel responsible. And now? Well, I can remind myself of things I saw and experienced by leafing through a book of Dali's paintings, or through *Visions 1*, the 1977 Pomegranate Press book by Bill Martin, *Garden of Life and Autumn*, and Gage Taylor's *The Creek*, immediately recall the kind of gestalt perception which made all the unsatisfactoriness worthwhile. So do fractals. But my days of dropping acid are over, man, I've still too many ideas to write, and who knows how much time?

A full Ramsey Campbell bibliography and information about his current projects, among a wealth of other information, can be found at: http://www.ramseycampbell.com

23

Psychedelics, Synchronicity & The Duck of Evidence

or

I Suppose a Duck's Out of the Question?

> *By doing certain things certain results follow;*
> *students are most earnestly warned against attributing*
> *objective reality or philosophic validity to any of them.*

> – Aleister Crowley

Those among you who have taken psychedelics with a questing nature and a weaving mind will, at some time, have undergone some pretty strange experiences. There is no end to the path of psychedelic practice, and we are always learning. However, once the initiate has assimilated the shock and awe of the psychedelic experience, become familiar navigating the kaleidoscopic visual challenges, accepted and embraced the somatic perceptions, and when the magnificence, depth, beauty and complexity of the multiverse has been revealed by super enhanced senses, they might then start to notice events that appear very hard to explain.

These singular occurrences seem to be manifested by the psychedelicised mind of the individual or group and appear to be linked, caused or summoned by the very act of taking psychedelics. Occasionally they can be further refined or directed by the will or desire of the celebrants. They are not consistent in nature or content and can be- often are—silly, surreal, just plain weird or frankly unbelievable. Equally, they can be freighted with tangible import and meaning relating to any aspect of the multiverse including your past, present or future or those of the lives of people you know. Sometimes they are a tangle of all these qualities, and more. But whatever these occurrences are, they are experienced by the percipients as being *real* and should not be ignored.

Sceptics, debunkers and those of a limited imagination will, of course, frame these experiences as 'coincidences', one dictionary definition being 'a remarkable concurrence of events or circumstances without apparent causal connection'. And well they might be, but here we're talking about events which at least appear to be linked, and categorising a series of apparently linked events as 'coincidence' (if only linked in the minds of the celebrants), in no way explains them and only serves to limit their possibility and potential.

So when such events take place it begs the question whether or not there is meaning to coincidence. Several contemporary cultural sages, themselves no stranger to psychedelics, have commented on this conundrum. Dylan, for instance, told us to 'Take what you need from coincidence', and Viv Stanshall (via Neil Innes) suggested, 'There are no coincidences but sometimes the pattern seems more obvious'. The grand old man of weirdness, William Burroughs, asserted that, 'In the magical universe there are no coincidences and there are no accidents. Nothing happens unless someone wills it to happen', which is particularly apt. If you believe we exist in a magical universe, that is!

But still, coincidences, eh? Let me tell you a story...

It's a lazy Sunday afternoon on the last day of the month of May. I've got no mind to worry, but instead of closing my eyes and drifting away, I am sat with two visiting sorcerers of my acquaintance, talking about acid weirdness, as you do. Earlier in the weekend similar conversations had taken place in which I'd explained that although not being a practitioner of magick I have, over the years, experienced several events in which psychedelics appeared to have connected me and the people I was tripping with to a completely different order of reality in which the unusual becomes usual, changes in consciousness are concomitant with changes in the physical world and, in the words of yet another psychedelic sage, the world becomes '*strangely strange, but oddly normal*'.

Previous essays in this Anthology describing occasions from the mid-1970s, including *Meddle(d)?*, and *Adventures in a Yorkshire Landscape*, describe similar events in which psychedelic synchronicity has resulted in consensually perceived high strangeness. And in later years I have used psychedelics with awareness and directed intent to increase the probability of finding (summoning?) certain desired physical objects while out walking and beachcombing. Many users of psychedelics have had similar experiences, and whether they can be described by philosophy, science or a combination of the two is immaterial. They occur and cannot, should not be, denied or ignored.

These experiences are broadly acknowledged, if not fully accepted or understood, by many psychiatrists including Stanislav Grof who has written at length about them as part of his 50 plus years of exploring non-ordinary states of consciousness noting, 'Lay self-experimenters with LSD frequently enter realms of experience that totally bewilder and puzzle practicing psychiatrists and psychologists…'. The bewilderment and puzzlement of the medical establishment does not, however, negate the reality or meaning of these experiences, nor should it affect the will to carry them out!

So there we were, discussing that sort of thing, whatever it is. Stories were being told, as they are when any psychonauts are gathered together. Let me tell you about this, I said, giving another, albeit long-winded, example of directed psychedelic synchronicity. The story starts several years ago, some months after my partner and I had started to beachcomb seriously. When I become interested in something I tend toward obsession and beachcombing was no exception. I read everything possible about the subject and during this literary immersion, came across several accounts of the loss at sea of the container ship *Ever Laurel*, sailing out of Hong Kong, bound for Washington, which sank in 1992 with its cargo of almost 28,800 plastic children's bath toys. Of this number, 7,200 of these toys were small yellow plastic ducks. The toys, and especially the ducks (surely there's *something* about ducks in Western culture; Donald Duck, Duckman, Daffy Duck, Duck Tape, Disco Duck, Count Duckula, the Ugly Duckling, Duck Soup, the list goes on!) became legendary. Oceanographers tracked their movement as they dispersed on the currents and logged the locations they washed up in. Before long the *Ever Laurel* ducks became the Holy Grail for beachcombers, a pointless but fun beach discovery which tied the finder into this legendary maritime disaster.

This event enthralled me and I *really* wanted to find one of these plastic ducks. Our beachcombing to date, almost exclusively on the Lleyn Peninsula,

Anglesey or on occasional trips to Scotland, had covered many miles of beaches but hadn't yielded any plastic children's bath toys. Within days of reading about the *Ever Laurel* I became obsessed with finding one of these sea borne mysteries.

Captain Ahab had his Moby Dick, I now had my Moby Duck. I decided, on our next beachcombing expedition, we *were* going to find one, and the agency for doing so was to be the applied use of psychedelics. I explained this theory to my patient and long suffering partner, who was sceptical about this kind of nonsense, despite having already seen evidence of it in other places at other times.

Saturday arrived and we turned on, tuned in and set off, I mentally re-affirming our desire for duck as we did so. The beaches of the northern Lleyn Peninsula were to be our initial target and we drove to a quiet, secluded, beach we hadn't previously visited. As we walked down the ramp to the beach, completely bare of all but a handful of sea-borne natural debris deposited as the early morning high tide receded, what did we see?

You guessed it, a small, yellow, plastic duck! Could we believe our eyes? We had no choice. It was there on the beach in front of us. We were mind-boggled. I picked the duck up and marvelled. It was solid, real and no figment of our illuminated state of mind. Clearly though, this was just one of those 'coincidences' and my intent multiplied by psychedelics had played no part in the finding of the duck! Maybe.

We pressed on to other beaches and to our astonishment found two more small yellow plastic ducks that day. These 'coincidental' ducks had clearly been hand delivered by one of the sea gods; Neptune, Poseidon or, as we were in Wales, most likely Llyr (working on behalf of Loki!). It was unlikely they had been dropped or left by holiday makers, at least not on that day, as we were the first people on those beaches after the, ahem, high tide. So why did they appear to us, there, then?

My mind was blown—I had found exactly what I wanted to find, when I wanted to find it, using the chosen method. The following week, excited and working under exactly the same set of criteria and experimental conditions, we found a further two small yellow plastic ducks; all similar but none identical. None were part of the famous 1992 'duck spillage'. That didn't matter, I realised I hadn't specifically *asked* to find ducks from the *Ever Laurel*, just to find small plastic yellow ducks! Maybe you only get what you ask for? All these ducks were duly rescued from their liminal mental and physical zones and brought home to adorn the 'wall of duck', in our back garden.

After that, nothing. In the years of intensive beachcombing all over north Wales and Scotland, since those magickal duck days (Robert Anton Wilson had his Dog Days, I had my Duck Days!), we have found hundreds of curiosities, natural and man-made, but no further small, plastic yellow ducks. The 'experiment' if you call it that, was successfully tried in respect of finding significant cetacean remains (a 15 metre long beached and dead Sperm Whale, answered the call, for instance) but was never tried again in respect of ducks again until...

My story to the Sorcerers was over and we all sagely nodded and agreed that weird shit often happens under the influence of psychedelics, and that what we laughingly call *reality* can, under certain circumstances, can be given a nudge, as if it were a cosmic fruit machine, to deliver if not exactly what you want, at least an approximation of that desire. The finding of the ducks, however ludicrous that may seem to you dear reader (the multiverse often reveals itself in preposterous ways to deter slavish belief, and, to encourage humour as a valid perspective on its manifestations) proved this to me, yet again.

As conversation faded and the tea pot emptied, we decided the afternoon was now bright and clear enough to go for a meander on a nearby beach. The promise of sea, sun, a tern colony and cobwebs being blown away appealed more than the gravitational pull of lounging the early evening away. A sacrament, appropriate in nature and dosage to the day was ingested and off we went...

Twenty minutes later we're walking the 300 yards or so across the dried salt marsh toward the beach. Although Talacre is frequently packed with tourists, the day had hitherto been dull, wet and windy and there were few people around.

There are several entrances to the beach and we headed for our usual one, an opening between the dunes, indicated by a tall wooden post. As we neared the gap I saw it first. A canary yellow object resting on its side at the base of the post, for all the world looking as if it had been intentionally placed. Other than marram grass, sea-holly and evening primrose, there was no other natural or man-made beach detritus and I immediately knew, but could hardly bring myself to accept, what the object was.

It was, of course, a small, bright yellow plastic duck. The type young children play with in the bath, the type we had found several of some years ago. Everyone else saw it seconds after I did, to various degrees of amazement.

The sorcerers with us that day were unsurprised either by my earlier stories or by the finding of the duck that bright last day of May. As one of them wisely summed the moment up, '*Tangible evidence, of a non-tangible theorem... you had to be there.*' That sort of stuff is, apparently, not unusual and fits into their general chaos magic paradigm. If plastic duck-conjuring is feasible who knows what else is possible!

As with all interesting finds the duck—immediately named and raised to the status of The Duck of Evidence—was carefully removed from its beach portal and given due acknowledgement, before being brought home and placed on the hearth altar with other wonders.

If you are still with me, you might be wondering why, if all this has any validity or relevance, I didn't find one of the original plastic ducks from the wreck of the *Ever Laurel* and not just any old small yellow plastic duck. Well, I suppose from a magical theory point of view, I didn't specifically *ask* to, I rather stupidly only asked to find small yellow plastic ducks and didn't specify where they originated from. A small detail, perhaps, but an important one.

Sceptics and debunkers will by now be laughing and sniggering; 'coincidence', 'selective attention', or, more likely, 'Roberts has finally gone mad'. Maybe, but you know I'm only playing, because all interpretations of the event are equally valid and 'true', some are just more interesting and useful than others. Carl Jung called these kinds of meaningful coincidences 'synchronicities' when they happened spontaneously; perhaps we need a term for them when they are actively sought after? One of the sorcerers involved has pointed out that 'spells' is probably the correct term, and I suspect she's right!

Some people just accept these strange happenings as, well, the sort of thing that happens when you take psychedelics. Others refuse to ascribe any meaning to them at all. But ignoring them misses the opportunity for the fun, thought and speculation that they offer. I suppose if I have to pin myself down to what they actually *mean*, to me at least, it would be that they offer revelations not of some divine pattern or truth but of what Robin Williamson has termed, 'the sheer unspeakable strangeness of being here at all'. That, more than anything else, everything revealed to me through the psychedelic experience seems to be the truth of the matter. We live in the heart of an unfathomable mystery and we need to be here now, absolutely and utterly aware, self-aware, and aware of being self-aware. And then see what happens!

No ducks were harmed during the course of these 'coincidences'.

24

The Acid King Dies

An obituary for Augustus Owsley Stanley III

19th January, 1935 – 12th March, 2011

A year ago this month, on 12th March, 2011, 76-year-old Augustus Owsley Stanley III drove his car into a ditch in a remote part of Queensland, Australia, killing himself and injuring his wife. In the years leading up to his death, Owsley Stanley had become a recluse on the other side of the world, a semi-mythical figure, refusing to give interviews and rarely photographed. To the media, Owsley, as he was simply and better known, was the world's first underground chemist, the first person to produce LSD outside government laboratories and the man who dosed the psychedelic revolution. He wasn't, of course, the *first* underground chemist, but such was his counter-culture cachet, especially in America, to all intents and purposes Owsley was up there with Tim Leary and Ken Kesey in the lysergic corruption of young minds.

Despite his prestigious background (his grandfather was Kentucky State Governor and a Democratic senator, his father a lawyer), Owsley's early family life was troubled: he responded by being completely unmanageable at school, while at the same time displaying intelligence way beyond his years. He was expelled from military prep school for getting his mates drunk, but even so, the headmaster later remembered him as a 'brainchild, a wunderkind, tremendously interested in science'.

After a short spell at the University of Virginia, a stint in the United States Air Force, and a period in which he studied Russian and French, and worked as a professional ballet dancer, he enrolled at the University of California where, in April 1964, he first tried LSD. He was impressed, 'I remember the first time I took acid and walked outside. The cars were kissing the parking meters.'

Until then, LSD had only been available to those undertaking serious medical research and all the early psychonauts like Ken Kesey and Allen Ginsberg took LSD as part of a federally funded volunteer programme. But there were always question marks over what drug they were actually being given and at what dosages.

In what might be seen as the original spirit of pioneering America, Owsley decided the only way to ensure the quality of what he took was to make it himself. At that time, LSD was still legal in America and Owsley was able to find a formula in the university library. He teamed up with Melissa Cargill, a chemistry student, and went into production. By May, 1965 Owsley had created his first batch of LSD, of a reasonably consistent dose of 200-300µg, more than enough for a full-blown psychedelic experience. On testing his first attempts at acid alchemy Owsley's housemate, Charles Perry, commented that it was "devastatingly strong in an almost heavy-handed way that recalled Owsley's own insistent manner". This comment echoed Owsley's belief that the state of mind of an LSD chemist affected the quality of the product and the consequent experience of the LSD user. At crucial stages of later LSD production runs, Owsley often phoned a radio DJ friend and asked for certain music to be played to help him get in the appropriate mood. Owsley believed that LSD chemistry, far from being a simple set of mechanistic procedures was actually much closer to acid alchemy, with science, art and intention combining in the correct circumstances to produce a substance that could change an individual for ever.

Owsley's fame spread and he met up with author and Merry Prankster Ken Kesey. He began supplying Kesey's notorious Acid Tests, LSD consumed in orange juice, famously chronicled by Tom Wolfe in *The Electric Kool Aid Acid Test*. But while Kesey and his cohorts wanted to be as stoned as possible on high dose LSD, Owsley knew they were playing a dangerous game. Equating the acid trip with the altered states of consciousness associated with magical rituals, he said to Kesey, "'You guys are fucking around with something people have known about forever... all the occult literature about ceremonial magic warns about being very careful when you start exploring these areas of the mind". And they laughed at me'.

It was at one of these gatherings, in 1965, that Owsley (also known as 'The Bear' because of his inordinately hairy chest) met The Grateful Dead, who were morphing from producing deranged Jug Band music to being the Bay Area's psychedelic dance band of choice. He soon began, by mutual and enthusiastic agreement, to use his LSD profits to further the band's career. He offered them accommodation, helped devise their famous 'skull and lightning bolt' logo and used his array of technical skills to build them a state of the art sound system for live performances that became the envy of every major rock band on the touring circuit.

That same year, he had his first run-in with the law. To help subsidise the costs of the raw chemicals for LSD, he had also been making bath-tub methamphetamine, and his lab was raided. Fortunately for Owsley, what was seized turned out to be LSD, legal at the time, so his lawyer, the vice mayor of Berkeley, successfully sued for the return of all Owsley's lab equipment.

LSD was outlawed in America on 28th October 1966, by which time, Owsley's name had become synonymous with cheap, high quality LSD. He produced 300,000 doses of what he called 'White Lightning' acid for the San Francisco Human Be-In event in January 1967, and in June, 'Monterey Purple' was consumed in some quantity backstage at the Monterey Pop Festival by the likes of Jimi Hendrix, Brian Jones and Pete Townsend. Owsley recalls: "Brian Jones had a photographer in his entourage who brought a telephoto lens which had been gutted. He took it back filled with Monterey Purple. I asked Brian to share the stash between his Stones and the Beatles. So far as I am aware he did so." So impressed was John Lennon that he allegedly bought a lifetime's supply of LSD from Owsley.

But the high life couldn't last and Owsley was arrested in late 1967, eventually serving three years in custody. On his release he kept a low profile, touring with the Grateful Dead and helping perfect their Wall of Sound concert system.

No-one, least of all Owsley, knows how much LSD he made but a reasonable estimate is over 1.25 million doses. The USA and Britain in the 1950s and early 1960s was a world of beige conformity as a generation craved peace and stability in the post-War period. The cultural revolution of the mid 1960s was an explosion of primary colours made possible by an elite group of musicians, artists, writers, photographers and fashion designers inspired by the impact of their own LSD experiences. Whatever one's view of the sixties, its political, social and cultural impact rumbles on; and so to that extent, the influence of Owsley Stanley is hard to exaggerate.

Yet he downplayed his influence, telling *Rolling Stone* magazine, "I just wanted to know the dose and purity of what I took into my own body. Almost before I realized what was happening, the whole affair had gotten completely out of hand. I was riding magic stallion. A Pegasus, I was not responsible for his wings, but they did carry me to all kinds of places".

In 1980, Owsley moved to Australia, driven by his belief that a new ice age was to engulf the northern hemisphere. He settled in the bush country near Cairns in Queensland, eventually becoming a naturalised Australian citizen. There he exercised his artistic talents, making and selling beautiful enamel jewellery and sculpture, a skill learnt in prison. The arrival of the internet enabled him to create a web site which allowed him to market his wares more widely and to publically espouse his unusual beliefs, producing essays on diet (he was a lifelong carnivore), exercise, war and drug prohibition, to name but a few.

But while he was only too aware of the potential dangers of hallucinogenic drugs—he once produced a batch of cosmically powerful STP from a recipe obtained from Alexander Shulgin—he was unrepentant over his life as the peoples' chemist. In a rare interview given to the *San Francisco Chronicle* in 2007, he said; 'I wound up doing time for something I should have been rewarded for. What I did was a community service, the way I look at it. I was punished for political reasons. Absolutely meaningless. Was I a criminal? No, I was a good member of society. Only my society, and the one making the laws, are different'.

I never knew Owsley personally. But during the writing of *Albion Dreaming* I contacted him by email to ask him various questions. He was quite a character, even via email! Irascible would, I think, be the best term to describe him, although it was often hard to tell by email whether he was living up to his reputation or genuinely believed his terse pronouncement.

When I reminded him that the psychedelic trickster Michael Hollingshead had wrote of how Bear and Richard Alpert (Baba Ram Dass) had visited Hollingshead in Wormwood Scrubs, bringing LSD filled grapes, he completely denied the event took place, saying he had never met or even heard of Hollingshead. He also railed pointlessly against the factual details of the Operation Julie LSD manufacturing and distribution ring with, 'I have always thought the 'Operation Julie' story was a hoax—it did not seem like any sort of acid reality I was familiar with.' And in between these bouts of digital sparring Owsley took me to task about my use of grammar suggesting I might like to 'engage the services of a competent editor for (your) book.' Yet he continued to respond to my relentless questions, and eventually I sensed a real ride in what he had done for the world as well as an interest in how far his infamy had spread; 'Is my name used today—on the street—over there?' he queried. He was clearly, albeit obliquely, pleased when I informed him that not only was the name Owsley widely known and respected among discerning British acid heads, but that he had entries in both the Encyclopaedia Britannica and the Oxford English Dictionary, where he is enshrined as: *Owsley, noun, An extremely potent, high quality type of LSD.* His wry comment when he heard of this was, 'Isn't that sort of surprising? I am like… 'Kleenex'! We will not see his like again. Farewell, Bear.

25

Afterword

On Coming Down

by Julian Vayne
Author & Sorcerer

The interviews, articles, stories and psychedelic travellers' tales in *Acid Drops* bear witness to a simple and profound truth; that, as Andy himself once explained to me, these substances are just 'so interesting'. Here we have molecules; specific arrangements of oxygen, carbon, nitrogen and the rest, in which dwell astonishing possibilities. One of the signature powers of these psychedelic substances is that they dissolve boundaries; the boundaries between heaven and hell, illumination and illusion, ourselves and the other. It is perhaps for this reason that this collection strides across history, autobiography, fiction and more. For the psychedelicised mind sees connections and relationships, it inspires interdisciplinary thought, radical re-imaginings of culture, and new styles of art. Novelist and Merry Prankster Ken Kesey explains it thus; "I believe that with the advent of acid, we discovered a new way to think, and it has to do with piecing together new thoughts in your mind."

However simply putting LSD (or any psychedelic for that matter) into a human brain is only part of the story. On acid we may experience the ineffable white-out peak, where all things become one and insights come thick and fast, crowding together at the event-horizon of awareness. Yet unless we can bring a little of this Promethean fire to earth, whether in the form of art, technical innovation, personal psychological transformation or what have you, we have only completed half of the journey. For coming down isn't the end of the trip, it's the start of the voyage of making sense, putting into practice, and allowing the psychedelic state to inform our ipseity.

Acid Drops grows from real-life experience of these powerful mind altering substances, and Andy has made his explorations manifest in writing. Furthermore, our author has brought to bear on these encounters the discerning eyes of the researcher. It's pretty easy to come down from being high with all manner of wild ideas but, after the drugs have worn off, these insights need to be tested. Facts are essential, especially to a historian like Andy, and while some evidence may be both strangely strange and yet oddly normal (like the synchronistic Duck of Evidence), corroboration and verification matter. It is the recognition and application of this truth that distinguishes the learned psychonaut from the deluded day-tripper.

While this book ranges across many subjects and styles, these are all part of one project. Like light on the facets of a crystal (probably produced by Owsley), each essay here is a partial reflection of the modern psychedelic landscape. These tales are created and curated by someone who in meeting these altered states asked; 'how can I make sense of this?' and, 'how can I communicate something of this experience and its importance to others?'.

As we come down from being high we can, like our author, record, reflect, edit, revise and share what we have learned. Perhaps the underlying message of this book is that no matter how high we get, afterwards we should ask ourselves; how does our experience enrich our own lives and that of people around us? There may be many answers to these questions, and as Andy demonstrates through this diverse collection, we may need many techniques to articulate the insights we discover when we take those tiny acid drops.

Notes

Chapter 3: Season of the Witch

1   Hansard. London. June 30 1966. Available from: http://hansard. millbanksystems.com/lords/1966/jun/30/drug-taking-by-young-people

2   Bedford, P. Cocktails will curb the boss's tantrums. *London Times.* 1960 October 17; 5

3   Hansard. London. December 11 1958. Available from: http://hansard. millbanksystems.com/commons/1958/dec/11/mescalin-and-lysergic-acid die thylamide#S5CV0597P0_19581211_HOC_26

4   Moorcock, M. Moorcock's Miscellany. 2 January 2007. Available from: http:// www.multiverse.org/fora/showthread.php?t=4892

5   Doctor's death mystery. *Daily Mirror.* 1963. February 19; 19

6   Hansard. London. May 11 1964. Available from: http://hansard.millbanksystems. com/lords/1966/may/11/control-of-drugs#S5LV0274P0_19660511_HOL_55

7   Fairlie, H. Political Commentary. *The Spectator.* 1955. September 23

8   Hollingshead, M. *The Man Who Turned On The World.* London. Blond & Briggs Ltd; 1973

9   Britain's first 'vision of hell' drugs case. *Daily Telegraph.* 1966. April 4

10   LSD: The Drug that could become a social peril. *London Life.* 1966. March 19

11   Gabbert, M. The men behind .LSD'- the drug that is menacing young lives. *The People.* 1966. March 20; 14-15

12   Sandell, C. Menace Of The 'Vision Of Hell'. *News of the World.* 1966. March 20; 9

13   Housego, M. Group plugs LSD and wins a rebuke. *Evening Standard*. 1966. March 23

14   LSD song: Home Office studies words. *Evening Standard*. 1966 March 25

15   Morning Glory 'drug' sold in Easter Cards. *The People*. 1966. April 3

16   Cassandra. The Cost Of LSD. *Daily Mirror.* 1966. April 4; 5

17   US firm to stop sale of LSD drug. *Manchester Guardian*. 1966. April 15; 1

18   Kempson, T. BBC In A Wild 'Drug Party' Sensation. *The People*. 1966. 1

19   LSD Drug Charges Man Convicted. *London Times*. 1966. April 28

20   Hansard. London. May 11 1966. Available from: http://hansard.millbanksystems. com/lords/1966/may/11/control-of drugs#S5LV0274P0_19660511_HOL_55

21   Drug case said to be 'trend setter'. *London Times*. 1966. May 11

22   Effects of LSD. *British Medical Journal*. 1966; issue no. 5502: 1495

23   Hansard. London. June 30 1966. Available from: http://hansard. millbanksystems.com/lords/1966/jun/30/drug-taking-by-young-people

24   Government move to stop misuse of the 'fantasy drug'. *Manchester Guardian*. 1966. July 22. 1

25   Pickard, C., Aitken, J. To LSD And Back Again. *Evening Standard*. London. 1966. September 8. 7

26   Young, W. The Truth About the Dream Drug. *Readers Digest*. 1966. October. 186-190

Chapter 6: No Imperfections in the Budded Mountain

1   *Telegraph*. "Marvellous McGough". 14 April, 2013: http://www.telegraph.co.uk/ culture/books/3649049/The-marvellous-McGough.html

2   Cunliffe, Barry. *Blackburn Brainswamp*. Bradford: Redbeck Press, 1991

3   Miles, Barry. *Allen Ginsberg Beat Poet*. 3rd ed. London: Virgin Books, 2010

4   Connors, Peter. *White Hand Society: The Psychedelic Partnership of Timothy Leary & Allen Ginsberg*. San Francisco: City Lights Books, 2010

Notes

5   PlosBlogs. "The Plot to Turn On the World: The Leary/Ginsberg Acid Conspiracy". 14 April 2013. http://blogs.plos.org/neurotribes/2011/04/21/the-plot-to-turn-on-the-world-the-learyginsberg-acid-conspiracy/

6   Sinclair, Iain. *The Kodak Mantra Diaries*, London: Albion Village Press, 1971

7   Maschler, Tom. *Publisher*. London: Picador, 2005

8   Sinclair, Iain. *The Kodak Mantra Diaries*, London: Albion Village Press, 1971

9   Ginsberg, Allen. *Wales Visitation*. London. Cape Goliard, 1968

10   Ginsberg, Allen. *Holy Soul Jelly Roll* (booklet to accompany CD box set). Rhino Word Beat R2 71693) 1994

11   Sinclair, Iain. *Landor's Tower*. 2nd edition. London: Granta, 2002

12   Portuges, Paul Cornel. *The Visionary Poetics of Allen Ginsberg*. San Diego: Blue Pacific Books, 1981

13   Sinclair, Iain. *The Kodak Mantra Diaries*. Coventry: Beat Scene, 2006 (re-print of 1971 edition with Postscript by Sinclair)

14   Firing Line. WOR-TV, 3 September 1968. http://www.youtube.com/watch?v=eKBAJYceQ54

15   Wales OnLine. "For sale: Allen Ginsberg poem written while on drugs in Wales". 14 April, 2013. http://www.walesonline.co.uk/news/wales-news/sale-allen-ginsberg-poem-written-2494407

Chapter 10: Glastonedbury

1   Hamish Millar and Paul Broadhurst, *The Sun and the Serpent*, Pendragon Press, Launceston, 1989, p 11

2   *Albion*, 1967, no. 1

3   For comprehensive histories of the early Glastonbury Fairs see: Crspin Aubrey and John Shearlaw, Glastonbury: an oral history, Ebury Press, London, 2004. George McKay, Glastonbury: a very English fair, Victor Gollancz, London, 2000

4   Aubrey and Shearlaw, ibid, p 25

5   Michael Clarke, *The Politics of Pop Festivals*, Junction Books, London, 1982

6   Interview with Andrew Kerr, 11 May 2007

7   Aubrey and Shearlaw, ibid, p 25

8   *The Observer*, 20 June 1971

9   McKay, 2000, op cit

10   Interview with Andrew Kerr, 11 May 2007

11   Tim Hargreaves. Personal communication

12   *The Observer music magazine*, June 2006, p 74

13   Email from William Bloom, 9 August 2007

14   Aubrey and Shearlaw, 2004, op cit, p 23

15   Interview with Andrew Kerr, 11 May 2007

16   http://www.mooncowhq.ch/Cornelius/Cornelius05.htm

17   Penny Marshall, *The God of Hellfire*, SAF, London 2005, p 116

18   Jeremy Sandford & Ron Reid, *Tomorrow's People*, JPC, London 1974, p 62

19   Mick Farren, *Give The Anarchist a Cigarette*, Jonathan Cape, London, 2001, p 32

20   *The Independent* 18 June 1995

Chapter 14: Francis Crick, DNA & LSD

1   http://www.hallucinogens.com/lsd/francis-crick.html

2   http://www.book-of-thoth.com/ftopict-6034.html

3   http://web.randi.org/swift/bushmans-deathbed-confessions

4   Hancock, Graham. *Supernatural*. Century. 2005. 469-70

5   http://www.grahamhancock.com/archive/supernatural/article_02.html

6   Lundborg, Patrick. *Psychedelia*, Lysergia 25-12. 2012. 514

7   But don't call me Shirley!

8   http://www.drugtext.org/library/articles/TimesAd.html

Notes

9   http://www.intuition.org/txt/crick2.htm

10   Ridley, Matt. *Francis Crick: Discoverer of the Genetic Code*, Harper Collins. 2006. 156

11   https://www.youtube.com/watch?v=oLTMavzWlgk

Chapter 21: Scale Green Birdman

1   http://www.davidkemp.uk.com/the-birdmans-hut-grizedale-forest/

Earth, water, fire and air,

Met together in a garden fair

Put in a basket bound with skin

If you answer this riddle you'll never begin...

– Robin Williamson